Study Guide

for

Sigelman and Rider's

Life-Span Human Development

Study Guide

for

Sigelman and Rider's

Life-Span Human Development

Fifth Edition

Elizabeth A. Rider
Elizabethtown College

THOMSON

WADSWORTH

Australia • Brazil • Canada • Mexico
Singapore • Spain • United Kingdom • United States

Printed in the United States of America
1 2 3 4 5 6 7 09 08 07 06 05

Printer: Thomson West

ISBN 0-495-03016-3
Credit image: (center image) © Banana Stock/age fotostock (clockwise from top) © Patrick Sheandell/age fotostock ; © Digital Vision/Getty ; © Stockbyte Gold/Getty Images ; © Photodisc ; © Ben Welsh/age fotostock ; © Banana Stock/age fotostock ; (leaf) © Royalty-free/CORBIS ; (daisies) © Royalty-free/CORBIS

Thomson Higher Education
10 Davis Drive
Belmont, CA 94002-3098
USA

For more information about our products, contact us at:
Thomson Learning Academic Resource Center
1-800-423-0563

For permission to use material from this text or product, submit a request online at
http://www.thomsonrights.com.
Any additional questions about permissions can be submitted by email to **thomsonrights@thomson.com.**

Contents

To The Student

This *Study Guide* was written to help you better understand and remember the material presented in *Life-Span Human Development*, fifth edition by Carol Sigelman and Elizabeth Rider. Many students believe that increasing their study time will increase their understanding of material. But *how* you study is just as important as how much time you spend studying. In thinking about studying and whether you truly understand material, it's useful to consider Bloom's taxonomy, which is a hierarchical , yet overlapping, set of learning objectives. Take a look at the following description of this hierarchy, which includes examples of questions that might be asked at each level.

1. ***Knowledge***—Reciting the definition of a term using the words from the text or your instructor.
   Example: Define "accommodation."

2. ***Comprehension***—Using your own words to define a term.
   Example: Explain "accommodation" in your own words.

3. ***Application***—Being able to use (apply) principles.
   Example: Indicate how accommodation relates to the process of equilibration. Or, use your understanding of learning principles to help a parent modify a child's inappropriate behavior.

4. ***Analysis***—Breaking a principle down into its parts and understanding how the parts relate.
   Example: Compare and contrast accommodation to assimilation. Or, discuss how Piaget's concept of nurture is different from Freud's concept of nurture.

5. ***Synthesis***—Putting old knowledge together in new ways.
   Example: In what ways would Piaget's description of the stage of preoperations need to be modified in order to better "fit" recent research in this area?

6. ***Evaluation***—Making judgments about material based on knowledge (not opinion).
   Example: Evaluate the usefulness of Piaget's concept equilibration. Provide justification for your response.

When you are in the process of learning material, ask yourself the extent to which you know this material.
   Can you give a definition?
   Can you explain this concept to someone else?
   Can you solve a real-life problem by applying this information?
   Can you compare this information to something you learned in an earlier chapter?
   Can you critically evaluate this material using one or more criteria?
The more of these questions you can answer—the better you understand the material.

Organization of the Study Guide

Each chapter of the Study Guide is written for a corresponding chapter in the Sigelman and Rider text and contains the following sections.

Chapter Overview—provides a general picture of each chapter. This is meant to orient you to the chapter and certainly does not replace reading the chapter. Read this before reading the corresponding chapter in the text.

Learning Objectives—questions that you should be able to answer after you have read and studied a chapter. For best results, read these before you begin a chapter in the text so that you have an idea of what to focus on as you read.

Summary and Guided Review—guides you through the main points in each chapter. As you read through the summary, fill in the blanks with terms that appropriately complete a sentence. There are questions in parentheses scattered throughout the summary; these are meant to encourage you to think actively as you are reading and connect this summary to the more detailed information provided in the text. The questions are in bold and italic type so that they stand out from the surrounding text. This will allow you to focus on the questions even if you do not fill-in the blanks of the guided review. Finally, each Summary and Guided Review uses the same headings and subheadings as the main text to help keep you oriented to the text material and allow you to work more easily on specific sections.

Review of Key Terms—designed to facilitate study of important terms that are in bold type in the main text. For each one, you need to complete the sentence with the appropriate key term.

Multiple Choice Self Test—allows you to check your understanding of material from the chapter. These 15 multiple choice questions in each chapter of your Study Guide are comparable to the multiple choice questions that are available to your instructor in the corresponding Test Bank and should serve as a good review in classes that use multiple choice tests.

Critical Thinking Questions—require you to think about the material on a fairly sophisticated level. You need to be able to discuss material in your own words, apply it to a problem of current interest, or synthesize and integrate several concepts to arrive at a new understanding of some problem. There are sample answers provided for three of the critical thinking questions in each chapter. These are provided as models of good answers, but keep in mind that there may be other ways to correctly answer the question. For the other critical thinking questions, you are given hints as to where to locate information in the main text that will help you check your understanding of the material. These questions are comparable to the essay questions available to your instructor in the corresponding Test Bank and should serve as a good review in classes that use essay tests.

Comparison or Additional Review of Material—provided in chapters where appropriate. Encourages you to see connections between material, or relate concepts to one another.

Answers—provided for the Summary and Guided Review, Key Terms, Multiple Choice Self-Test, and one Application question. Whenever you miss a question or term, go back to the textbook and review the relevant section so that you understand why your original answer was incorrect.

This is the fifth time that I have written the Study Guide for this text. I want to thank all the students in my Developmental Psychology classes who have used the Study Guide and given me feedback. Over the years, I have asked my students to give me honest appraisals about which sections were most helpful and which were less helpful so that I could tailor the Study Guide to how students actually study. Most gratifying to me were the comments at the end of the semester indicating how useful the Study Guide had been and how students believed it helped them understand the material. I hope you find it as helpful.

Elizabeth (Betty) Rider
March 2005

CHAPTER ONE

UNDERSTANDING LIFE-SPAN HUMAN DEVELOPMENT

OVERVIEW

     This chapter introduces the field of life-span human development and the nature/nurture issue that is so central to understanding development. The chapter begins by defining life span development and noting historical changes and cultural differences in conceptions of the life span. A large portion of the chapter is devoted to discussion of how developmentalists study life span changes. The goals of study include description, explanation, and optimization. Developmental study has progressed from the study of specific age groups to the study of the entire life span. There are seven assumptions of a life span perspective; these are described in this chapter and then echoed throughout the book.

     Developmental research is guided by the scientific method and its emphasis on systematic observations. Researchers collect their data through self-report measures or behavioral observations. They use experiments to establish cause and effect connections between variables, or they use correlational studies to show relationships or suggest connections among variables. Experiments and correlational studies have both advantages and disadvantages for developmental questions. An important part of this chapter is the description of three developmental designs and their strengths and weaknesses. These designs—cross-sectional, longitudinal, and sequential—are valuable tools for describing development. The chapter concludes by using Bronfenbrenner's bioecological model to consider several issues that arise in the study of development, namely the selection of participants and protecting participants' rights.

LEARNING OBJECTIVES

After reading and studying the material in this chapter, you should be able to answer the following questions.

1.   What is development? What processes underlie developmental changes across the life span?

2.   How has our understanding of different periods of the life-span changed historically? What cultural and subcultural differences exist in perspectives of the life span?

3.   What are the three goals of developmental psychology and the seven assumptions of the life-span perspective on human development?

4.   How is the scientific method used to study development?

5.   What are the important features of the experimental method?   What sorts of information can be gathered from an experimental study?

6.   What are the important features of the correlational method?   What sorts of information can be gathered from this type of study?

7.   What are the advantages and disadvantages of the cross-sectional and longitudinal designs and how does the sequential design resolve the weaknesses of the cross-sectional and longitudinal designs?

8.   What is the bioecological model of development?

9.   What problems or issues arise in studying development?

CHAPTER SUMMARY AND GUIDED REVIEW

The following summary provides an overview of the main points contained in this chapter of the text. Fill-in the blanks with terms that appropriately complete the sentence. Scattered throughout the summary are questions in parentheses. These are meant to encourage you to think actively as you are reading and connect this summary to the more detailed information provided in the text. You can answer these questions as you are filling in the blanks or you can complete all the blanks, then go back and reread the entire summary, addressing the questions in order to provide more depth of understanding.

HOW SHOULD WE THINK ABOUT DEVELOPMENT?

Defining Development

Development consists of systematic changes and continuities that occur in an individual between conception and death. Developmentalists are concerned with three general areas of change, including (1) _physical_, (2) _cognitive_, and (3) _psychosocial_ changes. Biologists typically define 4) _growth_ as physical changes occurring from conception to maturity and refer to the deterioration of an individual as (5) _biological aging_. Developmentalists, however, argue that both positive and negative changes occur throughout the lifespan, and that (6) _aging_ includes both positive and negative changes in the mature individual.

Conceptualizing the Life Span

The life span is typically divided into several distinct periods. The age group, or (7) _age grade_, to which a person belongs will in part determine the roles, privileges and responsibilities that person will be granted. Societal expectations or (8) _age norms_ define how people should behave at different ages. These provide a basis for the (9) _social clock_ or that sense of *when* life events should occur.

Framing the Nature/Nurture Issue

The nature/nurture issue concerns the question of how environmental factors—the (10) _nature_ side of the issue—interact with biological factors to make us who we are. Those who emphasize nature note that development is largely the result of genetically programmed biological unfolding of traits and behaviors, or (11) _maturation_. Those who emphasize nurture note how we change in response to the (12) _environment_. The relatively permanent change in behavior that occurs from environmental factors is called (13) _learning_.

WHAT IS THE SCIENCE OF LIFE-SPAN DEVELOPMENT?

Developmental psychology is the branch of psychology that studies the changes that occur between conception and death.

Goals of Study

One of the goals of life-span developmental psychology is the (14) _description_ of normal development and individual differences. In addition to this, developmentalists try to (15) _explain_, or understand why certain changes occur or do not occur. Finally, they try to (16) _optimize_ development by enhancing capabilities and minimizing problems. (***Can you give an example of each goal?***)

Themes of the Modern Life-Span Perspective

For a number of years, researchers tended to focus on a specific age group, such as the study of infants or the study of old age, known as (17) _gerontology_. Today, the study of development assumes a life-span perspective with seven assumptions:
1. Development is a (18) _lifelong_ process: We change throughout our entire life.
2. Development is (19) _multidirectional_, rather than following a single universal path.
3. Development includes both gains and losses at every age.

4. There is (20) _plasticity_ in human development, which means we can change in response to our experiences.
5. Development is shaped by the (21) _historical-cultural_ contexts in which it occurs.
6. Development is influenced by multiple factors.
7. Complete understanding of development requires input from multiple disciplines.

(***Can you give an example of each of these themes that illustrates the importance of the theme to the study of life-span development?***)

HOW IS DEVELOPMENTAL RESEARCH CONDUCTED?

The Scientific Method

Understanding development is best accomplished through the scientific method, which stresses that conclusions should be based on systematic, unbiased observations (data). To describe or explain a set of observations or facts, scientists develop a (22) _theory_, which consists of a set of concepts that might help us understand some experience. To test the validity of a theory, specific predictions or (23) _hypotheses_, can be generated and should hold true if the theory is in fact valid.

Methods of Data Collection

There are two general ways to measure behavior. People can be asked to provide information about themselves using several types of (24) _verbal reports_ such as interviews or questionnaires. (***What are several weaknesses of collecting data this way?***) Alternatively, researchers might use a kind of behavioral observation called (25) _naturalistic_ observation to directly measure people's behavior in their everyday surroundings. (***What are advantages and disadvantages of this measurement technique?***) Sometimes, researchers control some of the conditions under which they collect observations by using (26) _structured_ observations in hopes of eliciting the behavior of interest. They may also use (27) _physiological_ measures to assess internal variables such as heart rate and skin conductance.

The Experimental and Correlational Methods

In an effort to explain behavior or identify causes of developmental change, researchers often use an (28) _experiment_. The researcher manipulates or changes some aspect of the environment, called the (29) _independant_ variable, and measures the effect that this has on the (30) _dependant_ variable. In addition to manipulation of the variable of interest, participants in a true experiment must have an equal opportunity to end up in any of the groups, which is achieved through (31) _random assignment._ Finally, in a true experiment, all factors other than the independent variable must be held constant, a procedure called (32) _experimental control._ (***What are two major limitations of the experimental method?***) In some cases, when participants cannot be randomly assigned to groups, researchers might conduct a (33) _quasi experiment._

Some developmental questions cannot be answered by experimentally manipulating the environment. In these cases, researchers may use the (34) _correlational_ method, which involves determining whether two or more variables are related. (***Can you provide an example of a question studied with this method?***) The strength of the relationship between two variables is generally assessed with a (35) _correlation coefficient_ which can range in value from -1.00 to

+1.00. (*Can you describe a relationship that would have a large negative correlation and one that would have a large positive correlation?*) A major limitation of the correlational method is that it does not establish a (36) __causal__ relationship between the variables. (*Can you explain why the correlational method is not able to do this?*)

By combining multiple methods, we strengthen our understanding of development. A technique called (37) __meta-analysis__ allows the results from multiple studies on the same question to be synthesized into an overall conclusion.

Developmental Research Designs

There are three research designs frequently used to describe developmental change across the life span. In a (38) __cross-sectional__ design, the performances of people of different age groups are compared, which yields information about age (39) __differences__. In a (40) __longitudinal__ design, the performance of the same group of people is measured repeatedly over time, yielding information about age (41) __changes__. The findings of developmental studies can be influenced by three factors. (42) __age effects__ reflect the effects of getting older. Effects of (43) __cohort__ reflect the influences of being born in a particular historical context, and effects of (44) __time of measurement__ reflect the influences of particular events that occur at the time data are collected. In a cross-sectional study, findings may reflect (45) __cohort__ effects in addition to age effects because people of different ages are studied. Because people in a longitudinal design are repeatedly tested at different times, findings from this design may reflect changes due to (46) __time of measurement__ effects in addition to age effects. The (47) __sequential__ design combines the cross-sectional and longitudinal designs in a single study in order to disentangle effects due to age, cohort, and time of measurement. (*Can you describe situations where it would be appropriate to use each of these designs? What could you conclude about age effects from studies using each of these research designs?*)

WHAT ISSUES ARISE IN STUDYING DEVELOPMENT?
Appreciating the Ecology of Development

Urie Bronfenbrenner was concerned that researchers were not capturing *real* development because they were studying development out of its context. He developed a (48) __bioecological__ model that truly integrates nature and nurture. According to this theory, there are various environmental systems that interact with a person. The system closest to the individual is the (49) __microsystem__. A person's immediate environments are interrelated through the (50) __mesosystem__ so that events in one impact on behavior and events in another. Children can also be influenced by the (51) __exosystem__, which includes social settings that are not directly experienced but still influential. The broadest context in which development occurs is the (52) __macrosystem__. (*Can you provide an example of each type of environmental system?*) In addition to these, Bronfenbrenner used the concept of (53) __chronosystem__ to illustrate that changes in environmental systems occur throughout the lifespan in response to societal events.

The bioecological approach has various implications for research. For one, researchers cannot typically study all members of a population in which they are interested, so they select a (54) __sample__ from this population. Ideally, a (55) __random__ sample is selected so that all members of the population have an equal chance of being selected. This allows the researcher to generalize to other members of the population. One important ecological variable that can influence results of a study is a person's or family's (56) <u>socioeconomic status</u> which includes their income and educational background. (*What other factors should researchers consider in order to ensure that their research is ecologically valid?*)

<u>Protecting the Rights of Research Participants</u>

      Researchers need to protect their subjects from physical or psychological harm by following certain standards of (57) <u>research ethics</u>. This involves informing participants of what the research will involve so that they can provide (58) <u>informed consent</u>. It also means that the researcher will (59) <u>debrief</u> participants after the study to inform them of its true purpose. Finally, participants must be protected from harm and guaranteed that their responses will be (60) <u>confidential</u>.

REVIEW OF KEY TERMS

Below is a list of terms and concepts from this chapter. Use these to complete the following sentence definitions. You might also want to try writing definitions in your own words and then checking your definitions with those in the text.

adolescence
age effect
age grade
age norms
aging
baby boom generation
bioecological model
biological aging
centenarian
chronosystem
cohort effect
correlational method
correlation coefficient
cross-sectional design
dependent variable
development
ecosystem
environment
experiment
experimental control
gerontology
growth
hypothesis
independent variable

learning
life-span perspective
longitudinal design
macrosystem
maturation
meta-analysis
microsystem
naturalistic observation
nature/nurture issue
plasticity
population
quasi-experiment
random assignment
random sample
research ethics
sample
scientific method
sequential design
social clock
socioeconomic status
structured observation
theory
time of measurement effect

1.   The relatively permanent changes in behavior that result from experiences or practice are referred to as _learning_ .

2.   The _scientific method_ is a technique for systematically and objectively using observations to determine the merits of one's thinking.

3.   A(n) _experiment_ is a research technique in which some aspect of the subject's environment is manipulated or altered see if there is any change in the subject's behavior.

4.   People who are at least 100 years old are called _centenarian_ .

5.   A(n) _hypothesis_ is a testable prediction resulting from a theoretical position.

6.   Standards of conduct that investigators must ethically follow in order to protect subjects from harm are _research ethics_

7.   The _correlational method_ is a research design that involves determining whether two or more variables are related.

8.   A method that tests hypotheses by observing behaviors under naturally occurring conditions is called _naturalistic observation_

9.   Systematic changes in a person occurring between conception and death are collectively referred to as _development_ .

10.   A person's or family's position in society is often measured by their education level, occupational prestige and income in a composite measure called _socioeconomic status_

11.   A _sequential design_ is used to measure age-related change by studying participants from different age groups repeatedly over time.

12.   A person's _environment_ consists of all the external physical and social conditions that can influence the person.

13.   _Cohort effects_ result from being part of a group of people born about the same time and exposed to similar cultural and historical events.

14.   _Random sample_ is a technique that ensures that all research participants have an equal chance of being included in all experimental conditions.

15.   A _correlational coeff._ is a statistical value that represents the extent to which two variables are systematically related.

16. The physical changes that occur from conception to maturity are called _growth_.

17. _Age grades_ are distinctive periods of the life span, usually delineated by ages.

18. _Time of measurement_ refer to the historical events that occur when data are collected, which may influence findings.

19. In a _cross-sectional des,_ age-related differences are measured by simultaneously studying subjects from different age groups.

20. The _life-span persp_ is an approach to the study of development that focuses on changes occurring from conception to death of a person.

21. The deterioration of individuals that eventually leads to their death is referred to as _biological aging_

22. The _exosystem_ is a social setting that indirectly influences a child's development.

23. _Age norms_ are expectations about how people should act at different ages.

24. Changes that occur in a mature person are considered the _aging_ process.

25. _Maturation_ refers to a genetically programmed biological plan of development, relatively independent of effects of the environment.

26. The _baby boom generat_ refers to the large generation of people born from the end of WWII to about 1964.

27. The most immediate environment that a person experiences is the _microsystem_.

28. In an experiment, the _independant var._ is the aspect of the environment that the investigator deliberately manipulates in order to discover what effect this has on behavior.

29. Psychologists develop _age norms_, which are sets of rules or principles that describe and explain some behavior.

30. A subset of subjects from a larger population of interest is a _sample_.

31. A _quasi-experiment_ is similar to an experiment, but participants are not randomly assigned to groups.

32. A technique that ensures that all factors besides the independent variable are controlled or held constant is _experimental control_

33. _Gerontology_ is the study of aging and old age.

34. The _social clock_ refers to the sense that life events should occur at a particular time, according to a schedule dictated by age norms.

35. In a _longitudinal design_, age-related changes are measured by repeatedly studying the same individuals over time.

36. In an experiment, the _dependant variable_ is the aspect of a participant's behavior that is observed or measured in order to determine whether the independent variable had an effect.

37. A _random sample_ is when participants are drawn from the larger population of interest such that all members of the population have an equal chance of being selected for the sample.

38. In a _meta-analysis_, the results of multiple studies addressing the same question are synthesized to produce overall conclusions.

39. Researchers sometimes use the technique of _structured observation_ to create conditions that will elicit the behavior of interest.

40. _Plasticity_ refers to the ability to change in response to positive or negative experiences.

41. Researchers would like to be able to generalize their research findings to a _population_ after studying a subset of this group.

42. The interrelationships between two or more microsystems is the _chronosystem_ in Bronfenbrenner's bioecological model.

43. In research, the consequences of getting older are called _age effects_.

44. The _nature-nurture issue_ concerns the question of whether development is primarily the result of biological or environmental forces.

45. The _macrosystem_ is the largest cultural context in which development occurs.

46. The _bioecological_ model of development focuses on the influences of nature and nurture by examining a person's development within a series of environmental layers.

47. The transitional period between childhood and adulthood is known as the period of _adolescence_.

48. In Bronfenbrenner's bioecological model, the ~~chronosystem~~ characterizes the changes that occur in environmental systems over a person's lifetime.

MULTIPLE CHOICE SELF TEST

For each multiple choice question, read all alternatives and then select the best answer.

1. Development results from biologically programmed changes called _____ and from specific environmental experiences called _____.
   a. aging; learning
   b. learning; growth
   c. maturation; learning
   d. age changes; age differences

2. A 65-year-old woman who feels as though it is time for her to become a grandmother is feeling the influence of
   a. age grade.
   b. social clock.
   c. age norms.
   d. physiological needs.

3. The goals of developmental psychology are BEST described by which of the following?
   a. Developmental psychologists seek to modify behavior wherever possible.
   b. Developmental psychologists seek to identify behaviors that should be changed.
   c. Developmental psychologists seek to construct a single unifying theory to explain development.
   d. Developmental psychologists seek to describe and explain behavior, and where possible, optimize behavior.

4. One of the assumptions of the life-span perspective is that development is multidirectional. This means that
   a. development is caused by any number of factors and determining which cause is most influential can't be done.
   b. developmental changes are universal across most people.
   c. developmental outcomes can never be predicted.
   d. development at all ages consists of some gains and some losses, as well as some abilities that remain the same.

5. Another assumption of the life-span perspective is that there is plasticity in development. This means that
    a. most of our acquisition of new skills will occur during infancy when our brains are not fully developed.
    b. developmental changes can occur in response to our experiences across the life span.
    c. development is never really complete.
    d. all skills can be developed at any time of the life span.

6. Which of the following is an example of using naturalistic observation to collect data?
    a. watching how children behave on their playground
    b. asking participants to orally answer questions rather than fill out questionnaires
    c. asking parents to keep track of their children's TV viewing habits
    d. seeing how children behave when they are asked to play a game with unfamiliar children

7. Suppose you have one group of children role play (children assume the role of someone else) while another group of children does not role play. You then observe the level of empathy in children from both groups as they interact with other children. The independent variable would be
    a. whether children role played or not.
    b. children's level of empathy.
    c. the relationship between role playing and level of empathy.
    d. children's ability to role play.

8. A positive correlation between viewing televised violence and aggressive behavior would indicate that
    a. children who watch less televised violence tend to be more aggressive.
    b. children who watch more televised violence tend to be more aggressive.
    c. increases in aggression are caused by watching more televised violence.
    d. watching televised violence is not related to level of aggressive behavior.

9. The major disadvantage of correlational studies is that:
    a. they are costly and time-consuming.
    b. they do not allow researchers to make cause and effect conclusions.
    c. the conclusions are confounded by time-of-measurement effects.
    d. they have no clear dependent variables.

10. If you wanted to assess individual changes over time in prosocial behavior, you would need to use
    a. a longitudinal design.
    b. a cross-sectional design.
    c. a correlational design.
    d. an experimental design.

11. Cross-sectional designs provide information about age _____; longitudinal designs provide information about age _____.
    a. differences; changes
    b. changes; differences
    c. differences; differences
    d. changes; changes

12. Cross-sectional designs confound age effects with _____; longitudinal designs confound age effects with _____.
    a. cohort effects; cohort effects
    b. time of measurement effects; cohort effects
    c. cohort effects; type of measurement effects
    d. cohort effects; time of measurement effects

13. Ensuring that all subjects have an equal chance of participating in any of the experimental treatments is accomplished
    a. through experimental control.
    b. by selecting a random sample from the population.
    c. through random assignment to conditions.
    d. by administering a questionnaire.

14. Urie Bronfenbrenner's bioecological approach to development contends that
    a. development is influenced by interacting environmental systems.
    b. the home environment is the only really important influence on development.
    c. children have a passive role in development and are unable to shape their futures.
    d. the environment has a similar effect on all children.

15. According to the bioecological approach to development, a person's most immediate environment is the
    a. microsystem.
    b. mesosystem.
    c. exosystem.
    d. macrosystem.

COMPARE DEVELOPMENTAL RESEARCH DESIGNS

For each of the major developmental designs, indicate the procedure used to conduct the study, the type of information that can be gained, and the major advantages and disadvantages. Use Table 1.3 on page 20 of the text to check your answers.

	CROSS-SECTIONAL	LONGITUDINAL	SEQUENTIAL
Procedure			
Information Gained			
Advantages			
Disadvantages			

CRITICAL THINKING QUESTIONS

By answering the following questions, you will strengthen your understanding of the material in this chapter. These questions require higher level thinking skills such as integration and application of concepts. Sample answers are provided for three of the questions. These illustrate one possibility, but there are other answers you could provide that might be just as good. For the other questions, you can check yourself by referring to the text (a hint is provided), or by asking a peer or your instructor to review your answer.

1.   Many people in our society are interested in the possibility of "speeding up" some aspect of development, such as the ages when children can print or read. Similarly, parents are often concerned about providing appropriate learning experiences for their children to enhance their abilities. Design a study to test the possibility that some specific aspect of development can be accelerated. Indicate the type of design and the variables used to test this hypothesis.
[Sample answer provided]

2.   Another current concern is the effect of divorce on children of all ages. Design a study to assess whether divorce has a negative impact on children at different ages. Specify the type of design needed for this question and how you would measure the impact of

divorce.
[Sample answer provided]

3. The chapter notes that males, on average, are more aggressive than females. Using the framework of the nature/nurture issue, provide at least one possible explanation for the gender difference in aggression on both sides of the issue.
    [Sample answer provided]

4. Suppose you would like to study how nutrition, both before birth and after birth, affects the three major areas of development: physical, cognitive, and psychosocial. How would you ethically conduct this study? Discuss factors that would need to be considered when designing an ethical study and specify how you would define and measure your variables.
    [Hint: Review the section on "How do we protect the rights of research participants?" and the discussion of the limitations of correlational experimental methods in the subsection on "The correlational method."]

5. The age range for when it is considered appropriate to engage in various activities (e.g. sexual intercourse, marriage, settling down in career, having children, etc.) has changed over the years. How and why?
    [Hint: Review the section on "How Do We View the Life Span?" and consider the implications of historical events and cultural differences on our perception of the life span.]

ANSWERS

Chapter Summary and Guided Review (Fill-in the blank)

1.	physical	19.	multidirectional
2.	cognitive	20.	plasticity
3.	psychosocial	21.	historical/cultural
4.	growth	22.	theory
5.	biological aging	23.	hypotheses
6.	aging	24.	verbal reports
7.	age grade	25.	naturalistic
8.	age norms	26.	structured
9.	social clock	27.	physiological
10.	nurture	28.	experiment
11.	maturation	29.	independent
12.	environment	30.	dependent
13.	learning	31.	random assignment
14.	description	32.	experimental control
15.	explain	33.	quasi-experiment
16.	optimize	34.	correlational
17.	gerontology	35.	correlational coefficient
18.	lifelong	36.	causal

37.	meta-analysis	49.	microsystem
38.	cross-sectional	50.	mesosystem
39.	differences	51.	exosystem
40.	longitudinal	52.	macrosystem
41.	changes	53.	chronosystem
42.	age effects	54.	sample
43.	cohort	55.	random
44.	time of measurement	56.	socioeconomic status
45.	cohort	57.	research ethics
46.	time of measurement	58.	informed consent
47.	sequential	59.	debrief
48.	bioecological	60.	confidential

Review of Key Terms

1.	learning	25.	maturation
2.	scientific method	26.	baby boom generation
3.	experiment	27.	microsystem
4.	centenarians	28.	independent variable
5.	hypothesis	29.	theories
6.	research ethics	30.	sample
7.	correlational method	31.	quasi-experiment
8.	naturalistic observation	32.	experimental control
9.	development	33.	gerontology
10.	socioeconomic status	34.	social clock
11.	sequential design	35.	longitudinal design
12.	environment	36.	dependent variable
13.	cohort effects	37.	random sample
14.	random assignment	38.	meta-analysis
15.	correlation coefficient	39.	structured observation
16.	growth	40.	plasticity
17.	age grades	41.	population
18.	time of measurement effects	42.	mesosystem
19.	cross-sectional design	43.	age effects
20.	life-span perspective	44.	nature/nurture issue
21.	biological aging	45.	macrosystem
22.	exosystem	46.	bioecological
23.	age norms	47.	adolescence
24.	aging	48.	chronosystem

Multiple Choice Self Test

1.	C (p. 5)	6.	A (p. 12)	11.	A (pp. 18, 20)
2.	B (p. 3)	7.	A (p. 14)	12.	D (pp. 18-20)
3.	D (p. 8)	8.	B (p. 15)	13.	C (pp. 11-12)
4.	A (p. 9)	9.	B (p. 16)	14.	A (p. 22)
5.	D (p. 9)	10.	A (p. 19)	15.	A (p. 22)

Critical Thinking Questions

1.   *You would need to use a longitudinal or sequential design to determine whether development could be accelerated. Acceleration is really looking at whether or not some experience produces change over time. A cross-sectional design wouldn't work because this would provide information about age differences but not about whether individuals change over time as a result of their experiences. Further, if you wanted to show that acceleration was* <u>caused</u> *by a particular program, you would need to use an experiment.*

Suppose you're interested in speeding up the age at which children read. After selecting a group of representative participants, these participants would be randomly assigned to either a treatment condition or the control group. In the treatment condition, children would spend one hour every day in a special program designed to foster reading, while children in the control condition would not get any special treatment. Children would begin the program when they were 18 months old and continue for at least 8 years. Both groups of children would be tested on their reading progress every 6 months until they were 9 or 10 years old. If children in the treatment group read at an earlier age and/or progressed faster once they started reading, then we could conclude that this particular aspect of development could be accelerated by this particular type of treatment.

You could also use a correlational study to study this question if you couldn't randomly assign children to different groups. To do this, you might measure the performance of children who were already in a special reading program and compare them to children in a regular reading program to see if one group tends to have higher reading scores than the other. The problem with this is that children in the two groups might have been different to begin with, which may account for why some of them were in the special reading group and others were not. Also, you wouldn't have control over what was in the program or how long it lasted.

2.   *Researchers would not be able to study this experimentally because it's not possible to randomly assign children to different levels of the variable* <u>divorce</u>. *You can't randomly tell families that, for the purpose of your study, you want them to divorce or stay together. Researchers could use a correlational design to study this question. They could locate children who have experienced the divorce of their parents (or not), measure whatever aspects of behavior they are interested in, and then compare the responses or behaviors of the two groups. If the two groups are different, though, the researchers can't be sure that the divorce caused the differences because there are likely to be many of factors that differed between the two groups that were uncontrolled. And children whose parents end up getting divorced might have been different from the other kids even before the divorce. To determine this, researchers might start by testing a large number of children and then waiting to see if their parents get divorced at some point. The children could then be retested. This longitudinal study would allow researchers to compare pre- and post-measures of development in order to determine whether children of divorced parents end up being different from other kids after the divorce or whether they were different from other kids prior to the divorce.*

In order to determine how divorce affects children of different ages, researchers would need to include children from different age groups. Children could be grouped into several age groups (e.g., preschoolers, elementary-school aged children, adolescents) or children of all ages could be included and then researchers could look to see if age correlates with one of their other measures for the two groups of children (divorced and non-divorced).

The measures used to assess children would depend on what it is the researchers are really interested in. If they are interested in cognitive development, they might want to use classroom grades. If they are interested in behavior, they might use school records to see if children have gotten into trouble or they might have teachers and parents complete a behavior inventory that asks about problem behaviors.

The effects of divorce are always going to be difficult to assess because there are so many variables that go along with divorce that might influence development. For example, family income often drops after parents divorce and this might lead to changes in behavior rather than the divorce itself.

3.   *On the nature side, males may be more aggressive because something in their genes predisposes them to act more aggressively in response to certain conditions. Females, with their different genetic makeup (XX rather than XY chromosomes), respond less aggressively in the same situations. It may be that there are inherent chemical differences, such as greater testosterone in males, which lead to differences in expression of aggression. On the nurture side, parents and society expect males to be more aggressive, so perhaps they encourage and sanction greater aggression in boys than in girls. Parents may unintentionally (or even intentionally) reinforce their boys for their aggression, but punish their girls for behaving aggressively.*

CHAPTER TWO

THEORIES OF HUMAN DEVELOPMENT

OVERVIEW

This is an important foundational chapter for the rest of the text. The major developmental theories, which come up in most of the subsequent chapters, are introduced and evaluated here. Before getting into specific theories, the qualities of a good theory are discussed, as are the basic developmental issues that the theorists are trying to understand. These issues are: assumptions about human nature, nature and nurture, activity and passivity, continuity and discontinuity, and universality and context-specificity.

The chapter includes Freud's psychoanalytic theory with its psychosexual stages and three personality structures and Erikson's neo-Freudian psychoanalytic theory with its eight psychosocial stages. It covers the learning theories of Watson, Skinner, and Bandura, as well as Piaget's cognitive-developmental theory. Finally, the chapter introduces Vygotsky's sociocultural perspective and Gottlieb's evolutionary/epigenetic systems view of development. You should be able to describe the distinct features of each theory, compare and contrast issues among the theories, and evaluate the contributions of each theory. A good understanding of these theories will be important as you read other chapters in the text.

LEARNING OBJECTIVES

After reading and studying the material in this chapter, you should be able to answer the following questions.

1.   What are the five basic issues in human development? Where does each theorist stand on each of these issues?

2.   What are the distinct features of Freud's psychoanalytic theory? What are the strengths and weaknesses of the theory?

3.   How does Erikson's theory compare to Freud's theory? What crisis characterizes each of Erickson's psychosocial stages?

4.   What are the distinct features of Skinner's operant conditioning theory and Bandura's social-learning theory? What are the strengths and weaknesses of the learning theories?

5.   What is Piaget's basic perspective on cognitive development? What are the strengths and weaknesses of Piaget's theory?

6.   What are the essential elements of Vygotsky's sociocultural perspective and Gottlieb's evolutionary/epigenetic systems view of development?

7.   What are the strengths and weaknesses of the contextual and systems approaches to development?

CHAPTER SUMMARY AND GUIDED REVIEW

The following summary provides an overview of the main points contained in this chapter of the text. Fill-in the blanks with terms that appropriately complete the sentence. Scattered throughout the summary are questions in parentheses. These are meant to encourage you to think actively as you are reading and connect this summary to the more detailed information provided in the text. You can answer these questions as you are filling in the blanks or you can fill-in all the blanks, then go back and reread the entire summary, addressing the questions in order to provide more depth of understanding.

DEVELOPMENTAL THEORIES AND THE ISSUES THEY RAISE
Theories of human development try to organize and explain the facts and observations about a particular phenomenon. Some theories do a better job of this than others. The elements of a good theory should fit together logically, or possess (1) internally consistant. In addition, good theories can generate hypotheses that can be tested, either confirming or disconfirming the theory. This means the theory is (2)   falsifiable   . Good theories also should be supported by the research conducted on them.

There are five basic issues concerning what humans are like and how development occurs. (***Where do you stand on these issues and how do your views compare to the views of the major developmental theorists?***)

Nature and Nurture
Another basic issue concerns whether development results primarily from biological forces, called (3) ___nature___, or environmental experiences, called (4) ___nurture___. As noted in chapter 1, this is the most important and complex of the developmental issues.

The Goodness and Badness of Human Nature
One basic issue concerns our assumptions about human nature. In particular, are people

inherently good or bad, or are they born as (5) _tabula rasae_, meaning they are neither inherently good or bad but develop according to their experiences.

Activity and Passivity

A third issue concerns whether people actively produce developmental change or are more passively shaped by biological and/or environmental forces outside of their control.

Continuity and Discontinuity

A fourth issue is whether development is continuous or discontinuous. Continuity implies gradual and (6) _quantitative_ change, while discontinuity implies abrupt and (7) _qualitative_ change. Theorists who believe development is discontinuous often propose that development progresses through a series of (8) _developmental stages_, or phases that are qualitatively distinct from one another.

Universality and Context Specificity

A final developmental issue is whether we all follow a common or (9) _universal_ path of development or whether we each follow different, context specific paths of development.

FREUD: PSYCHOANALYTIC THEORY

Instincts and Unconscious Motives

Freud's psychoanalytic theory proposes that humans have inborn biological urges, called (10) _instincts_, that must be satisfied. We are often unaware that these instincts motivate behavior because they are (11) _unconscious motivation_

Id, Ego, and Superego

Freud believed that there were three personality components. At birth, the personality consists of only the (12) _id_, which seeks to satisfy a person's instincts. During infancy, the (13) _ego_ begins to develop and tries to realistically satisfy the demands of the id. The third component of the personality is the (14) _superego_, which begins to develop during early childhood and functions as a person's internalized moral standards. Problems may develop if the available (15) _psychic energy_ is not evenly distributed among the three personality structures.

Psychosexual Development

Freud believed that, as children mature, the psychic energy of the sex instinct, called the (16) _libido_, moves form one part of the body to another. These changes are reflected by progression through Freud's stages of (17) _psychosexual_ development. During the first stage, the libido seeks pleasure through (18) _oral_ activities. This focus shifts to (19) _anal_ activities during the second psychosexual stage of development. During the (20) _phallic_ stage of development, boys and girls become interested in their genitals and are influenced by the presence or absence of a penis. During the (21) _latent_ period, the psychic energy of the sex instinct becomes focused on socially appropriate activities such as schoolwork. The (22) _genital_ stage is the final psychosexual stage and occurs with the onset of puberty. It is characterized by mature love with the goal of biological reproduction.

Freud emphasized the influence of inborn biological drives but also recognized that early experiences could have a long-term effect on personality development. During any psychosexual stage, conflict among the personality components may create anxiety that is alleviated by use of (23) _defense mechanisms_. One example is (24) _fixation_, which occurs when the psychic energy remains tied to an early stage of development. Another example is (25) _regression_, which involves returning to an earlier, less traumatic stage of development.

Strengths and Weaknesses

One of the criticisms of Freud's theory is that many of the concepts cannot be tested, which means the theory is not (26) _falsifiable_. Freud also offered biased interpretations of many phenomenon. Freud's theory is valuable because it focused attention on unconscious motivation, early family experiences, and emotions.

ERIKSON: NEO-FREUDIAN PSYCHOANALYTIC THEORY

Erik Erikson was another psychoanalytic theorist, a neo-Freudian, who was distinct from Freud in several ways. Erikson focused less on sexual instincts than Freud and more on (27) _social_ forces. He also had a more positive view of human nature and believed that development continued through adulthood. Erikson also emphasized the rational ego more than the irrational id.

Psychosocial Stages

Erikson proposed that maturation and society together create eight life (28) _psychosocial stages_, which correspond to eight psychosocial stages of development. Each stage can be resolved positively or negatively and unresolved crises can have an effect on later development. For example, in the first psychosocial stage, infants must learn to develop a sense of (29) _trust_. Adolescents struggle to develop a sense of (30) _identity_ as they try to define who they are. Adolescents who have difficulty figuring out who they are experience (31) _role confusion_. Unlike Freud, Erikson extended his stages through adulthood. He believed that young adulthood is the time for establishing (32) _intimacy_ in a committed relationship. Middle aged adults are concerned with whether or not they have produced something meaningful that will live on after them, which is an issue of (33) _generativity_. In the last psychosocial stage, older adults try to find meaning in their lives and develop a sense of (34) _integrity_ rather than despair.

Strengths and Weaknesses

Like Freud, Erikson's theory has been criticized because it is difficult to test. Erikson also does not adequately explain development. The theory has been praised for focusing attention on adolescent and adult development.

LEARNING THEORIES
Watson: Classical Conditioning

John Watson believed it was not possible to study unconscious motivations or mental processes and developed a branch of psychology called (35) _behaviorism_. Watson believed that only overt behaviors were appropriate for study and that learned associations between a person's actions and external stimuli were the bases of human development. In classical conditioning, a stimulus that initially had no effect on an individual comes to elicit a response through its association with a stimulus that already produces the desired response. A stimulus that elicits the desired response without prior learning experiences is the (36) unconditioned stimulus. A stimulus that produces the desired response only after being associated with a stimulus that always elicits the response is the (37) conditioned stimulus. An unlearned response to an unlearned stimulus is the (38) unconditioned response, while a learned response to a conditioned stimulus is the (39) conditioned response. (*Can you provide an example of classical conditioning that is not in the text?*)

Skinner: Operant Conditioning

B.F. Skinner demonstrated that existing behaviors become more or less probable depending on the consequences of the behaviors. This form of learning is called operant conditioning. One possible consequence is (40) positive reinforcement, where something administered following a behavior strengthens that behavior. Behaviors could also be strengthened by removing something negative following the behavior, a process called (41) negative reinforcement. (*Can you provide an example of this?*) Decreasing the strength of a behavior is accomplished either by adding something unpleasant following a behavior, which is called (42) positive reinforcement, or removing something positive, which is (43) negative reinforcement. [*Hint: To remember whether reinforcement or punishment is positive or negative, think of the <u>action</u> being performed. When something is <u>added</u> to the situation, it is positive (reinforcement or punishment) and when something is <u>removed</u> from the situation, it is negative (reinforcement of punishment).*] (*Can you describe ways to make the use of punishment effective?*) Sometimes, a behavior is followed by no consequences, which eventually leads to (44) extinction because the behavior is not being reinforced.

Bandura: Social Cognitive Theory

Another learning theorist, one who emphasized the importance of cognition, is Albert Bandura. His social cognitive theory makes the claim that humans are active processors of environmental information. Bandura believes that (45) observational learning is the most important mechanism through which development occurs. The process of (46) vicarious reinforcement means that if the learner observes the model getting reinforced for his or her actions, the learner will be more likely to perform the behavior. Bandura has argued that humans exercise control over their environments and lives, a concept he calls (47) human agency. He also believes that development occurs through a constant give-and-take relationship between a person and the environment, called (48) reciprocal determinism

Strengths and Weaknesses

A strength of the learning theories is that precise hypotheses can be generated and tested. In addition, the principles apply to learning across the entire life span, and they are applicable to many developmental phenomenon. Learning theories have been criticized for not clearly showing that learning causes developmental changes and for oversimplifying developmental processes.

COGNITIVE DEVELOPMENTAL THEORY

Piaget's Constructivism

Piaget focused on cognitive development and proposed that children actively (49) constructivism their understanding of the world based on their experiences.

Cognitive development results from the interaction of maturation and environment. As children mature, they develop more complex (50) cognitive structures, which are organized patterns of thought or action that are used to interpret experiences.

Stages of Cognitive Development

Piaget proposed four stages of cognitive development, which form an (51) invariant sequence, meaning that children progress through the stages in order with no skipping. Infants are in the (52) sensorimotor stage because they learn about the world through their sensory experiences and their motoric responses to these experiences. Preschoolers are in the (53) preoperational stage, which is characterized by use of (54) perceptions and lack of logical thought. School-aged children are in the (55) concrete operational stage and can logically solve problems by applying a number of mental operations. They typically use a trial-and-error approach to solving problems. Adolescents are in the (56) formal operations stage, which is characterized by systematic hypothesis testing and logical reasoning on abstract problems.

Strengths and Weaknesses

Piaget's theory has been very influential. Piaget's descriptions of cognitive development have largely been supported by research. However, he has been criticized for not adequately considering the influence of social factors on cognitive development. In addition, research suggests that cognitive development is not nearly as stage-like as Piaget proposed.

CONTEXTUAL/SYSTEMS THEORIES

Contextual/systems theories propose that development results from the ongoing interrelationships between a changing person and a changing environment.

Vygotsky: A Sociocultural Perspective

Unlike Piaget, Vygotsky did not believe that humans progressed through common (57) stages of development. Instead, development is influenced by the (58) context in which it occurs. Cognitive development is really a (59) social process, not an individual process.

Gottlieb: An Evolutionary/Epigenetic Systems Perspective

Darwin's theory of evolution has inspired several theorists who have tried to understand development in terms of shared genetic endowment and evolved behaviors. Gottlieb's evolutionary/epigenetic systems approach views development as a complex interaction between biological and environmental forces. According to this perspective, we are predisposed through our (60) genes to certain developmental outcomes. The process through which nature and nurture interact is called the (61) epigenetic process. Gottlieb notes that genes do not determine behavior; behaviors only emerge through an interaction of genes and environments.

Strengths and Weaknesses

Contextual/systems theories are valuable for pointing out the importance of the context of development. Most, however, are broad and not fully developed. Indeed, it may not be possible to develop a specific contextual or systems theory because at the very heart of these theories is the notion that development depends on the unique and continuous interactions between a person and their world.

THEORIES IN PERSPECTIVE

Theories can be grouped according to the broad assumptions they make about human development. Theorists such as Freud, Erikson, and Piaget believed in universal (62) _____directions_____ whereas Watson, Skinner, and Bandura did not. Learning theorists focus more on the (63) _____environment_____ than the person. The contextual-systems theories focus on both factors. (***What are the implications of these basic assumptions for child rearing?***)

REVIEW OF KEY TERMS
_____

Below is a list of terms and concepts from this chapter. Use these to complete the following sentence definitions. You might also want to try writing definitions in your own words and then checking your definitions with those in the text.

activity/passivity issue
behaviorism
classical conditioning
concrete operations stage
conditioned response (CR)
conditioned stimulus (CS)
constructivism
contextual/systems theories
continuity/discontinuity issue
defense mechanisms
developmental stage
eclectic
ego
epigenetic process
ethology
extinction
evolutionary/epigenetic systems perspective
fixation
formal operations stage
human agency
id
instinct
libido

negative punishment
negative reinforcement
observational learning
operant conditioning
positive punishment
positive reinforcement
preoperational stage
psychoanalytic theory
psychosexual stages
psychosocial stages
reciprocal determinism
regression
sensorimotor stage
social cognitive theory
sociocultural perspective
superego
tabula rasa
unconditioned response (UCR)
unconditioned stimulus (UCS)
unconscious motivation
universality/context-specificity issue
vicarious reinforcement

1.   With the defense mechanism of ___regression___ , a person reverts to an earlier, less traumatic stage of development.

2.   Nature and nurture interact in the _epigenetic process_ to bring about development.

3. According to the school of psychology known as _behaviorism_, researchers and theorists should focus on observations of overt behavior rather than unobservable mental processes.

4. In Piaget's _concrete operations_ stage of cognitive development, school-aged children can reason logically about concrete problems.

5. According to _reciprocal determinism_ humans develop actively through a continuous reciprocal interaction between them and their environment, rather than being passively shaped by their environment.

6. The basic principle of _operant conditioning_ is that behaviors become more or less probable depending on the consequences they produce.

7. A form of learning in which a stimulus that initially had no effect on an individual comes to elicit a response through its association with a stimulus that already produces the desired response is _classical conditioning_

8. The study of how different species evolve in their natural environments is called _ethology_ .

9. The _activity/passivity_ concerns whether humans are actively involved in their development or passively influenced by factors beyond their control.

10. According to Freud, the _id_ is the most primitive component of personality, seeking immediate satisfaction of instincts.

11. A period of life characterized by a cohesive set of behaviors or abilities that are distinct from earlier or later periods is called a _developmental stage_

12. According to modern social cognitive theory, humans deliberately control their environments and lives through a concept Bandura calls _human agency_

13. In classical conditioning, a stimulus that elicits the desired response without learning experiences is the _unconditioned stimulus_

14. Unconscious techniques used by the ego to protect itself from anxiety are _defense mechanisms_

15. The _evolutionary epigenetic systems_ perspective on development argues that development is a product of complex interactions between biological and environmental forces.

16. _Tabula rasa_ is the belief that children have no inborn tendencies, but their outcome depends entirely on the environment in which they are raised.

17. Piaget's first stage of cognitive development during which infants learn about the world through their sensory experiences and their actions is the _sensorimotor_ stage.

18.   _Observational learning_ is a form of learning that results from watching the behavior of other people.

19.   In classical conditioning, an unlearned response to an unconditioned stimulus is the _unconditioned response_

20.   Theories stating that development arises from the ongoing interrelationships between a changing organism and a changing world are called _contextual sys. theory_

21.   We can decrease the likelihood of future responding with _negative punishment_ or removing something pleasant from the situation.

22.   Piaget believed in _constructivism_, the belief that children actively build their own understanding of the world.

23.   The question of whether development is smooth and gradual or somewhat abrupt is the focus of the _continuity / discontinuity issue_

24.   _Unconscious motiv_ refers to the influence of information that is in memory but is not recalled at a conscious level.

25.   Freud's term for the sex instinct's psychic energy is ___libido___.

26.   Erikson's theory proposes eight _psychosocial_ that represent conflicts between biological maturation and social demands.

27.   The defense mechanism of ___fixation___ is when development becomes arrested because part of the libido remains tied to an earlier stage of development.

28.   In Piaget's _preoperational_ stage of cognitive development, preschoolers are able to use symbols but lack logical reasoning.

29.   Vygotsky's _sociocultural_ of development maintains that cognitive development is shaped by the cultural context in which it occurs.

30.   The personality component that seeks to realistically satisfy instincts is called the ___ego___.

31.   Decreasing the likelihood of future responses by administering something unpleasant is called _positive punishment_

32.   In Piaget's _formal operational_ stage of cognitive development, adolescents can reason logically about abstract concepts and hypothetical ideas.

33.   The personality component that contains values and morals learned from parents and society is called the ___superego___.

34. In ___extinction___, a behavior is eliminated by removing its reinforcing consequences.

35. A person with an ___eclectic___ view believes that none of the major theories of human development can explain everything, but each has something to contribute to our understanding of human development.

36. The theory that humans are active processors of information from the environment, rather than passive recipients of information from the environment is the ___social cognitive theory___

37. An ___instinct___ is an inborn biological force that motivates behavior.

38. According to the ___psychoanalytic___ theory, humans are driven by unconscious motives and emotions and are shaped by early childhood experiences.

39. The ___context-specificity universality___ addresses whether developmental changes are common across people or are different for each person.

40. Children progress through the ___psychosexual stages___ as the libido shifts from one part of the body to another.

41. Any stimulus that increases the likelihood of a behavior occurring in the future when it is removed following the behavior is ___negative reinforcement___

42. A learned response to a conditioned stimulus is a ___conditioned response___

43. To increase the likelihood of a behavior in the future, we could use ___positive reinforcement by___ administering a pleasant stimulus following the behavior.

44. In classical conditioning, the ___conditioned stimul___produces the desired response only after it is associated with a stimulus that always elicits the response.

45. In the process of ___vicarious reinforcement___, children are influenced by observing another person receive reinforcement.

MULTIPLE CHOICE SELF TEST

For each multiple choice question, read all alternatives and then select the best answer.

1. A theorist who believes that humans progress through developmental stages is likely to believe in
    a. discontinuous changes.
    b. continuous changes.
    c. quantitative changes.
    d. multiple paths of development.

2.	The universality and context specificity issue concerns whether developmental changes
	a.	are quantitative or qualitative in nature.
	b.	are common to everyone or different from person to person.
	c.	are multiply caused.
	d.	follow universal paths determined by genetic factors or by environmental factors.

3.	According to Freud's theory, the _____ must find ways of realistically satisfying the demands of the _____.
	a.	superego, ego
	b.	superego, id
	c.	id, ego
	d.	ego, id

4.	Regression occurs when
	a.	a person reverts to an earlier stage of development.
	b.	a person pushes anxiety-provoking thoughts out of conscious awareness.
	c.	development becomes arrested because part of the libido remains tied to an earlier stage of development.
	d.	psychic energy is directed toward socially acceptable activities.

5.	Which statement BEST characterizes Erikson's position on the nature-nurture issue?
	a.	He emphasized nurture more than nature.
	b.	He emphasized nature more than nurture.
	c.	He emphasized nature and nurture equally.
	d.	He didn't really take a stand on this issue.

6.	According to Erikson, the main task facing adolescents is
	a.	developing a sense of identity.
	b.	achieving a sense of intimacy with another person.
	c.	mastering important academic tasks.
	d.	building a sense of self-confidence.

7.	You turn on the can opener to open the dog's food and the dog comes running into the room. In this example, food is the _____; the sound of the can opener is the _____; and running into the room in response to the sound is the _____.
	a.	unconditioned stimulus; conditioned stimulus; unconditioned response
	b.	conditioned stimulus; unconditioned stimulus; conditioned response
	c.	unconditioned stimulus; conditioned stimulus; conditioned response
	d.	conditioned stimulus; conditioned response; unconditioned response

8.	A stimulus can serve as reinforcement or as punishment depending on whether it
	a.	is pleasurable or not (negative) for the subject receiving it.
	b.	increases or decreases the frequency of the behavior it follows.
	c.	occurs before or after the behavior in question.
	d.	is administered or taken away from the person.

9.   Which of the following is an example of negative reinforcement?
       a.   giving a child dessert as a reward for eating his/her vegetables at dinner
       b.   paying a child for each "A" received on his or her report card
       c.   a parent stops nagging a child when the child finally cleans his or her room
       d.   cutting a child's television viewing by 30 minutes each time the child misbehaves

10.   Which of the following is <u>necessary</u> in order to learn through observation?
       a.   observing the model get a reward or punishment for his/her actions
       b.   being provided with an opportunity to imitate the model's actions immediately
             after the observation
       c.   hearing the model describe the consequences of his/her actions
       d.   observing and remembering the model's actions

11.   Which of the following explanations for developmental change would a social learning
      theorist be most likely to give?
       a.   Children are unconsciously motivated by internal conflict.
       b.   Children observe the world around them and actively process this information.
       c.   Children are passively influenced by environmental rewards and punishments.
       d.   Children actively construct an understanding of the world through interactions
             with their environment.

12.   Piaget would be most likely to make which one of the following statements?
       a.   Children learn best by observing people around them.
       b.   Children actively construct an understanding of the world by interacting with the
             world around them.
       c.   Children are genetically predisposed to act in certain ways and seek out
             environments that are compatible with their genetic make-ups.
       d.   Children are unconsciously propelled from one stage to another by maturational
             forces.

13.   A child in Piaget's preoperational stage is able to solve problems
       a.   that are concrete by using logical reasoning.
       b.   that are abstract by using logical reasoning.
       c.   using symbols.
       d.   through their sensory experiences and their actions.

14. Of the following, Piaget has been MOST criticized for his
    a. emphasis on sexual instincts during childhood.
    b. belief that children are actively involved in their development.
    c. description of cognitive development.
    d. belief that cognitive development occurs through an invariant sequence of coherent stages.

15. Which of the following theoretical perspectives places the greatest emphasis on the <u>interaction</u> of biological and environmental forces?
    a. Freud's psychoanalytic theory
    b. learning theory
    c. Vygotsky's sociocultural theory
    d. Gottlieb's evolutionary/epigenetic systems theory

COMPARE THEORIES ON BASIC DEVELOPMENTAL ISSUES

For this exercise, indicate each theory's position on the five basic issues of human development. Check yourself using Table 2.4 on page 52 of the text.

	PSYCHOANALYTIC THEORIES		LEARNING THEORIES	
	FREUD'S PSYCHOSEXUAL THEORY	ERIKSON'S PSYCHOSOCIAL THEORY	SKINNER'S LEARNING THEORY	BANDURA'S SOCIAL COGNITIVE THEORY
Nature— Nurture				
Goodness- Badness of Human Nature				
Activity— Passivity				
Continuity— Discontinuity				
Universality-- Context- Specificity				

	COGNITIVE-DEVELOPMENTAL THEORY: PIAGET'S CONSTRUCTIVISM	CONTEXTUAL THEORIES:	
		VYGOTSKY'S SOCIOCULTURAL THEORY	GOTTLIEB'S EVOLUTIONARY/ SYSTEMS THEORY
Nature— Nurture			
Goodness- Badness of Human Nature			
Activity— Passivity			
Continuity— Discontinuity			
Universality-- Context- Specificity			

CRITICAL THINKING QUESTIONS

By answering the following questions, you will strengthen your understanding of the material in this chapter. These questions require higher level thinking skills such as integration and application of concepts. Sample answers are provided for three of the questions. These illustrate one possibility, but there are other answers you could provide that might be just as good. For the other questions, you can check yourself by referring to the text (a hint is provided), or by asking a peer or your instructor to review your answer.

1. Consider the problem of shyness. Many children and adults in our society are socially shy to a significant degree and express anxiety in many everyday, social situations. How would each of the theorists in this chapter interpret or explain the development of this condition?
[Sample Answer provided]

2. In what ways do the learning theory explanations of development conflict with the psychoanalytic explanations of development?
[Sample Answer provided]

3. Piaget and Vygotsky were developing their theories at about the same time. How are the two theories similar and in what ways do they differ?
   [Sample Answer provided]

4. Freud and Piaget are often considered to be the "great stage theorists" of developmental psychology. Discuss ways in which Freud and Piaget are similar in their views of development and ways in which they differ.
   [Hint: Review the sections in the text on Freud's and Piaget's theories. This is another one of those "compare and contrast" questions in which you need to relate aspects of one theory to aspects of a second theory.]

5. Gottlieb's theory is called the evolutionary/epigenetic systems approach to development. What ideas about development are conveyed by this perspective?
   [Hint: Review the section on Gottlieb's theory, the Explorations box on Gottlieb's explanation of teenage pregnancy, and the final section of the chapter on "Theories in Perspective."]

ANSWERS

Chapter Summary and Guided Review (Fill-in the blank)

1.	internal consistency	26.	falsifiable
2.	falsifiable	27.	societal
3.	nature	28.	crises
4.	nurture	29.	trust
5.	tabula rasa	30.	identity
6.	quantitative	31.	role confusion
7.	qualitative	32.	intimacy
8.	stages	33.	generativity
9.	universal	34.	integrity
10.	instincts	35.	behaviorism
11.	unconscious	36.	unconditioned stimulus (UCS)
12.	id	37.	conditioned stimulus (CS)
13.	ego	38.	unconditioned response (UCR)
14.	superego	39.	conditioned response (CR)
15.	psychic energy	40.	positive reinforcement
16.	libido	41.	negative reinforcement
17.	psychosexual	42.	positive punishment
18.	oral	43.	negative punishment
19.	anal	44.	extinction
20.	phallic	45.	observational
21.	latency	46.	vicarious
22.	genital	47.	human agency
23.	defense mechanisms	48.	reciprocal determinism
24.	fixation	49.	construct
25.	regression	50.	cognitive structures

51.	invariant sequence	58.	context
52.	sensorimotor	59.	social
53.	preoperational	60.	genes or genetic endowment
54.	symbols	61.	epigenetic process
55.	concrete operations	62.	stages
56.	formal operations	63.	environment
57.	stages		

Review of Key Terms

1.	regression	24.	unconscious motivation
2.	epigenetic process	25.	libido
3.	behaviorism	26.	psychosocial stages
4.	concrete operations	27.	fixation
5.	reciprocal determinism	28.	preoperational stage
6.	operant conditioning	29.	sociocultural perspective
7.	classical conditioning	30.	ego
8.	ethology	31.	positive punishment
9.	activity/passivity issue	32.	formal operations
10.	id	33.	superego
11.	developmental stage	34.	extinction
12.	human agency	35.	eclectic
13.	unconditioned stimulus (UCS)	36.	social cognitive theory
14.	defense mechanisms	37.	instinct
15.	evolutionary/epigenetic systems	38.	psychoanalytic
16.	tabula rasa	39.	universality/context-specificity issue
17.	sensorimotor	40.	psychosexual stages
18.	observational learning	41.	negative reinforcement
19.	unconditioned response (UCR)	42.	conditioned response
20.	contextual/systems theories	43.	positive reinforcement
21.	negative punishment	44.	conditioned stimulus (CS)
22.	constructivism	45.	vicarious reinforcement
23.	continuity/discontinuity issue		

Multiple Choice Self Test

1.	A (p. 29)	6.	A (pp. 32, 34)	11.	B (p. 39-40)
2.	B (p. 30)	7.	A (p. 36)	12.	B (p. 42)
3.	D (p. 31)	8.	B (p. 38)	13.	C (p. 42)
4.	A (pp. 31-32)	9.	C (p. 38)	14.	D (pp. 43-44)
5.	C (p. 34)	10.	D (p. 39)	15.	D (p. 52)

Critical Thinking Questions

1. *Freud might say that shyness is used as a defense mechanism to protect the ego from anxiety caused by the superego. A shy child becomes inhibited through regression to early stages of development. Perhaps the shy child was punished for sucking his or her thumb too long in the oral stage or was punished for toilet training accidents during the anal stage. Early experiences may cause the child to develop a strong superego, which in turn leads the child to*

become inhibited and withdrawn in the quest to satisfy the need for perfection and acceptance in society. Whatever the specific cause, the child is not consciously aware of these motivating factors.

According to Erikson, a child may become shy as a result of not adequately resolving a life crisis in one of the eight psychosocial stages. For example, in the trust vs. mistrust stage, shyness could result because the parent is unresponsive to the child's needs and the child does not form a trusting relationship to others. In autonomy vs. shame and doubt, the child may not learn to be autonomous; instead, the child may feel doubtful of his/her abilities and not very comfortable trying new things. In initiative vs. guilt, the caregiver may have been too protective, inhibiting the child's initiative and interactive skills. The child may feel guilty whenever he/she tries to do something new and ends up not initiating things.

According to Piaget, children construct their own understanding of the world through their interactions with their environment. Thus, the child interprets their experiences in a way that leads the child to be shy. To avoid disequilibrium, people act in ways that are consistent with their cognitive understanding of events. The child decides that shyness is an adaptive way of interacting with their world. Perhaps the infant in the sensorimotor stage did not have adequate opportunity to explore the environment, leading to shyness because of lack of experience. Or a child in the preoperational stage who has had a bad experience may reason that all experiences are bad and withdraw from seeking new experiences.

Based on learning theories, people learn by forming associations between behaviors and consequences. Skinner would say that a person who is shy was either rewarded for being shy or punished for being outgoing. For example, the parent might reward the child for quiet activities like reading a book or punish child for being loud. According to Bandura, a child may model an adult who is shy and rewarded in some way.

Contextual/systems theorists believe that development arises from the ongoing interrelationships between a changing organism and a changing world: Changes in a person will affect his or her environment, and changes in the environment will affect that person. Vygotsky might focus on how the sociocultural context has affected the way children think about themselves in relation to others. According to Gottlieb, development results from a complex interaction of nature and nurture. Biological factors interact with environmental factors at both the species level and the individual level. We begin life with genetic predispositions that have been formed as a result of gene-environment interactions of previous generations. These genetic predispositions then interact with the individual's environments over a lifetime to determine outcomes. A person might be shy because they have been genetically predisposed to shyness and then ended up in environments that fostered this predisposition.

2.   Psychoanalytic theories place greater emphasis on nature than do the learning theories. According to Freud's psychoanalytic theory, development is driven by biology; children are propelled through the psychosexual stages according to a biological plan. Erikson, another psychoanalytic theorist, believed that biology interacts with environment to create the eight psychosocial conflicts that confront people throughout their lifespan. In contrast, the learning theorists focus almost exclusively on the role of the environment. Another difference between the two types of theories is their position on the continuity and discontinuity issue. The psychoanalytic theorists, Freud and Erikson, believe that development is discontinuous. They both propose that humans go through stages of development; during each stage, we are different from how we are in other stages. The learning theorists believe that development is continuous

over the lifespan. At different points of the lifespan, we may have more or less of something, but we are not qualitatively different. Another difference is their position on the universality and context specificity issue. The psychoanalytic theorists believe that there are universal changes in development, reflected in the stages that we all go through. Development, therefore, is somewhat predictable. The learning theorists believe that development is context specific; there are not universal stages that everyone goes through. Development depends very much on the specific experiences and environments that we each experience. Psychoanalytic theorists are likely to clash with learning theorists by claiming that development changes are: 1) influenced largely by nature (Freud) or by nature and nurture equally (Erikson); 2) stagelike; and 3) universal rather than specific to the individual.

3.   *Piaget and Vygotsky were developing their theories at about the same time, but Vygotsky had the misfortune to die young whereas Piaget worked on his theory for much of his 84 years. As a result, Piaget's theory is much more developed than Vygotsky's theory. Both theorists believed that children are actively involved in their development and in creating an understanding of the world. Piaget, though, focused more on the individual in isolation. That is, Piaget believed that children learned about their world by independently exploring it and interacting with physical objects. By interacting with toys, for example, they learn about the toys' properties. Vygotsky focused more on the social interactions of the person. Thus, Vygotsky believed that children learned more by interacting with others than they did by interacting with toys. Piaget believed that cognitive development was largely an internal process, whereas Vygotsky placed greater emphasis on the sociocultural context in which development occurred. Because of this focus on the culture, Vygotsky believed that development varies across social as well as historical contexts. Piaget believed that development is largely universal—it is the same across social and historical contexts.*

CHAPTER THREE

GENES, ENVIRONMENT, AND DEVELOPMENT

OVERVIEW

As the title suggests, this chapter is about both genetic and environmental contributions to development. In addition to describing how parents pass along their genes to their children, the chapter examines how genes interact with environments to make each of us unique with respect to intellectual and psychological attributes. Interestingly, genes can influence the kinds of environments we are exposed to, and environments can affect the expression of genetic factors. Note the point made in the second half of the chapter: people do not inherit traits, they inherit predispositions for traits that may or may not arise depending on the environmental influences.

One of the most interesting findings reported in the chapter is that siblings do not become similar to one another as a result of growing up in the same family and sharing similar experiences. Instead, nonshared environmental experiences are more important in creating individual differences among family members. This may help you understand why you and your siblings are so different from one another on some basic personality characteristics.

An important lesson from this chapter concerns the logic of the methods used to study genetic and environmental influences, and the pattern of the findings. The methods, including twin and adoption studies, can be used to demonstrate both genetic and environmental influences, not just genetic factors. You should understand the pattern of findings that would show a genetic influence, an environmental influence, and interaction effects, even if you do not know actual correlation coefficients or concordance values.

LEARNING OBJECTIVES

After reading and studying the material in this chapter, you should be able to answer the following questions.

1.   What do evolution and species heredity contribute to our understanding of universal patterns of development? What are the basic principles of Darwin's theory of evolution?

2.   What are the basic workings of individual heredity, including the contributions of genes, chromosomes, the zygote, and the processes of mitosis and meiosis? Note the difference between genotype and phenotype.

3. How are traits passed from parents to offspring? What is an example of how a child could inherit a trait through each of the mechanisms?

4. What tests are used to screen for genetic abnormalities? What are the advantages and disadvantages of using techniques like these to test for prenatal problems? Name several abnormalities that can currently be detected with prenatal screening.

5. What methods are used to assess the influences of heredity and environment on behavioral characteristics? Describe the logic of the methods, as well as strengths and weaknesses of each method.

6. How do genes, shared environmental, and nonshared environmental factors contribute to individual differences?

7. How do genes and environments contribute to individual differences in intellectual ability, personality and temperament, and psychological disorders?

8. What are three ways that genes and environments correlate to influence behavior?

CHAPTER SUMMARY AND GUIDED REVIEW

The following summary provides an overview of the main points contained in this chapter of the text. Fill-in the blanks with terms that appropriately complete the sentence. Scattered throughout the summary are questions in parentheses. These are meant to encourage you to think actively as you are reading and connect this summary to the more detailed information provided in the text. You can answer these questions as you are filling in the blanks or you can fill-in all the blanks, then go back and reread the entire summary, addressing the questions in order to provide more depth of understanding.

EVOLUTION AND SPECIES HEREDITY

Although people are quite different from one another, (1) _species heredity_ ensures that all members of a species share some commonalities. (***Can you provide examples of this common genetic endowment in humans?***) Charles Darwin's theory of evolution tries to explain how characteristics of species change or evolve over generations. His theory has three main points:

- Members of a species have different (2) _genes_ .
- Some genes are more adaptive than others.
- Those genes that are more adaptive will be passed along to offspring more so than genes that are less adaptive. This is the principle of (3) _natural selection_ .

Genes that are adaptive in one environment may not be adaptive in another environment.

INDIVIDUAL HEREDITY

Genes can contribute to differences between individuals through the process of individual heredity.

The Genetic Code

At conception, a woman's egg cell is fertilized by a man's sperm, resulting in a (4) _zygote_ . This new cell has 46 threadlike (5) _chromosomes_ , each made up of thousands of (6) _genes_ or segments of DNA molecules. Our understanding of genetics has been greatly enhanced by the (7) _human genome project_ designed to decipher the genetic code.

The single cell formed at conception begins to divide through a process called (8) _mitosis_ , which results in daughter cells with the same 46 chromosomes as the mother cell. The sperm and ova result from the process of (9) _meiosis_ so that they each have only 23, or half, of the original cell's chromosomes.

Although biological siblings share the same parents, their genetic makeup is unique, partly due to the phenomenon of (10) _crossing over_ in which parts of chromosomes are exchanged during cell division. Twins that are (11) _identical_ are exceptions because they develop from one zygote and so share 100% of their genes. On the other hand, twins that result from two separate ova fertilized by different sperm, called (12) _fraternal_ , are no more genetically similar than siblings. Siblings and fraternal twins share, on the average, half of their genes.

A child's sex is determined by whether or not the sperm that fertilizes the egg carries an X or Y chromosome. A female chromosome pattern is (13) _2X_ a male chromosome pattern is (14) _1X and 1Y_ .

Translation of the Genetic Code

Genes provide a flexible (15) _blueprint_ for development. Environmental factors exert a strong influence on how genes are expressed. A person's genetic makeup is called their (16) _genotype_ , while the actual outward characteristics a person shows are part of their (17) _phenotype_ .

Mechanisms of Inheritance

There are three main mechanisms of inheritance. One way to inherit is through a single pair of genes. Each gene of the pair can be either dominant or (18) _recessive_ . If one gene in the pair is (19) ___dominant___, the characteristic associated with this gene will express itself. In order for a (20) ___recessive___ trait to express itself, a person would need to receive a matched pair, one from each parent. (***What is an example of this?***)

Another pattern of inheritance occurs when a dominant gene in a pair does not completely mask the effects of the recessive gene. This pattern is called (21) ___incomplete dominance___. If neither gene dominates the other but both influence a trait, (22) ___codominance___ is said to be operating. (***Can you provide examples of characteristics inherited through each of these mechanisms?***)

Some traits are influenced by genes on the sex chromosomes, rather than on the other 22 pairs of chromosomes and are called (23) ___sex-linked___. (***Why are males more likely than females to inherit a trait through this mechanism?***) Many human characteristics are influenced by more than one pair of genes and so are transmitted through the mechanism of (24) ___polygenic___ inheritance. (***Can you provide examples of characteristics inherited through this mechanism?***)

Mutations

Occasionally, a new gene appears that was not passed from parent to child, but results from a mutation. Some mutations are actually beneficial and become more common through the process of (25) ___natural selection___. (***What is an example of a trait that probably started as a result of mutation?***)

Chromosome Abnormalities

Down syndrome is an example of a chromosomal abnormality that results from an extra (26) ___21___ chromosome. (***Why are older women at greater risk for having a child with chromosomal abnormalities such as Down syndrome?***) Females with a missing X chromosome have a condition known as (27) ___Turner___ syndrome. Males who inherit an extra X chromosome are said to have (28) ___Klinefelter___ syndrome. (***What characteristics are associated with each of these chromosomal abnormalities?***) A common sex-linked disorder that causes mental retardation is (29) ___fragile X syndrome___.

Genetic Diagnosis and Counseling

Genetic counseling provides information to parents who are concerned about the possibility of genetic birth defects. Genetic disorders that they might be tested for include (30) ___sickle cell___ disease, a recessive disorder that results from odd-shaped blood cells that deliver less oxygen than normal cells, leading to a number of debilitating symptoms. Individuals who have one dominant and one recessive gene for a recessive trait or disorder are called (31) ___carriers___. They do not express the trait but can pass it on to their offspring. Another disorder that parents might be concerned about is (32) ___Huntington's___ disease, caused by a single dominant gene and associated with motor problems, personality changes, and cognitive declines. (***What are the pros and cons of these screening techniques?***)

Prenatal detection of abnormalities often begins with an (33) ___ultrasound___, which constructs a visual image of the fetus by passing sound waves over the womb. In another procedure called (34) ___amniocentesis___, fetal cells are extracted from amniotic fluid and analyzed for chromosomal abnormalities. Similar information can be gained from a procedure called (35) ___Chorionic villus sampling___ in which fetal cells are extracted from the chorion membrane surrounding the fetus. For some couples, preimplantation genetic diagnosis can be used to screen for genetic abnormalities and then a healthy egg can be selected and implanted.

STUDYING GENETIC AND ENVIRONMENTAL INFLUENCES

The field of study concerned with the extent to which genetic and environmental differences among people are responsible for differences in their traits is (36) behavioral genetics Behavior geneticists often use (37) __heritability__ estimates, which provide information about the amount of variability between people that can be attributed to the genetic differences among those people. Even traits that are highly heritable are still influenced by environmental factors.

Experimental Breeding

One way to study the influence of genes on animal behavior is to deliberately mate animals and see whether certain traits are more or less likely following this (38) __selective breeding__. (*What have researchers learned from doing these sorts of studies?*)

Twin, Adoption, and Family Studies

Experimental breeding cannot be used with humans, so researchers use twin and adoption studies to study the influences of genes and environments. (*Can you identify some cautions regarding interpretation of findings from twin and adoption studies?*) If heredity influences a trait, (39) __identical__ twins should be more similar on the trait than (40) __fraternal__ twins. If adopted children resemble their adoptive parents more than they resemble their biological parents on some trait, then the trait must be influenced by (41) __environmental__ factors.

Estimating Influences

To estimate the influence of genetic and environmental factors on traits, researchers may calculate the (42) __concordance__ rate, which indicates the percentage of pairs who both have the trait if one of them has it. They may also use (43) correlation coefficients for traits that vary numerically, such as height or intelligence.

Behavioral geneticists try to estimate how various factors contribute to individual differences observed in a trait. Some variation may occur because of (44) __gene__ differences, as would be evident from findings showing that identical twins score more similarly on a trait than do fraternal twins. The fact that siblings raised together in the same home score more similarly on a trait than siblings raised apart would indicate the influence of the shared (45) __environment__. Finding that genetically identical pairs who are raised together are not perfectly similar would indicate the influence of (46) __nonshared__ factors.

Molecular Genetics

Molecular genetics is the analysis of specific genes and their effects. A major goal of molecular genetics is to determine how much variation in a trait is due to genes and how much is due to environment. For example, researchers are studying the apoE gene, which has been linked to (47) Alzheimer's disease.

ACCOUNTING FOR INDIVIDUAL DIFFERENCES

Intellectual Abilities

Research on intellectual abilities shows the influence of genes, the shared and nonshared environment. (***Can you describe the patterns of these findings?***) Identical twins tend to become more similar to one another in mental ability after 18 months of age and tend to follow the same course of mental development. Fraternal twins tend to become less similar to one another over the years. (***Can you explain why this pattern emerges?***) Overall, research shows that the most important environmental influence is the (48) _nonshared_ component.

Temperament and Personality

The tendency to respond in predictable ways is called temperament and is considered a precursor to later personality. Individual differences in temperament during infancy seem to be related to (49) _genetic_ differences among infants. In addition, the influence of (50) _nonshared_ environmental factors contribute to individual differences in temperament. (***What pattern of findings would support this conclusion?***) These influences help explain why siblings, who share, on average, 50% of their genes and grow up in the same home can be so different.

Psychological Disorders

Psychological problems are also influenced by genetic and environmental factors. Some individuals may be genetically predisposed to (51) _schizophrenia_, which involves disturbances in logical thinking and behavior. Psychological disorders are not inherited directly; people inherit (52) _predispositions_ to develop traits.

The Heritability of Different Traits

Although all traits are influenced to some extent by genes, some traits are more heritable than others. (***Which traits are more or less heritable?***)

Influences on Heritability

Estimates of heritability vary depending on the sample studied. Age and socioeconomic status influence heritability.

HEREDITY AND ENVIRONMENT CONSPIRING

Genes operate throughout a person's life span, interacting with environmental factors. Modern psychologists examine <u>how</u> heredity and environment work together.

Gene/Environment Interactions

The expression of a person's genotype depends on the person's environment, and how people respond to their environment depends on their genotype.

Gene/Environment (g/e) Correlations

There are three models for how genes and environments are correlated. In a (53) _passive_ g/e correlation, the child and the child's environment are both influenced by the parents' genotypes. In an (54) _evocative_ g/e correlation, a child's (55) _genotype_ triggers certain responses from other people. In an (56) _active_ g/e correlation, children actively seek out (57) _environments_ that suit their particular genotype. (***Can you provide examples of each type of correlation?***)

Genetic Influences on the Environment

Research shows that individuals can actively shape their environments, which in turn, influence them. Environmental and genetic factors constantly influence one another and are influenced by the other. Research on gene/environment correlations, summarized in the book *The Relationship Code*, suggests that the family is a vehicle for expressing the common genetic code of family members. ***(Can you give an example that illustrates what this means?)***

Controversies Surrounding Genetic Research

Some experts worry about potential dangers arises from genetic technology, such as cloning, or attempting to improve the human race by altering genetic traits. Others believe that the benefits of gene technology outweigh the pitfalls.

REVIEW OF KEY TERMS

Below is a list of terms and concepts from this chapter. Use these to complete the following sentence definitions. You might also want to try writing definitions in your own words and then checking your definitions with those in the text.

amniocentesis
behavioral genetics
carrier
chorionic villus sampling (CVS)
chromosome
chromosome abnormalities
codominance
conception
concordance rate
crossing over
cystic fibrosis
dominant gene
Down syndrome
Fragile X syndrome
fraternal twins
gene/environment correlation
gene/environment interaction
gene
gene therapy
genetic counseling
genotype
hemophilia
heritability
Human Genome Project
Huntington's disease
identical twins
incomplete dominance

karyotype
Klinefelter syndrome
meiosis
mitosis
molecular genetics
mutation
natural selection
nonshared environmental influences
phenotype
phenylketonuria (PKU)
polygenic trait
preimplantation genetic diagnosis
recessive gene
schizophrenia
selective breeding
sex-linked characteristic
shared environmental influences
sickle-cell disease
single gene-pair inheritance
species heredity
Tay-Sachs disease
temperament
Turner syndrome
ultrasound
X chromosome
Y chromosome
zygote

1. A person's _genotype_ consists of their genetic makeup.

2. Threadlike structures containing genetic material are called _chromosomes_.

3. A fertilized egg cell is a _zygote_.

4. The genetic endowment common to all members of a particular species is _species heredity_

5. Two individuals who develop as a result of one fertilized egg splitting in two are called _identical twins_.

6. _chromosome abnormalities_ occur when a child receives too many or too few chromosomes at conception.

7. A common caused of mental retardation resulting from an abnormality on the X chromosome is called _Fragile X syndrome_

8. The gene in a dissimilar pair that typically does not express itself in that person's phenotype is called the _recessive gene_.

9. The presence of the _Y chromosome_ determines whether the child will be male or female.

10. The field of _molecular genetics_ involves the analysis of specific genes and their effects.

11. Interventions that somehow alter a person's genetic makeup constitute _gene therapy_.

12. Two individuals who developed at the same time but from two different fertilized eggs are _fraternal twins_

13. The gene in a dissimilar pair that usually expresses itself phenotypically is called the _dominant gene_.

14. Cell division that results in two cells identical to the one original cell occurs through the process of _mitosis_.

15. Some couples undergo _preimplantation genetic diagnosis_ so that their physician can select and then implant only fertilized eggs that do not have chromosomal or genetic abnormalities.

16. A person's _phenotype_ reflects the expression of their genotype in conjunction with environmental influences.

17. According to _natural selection_, genes that promote adaptation to one's environment will be passed to offspring more often than genes that do not promote adaptation.

18. The moment when a woman's egg is fertilized by a man's sperm is called _conceptance_.

19. _Schizophrenia_ is a disorder involving disturbances in logical thinking, emotional expression and social behavior.

20. In a procedure called _amniocentesis_, fetal cells are removed from the amniotic sac by inserting a needle through the mother's abdomen in order to test chromosomal makeup.

21. The basic units of heredity are _genes_.

22. _Down syndrome_ is a chromosome disorder resulting from an extra 21st chromosome.

23. A female who receives only one X chromosome has a condition called _Turner syndrome_.

24. A _gene/environment correlation_ refers to the interrelationship between one's genes and one's environment.

25. _Genetic counseling_ provides information to people regarding the likelihood of genetically based problems in their unborn children.

26. A disorder resulting in dementia, emotional problems, loss of motor control, and premature death is _Huntington's disease_.

27. Cell division that results in four cells, each with half the number of chromosomes as in the one original cell, occurs through the process of _meiosis_.

28. According to the concept of _gene/environment interaction_, the influence of our genes depends on the experiences we have, and the experiences we have depend on the genes we have.

29. A _karyotype_ is a photograph of an individual's chromosomes organized into groups.

30. Experiences that are unique to an individual are called _nonshared environmental influences_

31. _Crossing over_ is a phenomenon in which parts of chromosomes are exchanged during cell division.

32. A _mutation_ results in a change in the structure or arrangement of one or more genes, resulting in a new phenotype.

33. _Single gene-pair inheritance_ occurs when one pair of genes determines the presence or absence of a trait.

34. A disorder in which blood cells cluster together and distribute less oxygen than normal cells is _Sickle-cell disease_

35. A male who receives an extra X chromosome has a condition called _Klinefelter syndrome_

36. _Shared environmental experiences_ are experiences that individuals have in common because they live in the same home environment.

37. In the inheritance pattern of _incomplete dom._, the dominant gene in a pair is not able to totally mask the effects of the recessive gene.

38. The _heritability_ statistic represents the amount of variability in a trait within a large group of people that can be linked to genetic differences among those people.

39. _Selective breeding_ involves deliberately mating animals with certain genotypes in order to determine if it is possible to produce offspring with certain characteristics.

40. In the inheritance pattern of _codominance_, neither gene in a pair is able to completely dominate the other and both express themselves.

41. A trait that is influenced by single genes located on the sex chromosomes is referred to as a _sex-linked characteristic_

42. A characteristic that is influenced by multiple genes is called a _polygenic trait_

43. Individuals who are _carriers_ do not express a trait but can pass the trait on to their offspring.

44. _PKU_ is a disorder in which a critical enzyme needed to metabolize phenylalanine is missing.

45. In a procedure called _CVS_, fetal cells from the chorion are removed by inserting a catheter through the mother's vagina in order to test chromosomal makeup.

46. The _X chromosome_ is a sex chromosome that, when matched with another like it, results in a female child.

47. The tendency to respond in predictable ways is part of a person's _temperament_.

48. _Concordance rate_ represents the probability that one of a pair of twins will show a given characteristic, given that the other twin has the characteristic.

49. A genetic disorder that causes gradual deterioration of the nervous system is called _Tay-Sachs disease_

50. A(n) _ultrasound_ is a procedure to detect fetal growth and characteristics by passing sound waves over the mother's abdomen.

51. _Behavioral genetics_ refers to the scientific study of the extent to which genetic and environmental differences within a species are responsible for differences in traits.

52. _cystic fibrosis_ is a disease that leads to a buildup of sticky mucus in the lungs, shortening a person's life span.

53. A sex-linked disorder that limits the blood's ability to clot is called _hemophilia_.

54. The _Human Genome Project_ is a massive attempt to decipher the human genetic code.

MULTIPLE CHOICE SELF TEST

For each multiple choice question, read all alternatives and then select the best answer.

1. All children tend to walk and talk at about 12 months of age. This universal pattern of development results from
   a. the crossing over phenomenon.
   b. societal expectations.
   c. species heredity.
   d. single gene-pair inheritance.

2. A zygote
   a. merges with a sperm cell at conception to form a fertilized cell.
   b. is a cell that will split and develop into fraternal twins.
   c. contains only the sex chromosomes.
   d. is a fertilized egg cell.

3. A person's phenotype is most accurately described as
   a. a person's genetic inheritance.
   b. the outcome of the interaction between a person's genotype and a particular environment.
   c. the result of the union between a sperm cell and egg cell.
   d. those characteristics that do not have a genetic basis.

4. Suppose two people are carriers for thin lips, which is a recessive trait. Each one of their children would have a _____ chance of expressing this trait in their phenotype.
    a. 25%
    b. 50%
    c. 75%
    d. 100%

5. Incomplete dominance results when
    a. two different genes in a pair are both expressed in a compromise of the two genes.
    b. one gene in a pair cannot completely mask the effects of the other gene.
    c. several gene pairs contribute to the expression of a trait.
    d. both parents are carriers for a particular trait.

6. A person is a carrier for a genetic disorder if she/he
    a. does not show the disorder and cannot pass on the disorder to offspring.
    b. does not show the disorder but can pass on the disorder to offspring.
    c. shows the disorder but cannot pass on the disorder to offspring.
    d. shows the disorder and can pass on the disorder to offspring.

7. In X-linked traits
    a. males and females are equally likely to express (i.e., have or show) the trait.
    b. males are carriers of the trait but do not always express the trait.
    c. females can express the trait but do so much less often than males.
    d. females and males typically carry but do not express the trait.

8. Down syndrome occurs when
    a. a child receives too few chromosomes.
    b. a male receives an extra X chromosome.
    c. there is an abnormality associated with one of the sex chromosomes.
    d. a child receives an extra 21st chromosome.

9. Heritability refers to
    a. the amount of variability in a group's trait that is due to genetic differences between people in the group.
    b. the degree to which an individual's characteristics are determined by genetics.
    c. the degree of relationship between pairs of individuals.
    d. a person's genetic makeup.

10. Some people have criticized the logic of twin studies because
    a. identical twins are always the same biological sex while fraternal twins are not.
    b. identical twins are more likely to participate in this type of study than fraternals.
    c. identical twins are treated more similarly than fraternal twins, making it difficult to separate environmental from genetic factors.
    d. it is not always possible to accurately identify twins as fraternal or identical.

11. Which of the following statements is FALSE regarding genetics and intellectual ability?
    a. Intellectual development in infancy is only weakly influenced by individual heredity and environment.
    b. Identical twins become more similar with age in their intellectual performance while fraternal twins become less similar.
    c. Both identical and fraternal twins become more similar in intellectual performance with increasing age.
    d. Genes influence the <u>course</u> of intellectual development.

12. With regard to individual differences in intellectual ability, research suggests that
    a. genes, shared environmental influences, and nonshared environmental influences contribute equally across the life span.
    b. shared environmental influences have the greatest impact at all stages of the life span.
    c. genetic influences become more influential and shared environmental influences become less influential with age.
    d. shared and nonshared environmental influences become more influential and genes become less influential with age.

13. The concept of an evocative genotype/environment correlation suggests that
    a. parents select environments for their children and their selection is determined by genetic factors.
    b. children's genotypes trigger certain reactions from other people.
    c. children seek out environments that suit their particular genotypes.
    d. genotypes limit the range of possible phenotypic outcomes.

14. Research shows that
    a. people directly inherit many psychological disorders.
    b. people inherit predispositions to develop psychological disorders.
    c. psychological disorders have no genetic basis.
    d. having a parent with a psychological disorder means that the child of that person will also have the disorder.

15. The goals of genetic counseling include all of the following EXCEPT
    a. identify traits that parents might be carrying.
    b. calculate probabilities that a particular trait might be transmitted to children.
    c. make decisions for the couple about whether to terminate or continue a pregnancy.
    d. provide information about characteristics and treatment of genetic disorders.

REVIEW GENETIC AND ENVIRONMENTAL CONTRIBUTIONS TO TRAITS

This exercise helps you interpret data concerning genetic and environmental contributions to human traits. Review the section on "Intellectual Abilities" on page 72 of the text and take a look at the following table of correlations on intelligence scores (from Table 3.4 of the text) to help answer the questions.

1. Which correlation(s) show a genetic influence? Would you characterize this influence as slight, moderate, or strong? Why?

2. Which correlation(s) show the influence of the environment on intelligence? Would you characterize this influence as slight, moderate, or strong? Why?

3. Are genetic or environmental forces more evident in IQ differences? Use the correlations to support your answer.

4. How do shared and nonshared environmental influences on intelligence change across the lifespan?

5. Do genetic influences on variations in IQ increase or decrease with age?

Relationship between pairs	Raised together	Raised apart
Identical Twins	.86	.72
Fraternal Twins	.60	.52
Biological Parent & Child	.42	.22
Adopted Parent & Child	.19	—

CRITICAL THINKING QUESTIONS

By answering the following questions, you will strengthen your understanding of the material in this chapter. These questions require higher level thinking skills such as integration and application of concepts. Sample answers are provided for three of the questions. These illustrate one possibility, but there are other answers you could provide that might be just as good. For the other questions, you can check yourself by referring to the text (a hint is provided), or by asking a peer or your instructor to review your answer.

1. Consider a characteristic such as humor. What evidence would you need to collect to convince someone that this trait is influenced by genetic factors? What evidence would you need to show the effects of shared and nonshared environmental influences on humor?
[Sample answer provided.]

2. How can you account for the findings that identical twins become more similar to one another in mental ability as they get older, and fraternal twins become less similar to one another in mental ability as they get older?
    [Sample answer provided.]

3. What measures are currently available to screen for chromosomal and genetic abnormalities? Evaluate the pros and cons of these techniques for couples considering having a baby.
    [Sample answer provided.]

4. How can you explain the intriguing finding that siblings, who share some common genetic material and who grow up in the same home, turn out to have such different personalities?
    [Hint: Review the section in the text on "Temperament and personality."]

5. How can genes influence the environments that people live in and how can environments influence genes?
    [Review the section on "Heredity and environment conspiring."]

ANSWERS

Chapter Summary and Guided Review (Fill-in the blank)

1.	species heredity	24.	polygenic
2.	genes or genetic make-ups	25.	natural selection
3.	natural selection	26.	21st
4.	zygote	27.	Turner
5.	chromosomes	28.	Klinefelter
6.	genes	29.	Fragile-X syndrome
7.	Human Genome Project	30.	sickle cell
8.	mitosis	31.	carriers
9.	meiosis	32.	Huntington's
10.	crossing over	33.	ultrasound
11.	identical	34.	amniocentesis
12.	fraternal	35.	chorionic villus sampling (CVS)
13.	2 X	36.	behavioral genetics
14.	1 X and 1 Y	37.	heritability
15.	blueprint	38.	selective breeding
16.	genotype	39.	identical
17.	phenotype	40.	fraternal
18.	recessive	41.	environmental
19.	dominant	42.	concordance
20.	recessive	43.	correlation coefficients
21.	incomplete dominance	44.	genetic
22.	codominance	45.	shared environment
23.	sex-linked	46.	nonshared environmental

47.	Alzheimer's disease	53.	passive
48.	nonshared	54.	evocative
49.	genetic	55.	genotype
50.	nonshared	56.	active
51.	schizophrenia	57.	environments
52.	predispositions		

Review of Key Terms

1.	genotype	28.	gene/environment interaction
2.	chromosomes	29.	karyotype
3.	zygote	30.	nonshared environmental influences
4.	species heredity	31.	crossing over
5.	identical twins	32.	mutation
6.	chromosome abnormalities	33.	single gene-pair inheritance
7.	Fragile-X syndrome	34.	sickle cell disease
8.	recessive gene	35.	Klinefelter syndrome
9.	Y chromosome	36.	shared environmental influences
10.	molecular genetics	37.	incomplete dominance
11.	gene therapy	38.	heritability
12.	fraternal twins	39.	selective breeding
13.	dominant gene	40.	codominance
14.	mitosis	41.	sex-linked characteristic
15.	preimplantation genetic diagnosis	42.	polygenic trait
16.	phenotype	43.	carriers
17.	natural selection	44.	phenylketonuria (PKU)
18.	conception	45.	chorionic villus sampling (CVS)
19.	schizophrenia	46.	X chromosome
20.	amniocentesis	47.	temperament
21.	genes	48.	concordance rate
22.	Down syndrome	49.	Tay-Sachs disease
23.	Turner syndrome	50.	ultrasound
24.	gene/environment correlation	51.	behavioral genetics
25.	genetic counseling	52.	cystic fibrosis
26.	Huntington's disease	53.	hemophilia
27.	meiosis	54.	Human Genome Project

Multiple Choice Self Test

1.	C (p. 52)	6.	B (p. 61)	11.	C (p. 72)		
2.	D (p. 57)	7.	C (p. 62)	12.	C (p. 72)		
3.	B (p. 61)	8.	D (p. 63)	13.	B (p. 77)		
4.	A (p. 61)	9.	A (p. 68)	14.	B (p. 74)		
5.	B (p. 61)	10.	C (p. 69)	15.	C (pp. 65-66)		

Critical Thinking Questions

1.   *To show that humor is influenced by genetic factors, you could show that identical twins raised apart are similar to one another on some measure of humor, and more similar than fraternal twins or other siblings who are raised together. Because the only thing the identical twins raised apart have in common is their genetic makeup, any similarities among them must be due to their genetic similarity. One way to demonstrate influences of the shared environment is to show that sibling pairs raised together are more similar to one another than sibling pairs raised apart. The influence of nonshared environmental influences would be evident if identical twins raised together were dissimilar on humor.*

2.   *Research on intellectual ability suggests that genetic influences actually increase over the lifespan rather than decrease. During infancy, fraternal twins are about as similar to one another on mental ability as identical twins are to one another. This is true despite the fact that identical twins share 100% of the same genetic material, whereas fraternal twins share, on average, 50% of the same genetic material. Starting around 18 months of age, identical twins become more similar to one another, with correlations of about 0.85 in childhood and adolescence. In contrast, fraternal twins become less similar to one another, with correlations of about 0.54 in adolescence. This difference in the pattern of scores for fraternal and identical twins indicates that heritability of mental ability increases. Genetic differences between people in a group play a large role in observed differences in their mental ability.*

       At the same time, shared environmental influences decrease in importance across the lifespan. Siblings growing up in the same home often seem similar to one another because they are strongly influenced by their parents. Their parents determine what they wear, what their rooms look like, what they do, etc. Young children's lives are strongly controlled by their parents. But as they get older, this parental (shared environmental) influence lessens. This may happen because children begin to express their unique, and genetically influenced, personalities and intellects. They seek out environments that are most compatible with their true selves. They no longer go to music classes because their parents want them to and take them, but they sign themselves up for soccer or computer camp because that's what they enjoy or are good at. Identical twins are likely to select similar environments for themselves because the same genes are influencing their choices. Fraternal twins are less likely to seek out similar environments because of their greater genetic variability. The different experiences make fraternal twins (and other siblings) increasingly different from one another.

3.   *There are several tests used during pregnancy that can assess for some genetic conditions. Many pregnancies are monitored with ultrasound, which uses sound waves to scan the womb and create a visual image of the developing fetus. Physical abnormalities and growth problems may be detected with an ultrasound. Some women undergo amniocentesis in which a needle is inserted into the abdomen and cells are extracted from the amniotic fluid. These cells can be examined microscopically to determine the sex of the fetus as well as abnormalities of the chromosomes. Amniocentesis, for example, can indicate whether a fetus has the normal array of 46 chromosomes, arranged in 23 pairs. A third 21st chromosome indicates the presence of Down Syndrome. Because of safety concerns, amniocentesis can't be performed until at least the fifteenth week of pregnancy. The same information can be derived a little earlier in pregnancy by using chorionic villus sampling, which involves collecting cells from the chorion by going through the mother's vagina and cervix. For parents who are worried that they will pass along*

a known genetic defect to their children, preimplantation genetic diagnosis is an option. This involves fertilizing an egg with a sperm in a laboratory and then conducting DNA tests on the fertilized egg. Eggs that don't contain the genetic abnormality can then be implanted in the mother's womb. Many people have concerns about preimplantation genetic diagnosis because parents might use it just to eliminate traits they don't like rather than traits that are life-threatening or harmful. Testing the mother's blood might also yield some information about fetal development. The mother's blood might contain fetal cells that have slipped through the placenta, but then again, it might not, or it might contain cells from a previous pregnancy. This form of testing is best when combined with other indicators of genetic defects.

CHAPTER FOUR

PRENATAL DEVELOPMENT AND BIRTH

OVERVIEW

This chapter begins by discussing the dramatic changes that take place during the prenatal period and the environmental factors that can influence prenatal development. These include maternal conditions such as age, emotional state and nutritional condition, and outside factors—called teratogens—that can adversely affect development. The environment surrounding birth (the perinatal period) is also discussed, with attention to complicating factors and to the parent's experience of the birth process. As you read about all the things that could potentially harm a developing fetus, keep in mind that the vast majority of pregnancies and deliveries are normal, with no complications. Finally, the early environment of the infant (the neonatal period) is considered, including risks to development such as low-birth-weight as well as factors associated with resilience.

LEARNING OBJECTIVES

After reading and studying the material in this chapter, you should be able to answer the following questions.

1.   How does development proceed during the prenatal period? How does prenatal behavior of the fetus relate to postnatal behavior of the infant?

2.   How do mother's age, emotional state, and nutrition affect prenatal and neonatal development?

3.   How and when do various teratogens affect the developing fetus?

4.   What is the perinatal environment like? What hazards can occur during the birth process?

5.   What is the birth experience like from the mother's and father's perspectives, and from different cultural perspectives?

6.   To what extent are the effects of the prenatal and perinatal environments long lasting? What factors influence whether effects are lasting?

CHAPTER SUMMARY AND GUIDED REVIEW

The following summary provides an overview of the main points contained in this chapter of the text. Fill-in the blanks with terms that appropriately complete the sentence. Scattered throughout the summary are questions in parentheses. These are meant to encourage you to think actively as you are reading and connect this summary to the more detailed information provided in the text. You can answer these questions as you are filling in the blanks or you can complete all the blanks, then go back and reread the entire summary, addressing the questions in order to provide more depth of understanding.

PRENATAL DEVELOPMENT
The mother's womb is the physical environment prior to birth. The prenatal environment can have lasting effects on development, both negative and positive.

Conception
    Conception occurs when a sperm fertilizes an egg cell, forming a single cell called a
(1) _____, which begins to divide and replicate.

Prenatal Stages
    Prenatal development is divided into three stages. The first is the
(2) _____ period, which lasts from conception until implantation of the
(3) _____ in the wall of the uterus. At this point, the period of the
(4) _____ begins and lasts through the eighth week of prenatal development.
During this time, every major organ forms in a process called (5) _____.
The layers of the embryo become distinct, with an outer layer forming the amnion and the
(6) _____, which attaches to the uterine wall. Eventually, this becomes the
lining of the (7) _____, a tissue that is fed by blood vessels from the mother.
This tissue connects the embryo to the (8) _____, and together these structures
provide nutrients and oxygen for the embryo. The brain begins to emerge at 3-4 weeks when the
neural plate folds up to form the (9) _____. Problems with this process can
lead to (10) _____ in which the spinal cord is not fully encased by the
protective spinal column.
    The process of sexual differentiation begins during the seventh and eighth prenatal weeks
with development of male testes or female ovaries from an undifferentiated tissue. The testes

will then secrete (11) _____, which will stimulate development of a male internal reproduction system, or in its absence, the internal reproduction system of a female.

The third stage of prenatal development is the (12) _____, which lasts from the ninth week of pregnancy until birth. The number of neurons increases dramatically during this period. They migrate to their final location and take on specialized functions. Before becoming specialized, cells are called (13) _____ and have the potential to take on any function. At about 24 weeks, the fetus may be able to survive outside the womb, making this the age of (14) _____. The last trimester brings rapid weight gain for the fetus; brain cells increase in number and size and some develop an insulating cover called (15) _____. Fetal behavior becomes increasingly organized, resembling organized patterns of waking and sleeping known as (16) _____. Prenatal behavior patterns correlate with later infant patterns, demonstrating continuity in development.

PRENATAL ENVIRONMENT
Teratogens
A teratogen is any environmental agent that can produce abnormalities in a developing fetus. A time when the developing embryo or fetus is particularly sensitive to environmental influences is called a (17) critical period. Effects of teratogens are worse with greater exposure. Outcomes are influenced by genetic makeup as well as quality of pre- and post- natal environments.

One category of teratogens includes drugs. A mild tranquilizer called (18) thalidomide, which was used years ago to combat morning sickness, caused serious deformities that varied depending on when the drug was taken during pregnancy. Smoking, and even exposure to second-hand smoke, can lead to growth retardation and other developmental delays. Smoking also increases the risk of (19) sudden infant death syndrome Children whose mothers drank alcohol during pregnancy may exhibit a cluster of symptoms called (20) fetal alcohol syndrome. There is no known amount of alcohol that is entirely safe to consume during pregnancy, although the severity of FAS symptoms depends on the amount of alcohol consumed. The illegal drug (21) cocaine also leads to a number of prenatal and postnatal complications, including possible long-term deficits in cognitive, language, and social development. (*What other environmental conditions or maternal conditions can adversely affect prenatal development?*)

Like drugs consumed prenatally, diseases can also adversely affect development. German measles or (22) rubella is a disease that is most damaging to the developing organism during the first trimester and can cause a variety of defects. A sexually transmitted disease called (23) syphilis results in similar problems but has its greatest impact on development during the middle and later stages of pregnancy. Another sexually transmitted disease is (24) AIDS and can be passed from mother to infant prior to, during, or after birth.

A number of environmental hazards, such as radiation and pollutants, can also adversely affect prenatal development. Some pollutants known to be hazardous have been restricted, but still exist in the environment. For example, older houses may expose children to high levels of (25) lead in paint.

The Mother's State

A number of factors associated with the prenatal environment can influence growth and development. Mothers who are younger than 17 years or older than about 40 years are more likely to experience complications. (***What is one possible reason for this increased risk associated with mother's age?***) Mothers who experience prolonged and severe (26) __emotional stress__ during their pregnancies increase the risk of harm to the fetus. (***What mechanisms might explain how this factor influences fetal development?***) Maternal nutrition can also impact negatively on the developing fetus, particularly if malnutrition occurs during the (27) __first__ trimester of pregnancy.

The Father's State

A father's (28) __age__ can influence the quality and quantity of his sperm, leading to fertility problems and genetic defects.

PERINATAL ENVIRONMENT

The perinatal environment is the environment surrounding birth and includes drugs administered to the mother, delivery practices, and the immediate social environment following birth. Birth consists of three stages that are, in order of occurrence, (29) _____, (30) _____, and (31) _____.

Possible Hazards

During birth, lack of adequate oxygen or (32) _____ can result in brain damage or a neurological condition called (33) _____ that is associated with trouble controlling muscle movements. (***What are some of the potential outcomes for an infant/child who experienced lack of oxygen at birth?***) Another birth complication can result if the fetus is not positioned in the typical head-down position, but instead is positioned feet or buttocks first, called a (34) _____ presentation. Some fetuses are delivered by a (35) _____ in which an incision is made in the mother's abdomen and uterus so that the fetus can be removed. Delivery methods and medications administered to the mother during delivery can impact on the outcome of the delivery process.

The Mother's Experience

The cultural and social environment surrounding birth can have an impact on mother's experience of birth. Mothers who receive (36) _____ and are prepared for the birth generally have a more positive experience than other mothers.

Some mothers may experience (37) _____, or feelings of sadness, irritability, and depression following a birth. (***What are possible explanations for these feelings, and what are the effects on the infant?***)

The Father's Experience

Like mothers, fathers experience the birth of a baby as a significant life event, and often feel stressed during delivery and engrossed by the baby after birth.

NEONATAL ENVIRONMENT

The first month after birth is referred to as the (38) _____ period.

There are large cultural differences in how parents interact with their babies during this period.

Identifying At-Risk Newborns

Some newborns are thought to be (39) _____ or in jeopardy for some reason. To measure general well-being of an infant, the (40) _____ test is administered immediately and at five minutes after birth. (**Can you list the five characteristics assessed by this test?**)

One group of at-risk infants are those born small or with (41) _____. Low birth weight is associated with certain teratogens, poverty, and births of multiples. These babies may experience respiratory problems because their premature lungs have not yet produced enough (42) _____ to function normally.

Risk and Resilience

Even if infants experience prenatal or perinatal complications, studies show that some are (43) _____; they can get back on track and develop normally. There may be some (44) _____ factors that help prevent at-risk infants from developing problems. Success seems to depend on the child's personal resources or (45) _____ makeup as well as having a favorable postnatal (46) _____. (**What does research indicate with respect to outcomes for these infants?**)

REVIEW OF KEY TERMS

Below is a list of terms and concepts from this chapter. Use these to complete the following sentence definitions. You might also want to try writing definitions in your own words and then checking your definitions with those in the text.

acquired immune deficiency syndrome (AIDS)
age of viability
amnion
anoxia
Apgar test
artificial insemination
assisted reproductive technologies (ART)
at-risk
blastocyst
breech presentation
cerebral palsy
cesarean section
chorion
critical period
embryonic period
environment
fetal alcohol syndrome (FAS)

fetal period
germinal period
infant states
in vitro fertilization (IVF)
Lamaze method
neonatal
organogenesis
perinatal period
placenta
postnatal depression
prenatal environment
protective factors
resilience
rubella
stem cells
sudden infant death syndrome (SIDS)
surfactant

syphilis   thalidomide
teratogen   umbilical cord
testosterone

1.   During the process of _____, all major organs begin to take shape.

2.   _____ refers to the tendency to get back on track and recover from early
      disadvantages.

3.   Thalidomide is the name of a mild tranquilizer that, when taken during pregnancy,
      results in birth defects.

4.   Symptoms in children whose mothers drank alcohol during their pregnancy are
      collectively referred to as FAS.

5.   Organized sleep-wake patterns of babies are called _____.

6.   Often caused by anoxia, _____ is a neurological problem associated with
      trouble controlling muscle movements.

7.   The _____ is the third prenatal phase, lasting from the ninth week until birth.

8.   Personal resources and supportive environment are two types of _____ that
      may prevent developmental problems.

9.   Failure of the respiratory system causing the death of a sleeping baby is known as
      SIDS.

10.   Before cells become specialized for particular functions, they are known as
      _____ and are capable of developing into any type of cell.

11.   A substance that helps infants breathe by preventing the air sacs of the lungs from
      sticking together is _____.

12.   In a procedure called _____, sperm are injected into a woman's uterus.

13.   In a procedure called _____, sperm fertilize eggs in a laboratory and are then
      placed in a woman's uterus.

14.   The _____ is the first prenatal period, lasting from conception to
      implantation of the blastula in the wall of the uterus.

15.   _____ is a membrane surrounding the amnion that attaches to the uterine
      lining to gather nourishment for the embryo.

16. The point at about 24 weeks prenatal development when survival outside the uterus may be possible is the _age of viability_

17. The weeks following the birth of a baby is referred to as the _____ period.

18. The disease caused by the HIV virus that destroys the immune system is called

_____.

19. A period of time during which the developing organism is particularly sensitive to environmental influences is a _critical period_

20. ___Rubella___ is a viral infection that can cause a number of serious birth defects if contracted by the mother during the first trimester of pregnancy.

21. The primary male hormone secreted by the testes is _testosterone_.

22. _____ is a hollow ball of cells formed from the repeated cell division of the zygote.

23. _____ is any environmental agent that can produce abnormalities in a developing embryo or fetus.

24. A test used to assess the newborn's heart rate, respiration, color, muscle tone, and reflexes immediately after and five minutes after birth is the _____.

25. _____ consists of a cluster of symptoms, including feelings of sadness, irritability, resentment, and depression, that some new mothers experience shortly after a birth.

26. The physical environment of the womb is the _prenatal environment_

27. _Umbilical cord_ is a tissue connecting the mother and embryo that provides oxygen and nutrients and eliminates waste products.

28. _____ is a fluid-filled, watertight membrane surrounding the embryo.

29. ___Syphilis___ is a sexually transmitted disease that is most damaging during the middle and later stages of pregnancy and can result in blindness, deafness, heart problems, or brain damage.

30. In a _____, a baby is born feet or buttocks first.

31. The time frame of events surrounding birth is referred to as the _____.

32. The _____ connects the embryo to the placenta, and contains blood vessels that nourish the fetus and eliminate wastes.

33. _____ refers to lack of adequate oxygen to the brain, which can result in brain damage.

34. _____ is the second prenatal period, lasting from implantation of the blastula to the end of the eighth week of prenatal development.

35. Some babies are delivered by _____, a surgical procedure in which an incision is made in the mother's abdomen and uterus so that the baby can be removed.

36. _____ is a method of prepared childbirth in which parents learn a set of mental exercises and relaxation techniques.

37. Infants who are thought to be likely candidates for developing problems make-up the category of _____ infants.

MULTIPLE CHOICE SELF TEST

For each multiple choice question, read all alternatives and then select the best answer.

1. Research on reproductive technologies shows that children who are born as a result of their parents using one of these procedures:
   a. are more likely to be low birth weight or premature than other children.
   b. are more likely to be resentful about their atypical origins.
   c. have parents who are more stressed and negative about their circumstances.
   d. are equal to other groups of children in emotional adjustment and other developmental outcomes.

2. The single cell that is formed by the union of a sperm cell and egg cell is called a(n)
   a. blastocyst.
   b. embryo.
   c. zygote.
   d. germ cell.

3. All major organs begin to form between the second and the eighth week after conception. This period of time is called the
   a. embryonic period.
   b. germinal period.
   c. fetal period.
   d. age of viability.

4.   The placental barrier
   a.   supports the developing embryo with oxygen and nutrients from the mother.
   b.   blocks dangerous substances from reaching the developing embryo.
   c.   allows maternal blood to pass to the developing embryo.
   d.   is replaced by the umbilical cord at the end of the germinal period.

5.   Which of the following accurately represents the process of sex differentiation during the prenatal period?
   a.   Sex differentiation is determined at conception by the inheritance of X and Y chromosomes.
   b.   Males and females begin with different tissue at conception that evolves into different reproductive systems.
   c.   Sex differentiation begins around the 7th or 8th week with the development of male and female external genitalia.
   d.   Males and females begin with identical tissue that can evolve into male or female reproductive systems depending on genetic and hormonal factors.

6.   The presence or absence of testosterone affects the process of sexual differentiation in
   a.   males only.
   b.   females only.
   c.   males and females.
   d.   neither males or females.

7.   The age of viability refers to
   a.   the age at which a woman is still able to conceive.
   b.   the point at which a fetus has a reasonable chance of survival outside the womb.
   c.   the point at which the brain and respiratory system are completely formed and functional.
   d.   the point at which all the major organs can be identified.

8.   Prolonged and severe emotional strain experienced by a mother during pregnancy can result in
   a.   a miscarriage.
   b.   prolonged and painful labor.
   c.   a baby who is irritable and has irregular habits.
   d.   all of the above.

9.   It is most important for mothers to consume ample amounts of protein, vitamins and calories during
   a.   the first trimester.
   b.   the second trimester.
   c.   the third trimester.
   d.   before becoming pregnant.

10. A critical period is a time when
    a.   a fetus can survive outside the womb.
    b.   conception occurs.
    c.   the brain forms.
    d.   a developing organ is particularly sensitive to environmental influences.

11. Mothers who contract rubella (German measles) during the first trimester of pregnancy often have children who have problems such as
    a.   deafness, blindness, heart defects, and mental retardation.
    b.   missing or malformed limbs.
    c.   small head size and malformations of face, heart, and limbs.
    d.   slow growth and low birth weight.

12. Which of the following is NOT a generalization about the effects of teratogens?
    a.   The greater the exposure to a teratogen, the more likely that serious damage will occur.
    b.   The effects of teratogens are worse during the time when organs are rapidly developing.
    c.   Effects of teratogens are not affected by the quality of the postnatal environment.
    d.   Not all fetuses are equally affected by the same teratogen.

13. Serious anoxia during the birth process is associated with
    a.   low birth weight.
    b.   cerebral palsy.
    c.   sudden infant death syndrome.
    d.   irritability at birth and mild cognitive deficits.

14. The experience of childbirth
    a.   is universal.
    b.   is influenced by cultural factors.
    c.   determines the quality of postnatal life.
    d.   can be predicted by the experience of pregnancy.

15. Longitudinal studies of at-risk babies
    a.   show that most of these babies continue to have problems throughout their lives.
    b.   show that most of these children never develop any problems regardless of their experiences.
    c.   show that babies at greater risk have a better prognosis because they receive more medical care than babies at less risk.
    d.   suggest that children can outgrow their problems when placed in favorable. environments

CRITICAL THINKING QUESTIONS

By answering the following questions, you will strengthen your understanding of the material in this chapter. These questions require higher level thinking skills such as integration and application of concepts. Sample answers are provided for three of the questions. These illustrate one possibility, but there are other answers you could provide that might be just as good. For the other questions, you can check yourself by referring to the text (a hint is provided), or by asking a peer or your instructor to review your answer.

1. What advice concerning prenatal care would you give to a woman who has just learned that she is two months pregnant? Provide justification for your answer.
   [Sample answer provided]

2. How can the material in this chapter be used to illustrate the <u>interaction</u> of nature and nurture?
   [Sample answer provided]

3. Outline the basic developments occurring during each trimester of pregnancy.
   [Sample answer provided]

3. How can we structure the environment to optimize development?
   [Hint: There is information about this throughout the chapter, including things that mothers can do (or avoid) while pregnant and things that can be done during and after birth. Also review the section on "Risk and Resilience."]

4. In 2004, a 57-year-old woman gave birth to healthy fraternal twins by cesarean section. Considering material covered in Chapters 3 and 4, what odds must have been overcome for this to have occurred?
   [Hint: You will want to review the sections on "Chromosome abnormalities" and "Genetic diagnosis and counseling" from chapter 3 as well as the sections on "Conception" and "Prenatal environment" from chapter 4. In particular, note the research on how mother's age influences her pregnancy.]

ANSWERS

Chapter Summary and Guided Review (Fill-in the blank)

1.	zygote	8.	umbilical cord
2.	germinal	9.	neural tube
3.	blastula	10.	spina bifida
4.	embryo	11.	testosterone
5.	organogenesis	12.	fetal period
6.	chorion	13.	stem cells
7.	placenta	14.	viability

15. myelin
16. infant states
17. critical period
18. thalidomide
19. sudden infant death syndrome
20. fetal alcohol syndrome
21. cocaine
22. rubella
23. syphilis
24. AIDS
25. lead
26. stress
27. third (or last)
28. age
29 contractions
30. delivery of baby

31. delivery of placenta
32. anoxia
33. cerebral palsy
34. breech
35. cesarean section
36. social support
37. postpartum depression
38. neonatal
39. at-risk
40. Apgar
41. low birth weight
42. surfactant
43. resilient
44. protective
45. genetic
46. environment

Review of Key Terms
1. organogenesis
2. resilience
3. thalidomide
4. fetal alcohol syndrome
5. infant states
6. cerebral palsy
7. fetal period
8. protective factors
9. sudden infant death syndrome
10. stem cells
11. surfactant
12. artificial insemination
13. in vitro fertilization (IVF)
14. germinal period
15. chorion
16. age of viability
17. neonatal
18. acquired immune deficiency syndrome
19. critical period

20. rubella
21. testosterone
22. blastocyst
23. teratogen
24. Apgar test
25. postpartum depression
26. prenatal environment
27. placenta
28. amnion
29. syphilis
30. breech presentation
31. perinatal period
32. umbilical cord
33. anoxia
34. embryonic period
35. cesarean section
36. Lamaze method
37. at-risk

Multiple Choice Self Test
1. D (p. 85)
2. C (pp. 85-86)
3. A (pp. 85-86)
4. A (pp. 85-86)
5. D (p. 87)

6. C (p. 87)
7. B (p. 89)
8. D (p. 99)
9. C (pp. 99-100)
10. D (p. 91)

11. A (pp. 100-102)
12. C (p. 91)
13. B (pp. 101-102)
14. B (p. 104)
15. D (pp. 106-108)

<u>Critical Thinking Questions</u>

1. *I would first note that the vast majority of pregnancies and deliveries are without complications. However, there are a number of things that a woman should be aware of that may affect prenatal development. The first three months are especially important because this is when all the major fetal organs develop (organogenesis). Diseases, such as rubella and drugs such as the prescription thalidomide or the illegal cocaine, can adversely affect the fetus, leading to long-term problems. Maternal nutrition is important, especially during the third trimester when the fetus should be putting on weight and brain development is taking place. Heavy alcohol consumption can lead to a cluster of symptoms, both physical and behavioral that can plague a child for years. Other factors can influence prenatal development, but women do not always have control of these factors, such as pollution in the air or water and their own age. Finally, these things are risk factors and do not automatically lead to developmental problems. There are large individual differences in their effects, which are influenced by the child's personal resources (e.g., genetic makeup) and the postnatal environment.*

2. *The material on prenatal development provides a good illustration of the interaction of nature and nurture. There are many environmental factors that have the potential to adversely affect development during the prenatal period. Whether, and to what extent, these factors affect a particular fetus can depend on the <u>nature</u> (e.g., the genetic makeup) of the mother and her unborn child. For example, drinking alcohol during pregnancy can have serious health consequences such as fetal alcohol syndrome (FAS). But there is no single amount of alcohol that is safe for all women. Some babies might exhibit signs of FAS after their mothers consumed small amounts of alcohol during the first trimester. Another baby may be unaffected even though his mother consumed larger amounts of alcohol throughout pregnancy. Some women and their unborn babies may have genetic makeups that are more resistant to the harmful by-products of alcohol.*

   Another example is stress. High levels of stress during pregnancy could potentially influence the growth of the fetus because stress releases different levels of hormones in the mother's body. But the same environmental stress might debilitate one woman yet have little effect on another woman. One woman may have inherited a personality that is resistant to stress—she is sturdy and stoic in the face of problems. But another woman might have inherited a personality that leads her to "fall to pieces" at the slightest problem.

   So while there are many environmental factors that could influence prenatal development, the nature of the mother and the fetus play a large role in how these factors express themselves. For this reason, it is difficult to say that one factor will affect all pregnancies the same way.

3. *Pregnancy can be divided into three trimesters and each is characterized by amazing changes in the developing child.*
First trimester
   - *Includes the germinal period*
      - *Conception (egg is fertilized by a sperm cell) and implantation into the wall of the uterus*
      - *Rapid cell division*
   - *Includes the embryonic period*

- o *Formation of all major organs during a process of organogenesis (approximately weeks 3 to 8 after conception)*
- o *Heart begins to beat*
- o *The brain is formed from the neural tube*
- o *Sexual differentiation takes place leading to different sex organs for males and females*

Second trimester
- *Continued proliferation and differentiation of neurons*
- *Fetus begins to be more active and mother may begin to feel fetal movements*
- *Sensory organs begin to function by end of second trimester*
- *Reaches the age of viability toward the end of the second trimester; survival outside the womb might be possible*

Third trimester
- *Fetus increases in size, puts on weight*
- *Much brain growth occurs during the final trimester; important neural connections are made*
- *Behavior is increasingly organized*

CHAPTER FIVE

THE PHYSICAL SELF

OVERVIEW

This chapter has a great deal of useful information about physical changes across the life span. It provides an overview of the endocrine and nervous systems, which act in concert to produce physical growth and facilitate physical behavior. You will learn that there is a tremendous amount of brain growth during the prenatal period and the first two years of life. Brain development, though, is by no means "set in stone" at the end of infancy. The brain continues to be responsive to experiences, and can change to adapt to these experiences, across the life span.

This chapter covers the maturation of the reproductive system during adolescence and its changes during adulthood. The discussion of how adolescents interpret and react to the changes of puberty is particularly interesting. Physical behaviors across the life span, including motor skills, are also explored in this chapter. One of the most valuable lessons about physical behavior may be one regarding adults: healthy, active adults show little decline in physical and psychological functioning. This contradicts stereotypes of older adults as physically unfit.

LEARNING OBJECTIVES

After reading and studying the material in this chapter, you should be able to answer the following questions.

1. How do the workings of the endocrine and nervous systems contribute to growth and development across the life span?

2. To what extent are cells responsive to the effects of experience?

3. What is lateralization? How does it affect behavior?

4. How does the brain change with aging?

5. What principles underlie growth? What are examples of each principle?

6.   What is the difference between survival and primitive reflexes? What are examples of each type of reflex? What other capabilities do newborns have?

7.   How do locomotion and manipulation of objects evolve during infancy? What factors influence the development of infant's motor skills?

8.   How are children's motor skills advanced relative to those of infants?

9.   What physical changes occur during adolescence? What factors contribute to sexual maturity of males and females? What psychological reactions accompany variations in growth spurt and the timing of puberty?

10. What physical changes occur during adulthood? What are the psychological implications of the physical changes that occur with aging?

CHAPTER SUMMARY AND GUIDED REVIEW

The following summary provides an overview of the main points contained in this chapter of the text. Fill-in the blanks with terms that appropriately complete the sentence. Scattered throughout the summary are questions in parentheses. These are meant to encourage you to think actively as you are reading and connect this summary to the more detailed information provided in the text. You can answer these questions as you are filling in the blanks or you can complete all the blanks, then go back and reread the entire summary, addressing the questions in order to provide more depth of understanding.

BUILDING BLOCKS OF GROWTH AND DEVELOPMENT

Growth is influenced by both genetic and environmental factors. Children who have been malnourished can get back of track, or experience (1) catch-up growth with appropriate treatment.

The Endocrine System

Physical development in humans is driven by the endocrine and nervous systems. The endocrine glands secrete chemical substances called (2) hormones directly into the bloodstream. These substances regulate growth and development. The

(3) ___pituitary___ gland regulates other glands and secretes
(4) ___growth___ hormone, which stimulates rapid growth and development of body cells. Growth and development are also influenced by the (5) ___thyroid___ gland.

    A male fetus develops male reproductive organs when a gene on his Y chromosome triggers development of testes, which in turn secrete a male hormone called
(6) ___testosterone___. This hormone, along with others that are collectively called
(7) ___androgens___, stimulate the adolescent growth spurt and development of male sex organs. In females, the ovaries produce larger quantities of (8) ___estrogen___, the primary female hormone, which along with progesterone, is responsible for development of female sex organs and for regulating menstrual cycles. In addition, the
(9) ___adrenal___ glands secrete androgen-like hormones that contribute to the maturation of bones and muscles.

The Nervous System
    The nervous system is made-up of billions of nerve cells or
(10) ___neurons___. The connection point between neurons is called a
(11) ___synapse___. By releasing neurotransmitters across this space, neurons can stimulate or inhibit another neuron's action. During development axons of some neurons become covered by (12) ___myelin sheath___, which improves transmission of neural impulses. Early in life, the brain exhibits responsivity or (13) ___plasticity___ in response to experiences. (***How can normal and abnormal experiences affect the brain?***)

    Brain growth continues beyond infancy, with increased myelination of neurons and specialization. Specialization of the two hemispheres of the cerebral cortex is called
(14) ___lateralization___. Specialization of the brain is evident at birth and becomes stronger throughout childhood. (***What is an example of specialization of the hemispheres?***) Brain development continues through adolescence and may be responsible for advances in adolescent thinking. Changes in the brain during adolescence may also contribute to the increased (15) ___risk-taking___ seen during this period.

    There is some degeneration of the nervous system with aging. Loss of neurons and slower transmission of signals contribute to slower information processing in older adults. The aging brain also shows some (16) ___plasticity___ or the ability to change in response to experiences and develop new abilities.

Principles of Growth
    Several principles underlie the pattern of growth. Growth occurs in a
(17) ___cephalocaudal___ direction, meaning from the head to the tail. As a result, the head of a newborn is more fully developed than the trunk and legs. Growth also proceeds from the center outward, or in a (18) ___proximodistal___ direction. (***What is an example of this principle of growth?***) According to the (19) ___orthogenetic___ principle, physical development proceeds from responses that are global to ones that are differentiated and integrated.

THE INFANT

Rapid Growth

Physical growth during infancy is rapid and occurs in bursts.

Newborn Capabilities

Newborns can produce a number of unlearned and automatic responses to stimuli called (20) _reflexes_. (***Can you provide examples of some unlearned responses that are essential to survival?***) Some (21) _primitive_ reflexes do not seem to have functional value in our culture and typically disappear during the first year of life. (***Can you provide examples of this type of reflex? What is the significance of the presence and then the absence of these reflexes?***)

Another strength of newborns is the presence of organized patterns of daily activity such as sleep-week cycles. There are individual differences in how much time infants spend in each state, although newborns spend about (22) _70%_ of their time asleep and only 2-3 hours a day actively taking in their environments. Half of a newborn's sleep time is spent in active, irregular sleep called (23) _REM_ sleep. This percentage decreases across the life span to about 20%. (***What are possible explanations for this change across the life span?***) Newborns also have well developed sensory systems and can learn from their experiences.

Physical Behavior

The average age when half of infants have mastered a skill is the (24) _developmental norm_ for the skill. Motor behaviors develop according to the cephalocaudal and proximodistal principles, so infants will be able to sit before they walk. They master (25) _gross motor_ skills using large muscle groups before (26) _fine motor_ skills that require precise motor control. (***What are some examples of how the orthogenetic principle guides the development of motor skills?***)

Most infants begin to crawl around (27) _7_ months and begin to walk at about (28) _12_ months. Around 9 to 12 months, infants can use a (29) _pincer grasp_ to pick up objects using only their thumb and one other finger. This development occurs sometime after infants have gained control of their arms and hands and thus is an example of the (30) _proximodistal_ direction of development. Acquisition of motor skills is largely directed by (31) _maturation_. Experience affects the (32) _rate_ at which infants progress through the sequence of motor milestones.

According to the (33) _dynamic systems_ approach, motor development is also influenced by infants' use of feedback from different movements. Before a new motor skill emerges, infants often engage in (34) _rhythmic stereotypies_ when they repeat individual components of the skill. In this view, motor skills emerge from a combination of maturation and experience.

THE CHILD

Steady Growth

Growth from infancy to adolescence is slow but steady, and continues to be guided by cephalocaudal and proximodistal principles.

Physical Behavior

Children learn to control their movements in a changing environment, extending earlier skills mastered in a stationary environment. Motor skills are refined during childhood and eye/hand coordination improves. Children also respond faster, or have better (35) _reaction times_ as they develop.

THE ADOLESCENT
Growth Spurt

Adolescents experience rapid growth, called the (36) _adolescent growth spurt_ Females typically begin their growth spurt about two years before males. (***What are the typical ages of rapid growth for males and females?***)

Sexual Maturation

Puberty for girls is marked by (37) _menarche_, their first menstruation, at about 12 or 13 years of age. For boys, the event that is typically used to mark puberty is (38) _semenarche_, or first ejaculation, which occurs around 13 or 14 years of age. There is large variation in the timing of sexual maturation. Rate of development is largely determined by (39) _genetic_ factors although environment also plays a role in timing of maturation, as indicated by the (40) _secular trend_ or the tendency in industrialized societies for earlier maturation and larger body size. (***What factors contribute to this trend?***)

Emotional responses to puberty are mixed for males and females, but tend to be stronger in females. (***How do pubertal changes affect parent-child relations?***) The psychological impact of being an early versus a late developer is different for males and females. Early maturing (41) _males_ are often found to have advantages over their later maturing peers. (***What are some of these advantages and are they long-lasting?***) Early development is not really an advantage for girls and may in fact be a disadvantage. Late-maturers of both sexes often experience some anxiety, but late-maturing (42) _males_ seem to experience the most disadvantages.

Physical Behavior

Advances in strength and physical competence continue throughout adolescence. Gender differences emerge as boys' physical performance continues to increase while girls' physical performance levels off or declines. Biological differences in muscle mass may account for some of this difference, but gender-role socialization also contributes.

THE ADULT
Physical Changes

Although physical aging occurs over most of the life span, outward signs are often not noticed until one's (43) _40's_. Wrinkles, thinning and graying hair, and extra weight are common physical changes in middle age. Older adults lose muscle mass, largely because they are less active than younger adults. Some older adults may experience (44) _osteoporosis_, extreme bone loss leaving bones fragile. (***What can be done to prevent this disease?***) Other adults have a joint problem called (45) _osteoarthritis_ that may limit their activities.

The average older adult has poorer physical functioning than younger adults, although not all older people experience declines in physical functioning. Many organ systems show a decrease in (46) _reserve capacity_, which is the ability to respond to demands for above-normal output. A majority of adults over the age of 65 have some sort of chronic impairment. Nonetheless, most older adults report that they are in good health.

Negative stereotypes about older adults can lead to prejudice against them or (47) _ageism_. Older adults strive to avoid being classified in the "old" category. Despite some physical declines, most older adults have a good sense of well being.

The Reproductive System

Hormone levels fluctuate in both sexes across the life span, although hormone changes typically affect women more than men. Some women report experiencing (48) _PMS_, a cluster of symptoms including breast tenderness and irritability just before menstruation. Both premenstrual and menstrual symptoms are affected by biological factors such as hormone changes, and by social factors. (***Can you describe some of the social factors that contribute to symptoms?***)

The end of menstrual periods occurs sometime during mid-life and is called (49) _menopause_. The lower levels of female hormones that are produced may result in vaginal dryness and (50) _hot flashes_ for some women. Some women experience psychological symptoms such as irritability and depression in connection with menopause. (***How does the experience of menopause differ cross culturally?***) In our culture, doctors often recommend (51) _hormone replacement therapy_ to treat the symptoms of menopause.

Men also experience loss of reproductive capacity, but more gradually than women, during a period of time referred to as (52) _andropause_.

Physical Behavior

A number of physical behaviors are carried out at a (53) _slower_ pace as we get older. (***What explanation is given for this slowing of the nervous system and motor performance?***) This is variable among adults and relates to exercise of physical skills.

Chronic disease often contributes to some of the declines among older adults. In addition, declines in physical functioning may relate to (54) _disuse_ of the body, as well as to abuses of the body.

REVIEW OF KEY TERMS

Below is a list of terms and concepts from this chapter. Use these to complete the following sentence definitions. You might also want to try writing definitions in your own words and then checking your definitions with those in the text.

adolescent growth spurt

ageism

androgens

andropause

catch-up growth

cephalocaudal principle

developmental norm

dynamic systems approach

endocrine gland

estrogen

fine motor skills

gross motor skills

growth hormone

hormone replacement therapy (HRT)

hot flashes

lateralization

menarche

menopause

myelin

neuron

orthogenetic principle

osteoarthritis

osteoporosis

pincer grasp

pituitary gland

plasticity

premenstrual syndrome (PMS)

proximodistal principle

puberty

reaction time

reflex(es)

REM sleep

reserve capacity

rhythmic stereotypies

secular trend

semenarche

synapse

testosterone

1.   Male hormones, including testosterone, which trigger the adolescent growth spurt and development of male sex organs are collectively called _androgens_ .

2.   Unlearned and automatic responses to stimuli are called _reflex(es)_ .

3.   Children show mastery of _fine motor skills_ when they engage in movements that require precise control of their hands or feet.

4.   Located at the base of the brain, the _pituitary gland_ is an endocrine gland that is responsible for regulating other glands and producing growth hormone.

5.   According to the _cephalocaudel principle_, growth proceeds in a head to tail direction.

6.   Cells that have not yet been committed to a particular function and have the capacity to be shaped by experience are said to be in a state of _plasticity_ .

7.   Specialization of the left and right hemispheres of the cerebral cortex is referred to as _lateralization_

8.   The rapid increase in growth at the end of childhood is the _adolescent growth spurt_

9.   Aging of the male reproductive system is known as _andropause_.

10.   The _secular trend_ is the tendency for earlier maturation and larger body size in industrialized societies over time.

11. Osteoporosis is a disease resulting from a loss of minerals, which causes deterioration of bone tissue.

12. Some women experience PMS, a cluster of symptoms including breast tenderness, a bloated feeling, irritability and moodiness that occur just before menstruation.

13. Growth hormone is secreted by the pituitary gland and stimulates growth and development of body cells.

14. Catch-up growth occurs after a growth deficit and gets a person back on his/her genetically programmed growth course.

15. Some women may experience hot flashes, which are sudden, brief, and unpredictable sensations of warmth that may be followed by a cold shiver.

16. A(n) endocrine gland is a ductless gland that secretes hormones directly into the bloodstream.

17. A female hormone secreted by the ovaries that stimulates development of female sex organs and regulates menstrual cycles is estrogen.

18. According to the proximodistal principle, growth proceeds from the central portions of the body to the extremities.

19. The pincer grasp is evident when children use their thumb in opposition to one other finger in order to pick up and manipulate objects.

20. The point when a person reaches sexual maturity and acquires secondary sexual characteristics is called puberty.

21. A neuron is the basic cell of the nervous system that transmits and receives signals.

22. A developmental norm represents the average age when half of all infants can master a particular skill.

23. Menarche is defined as a girl's first menstrual period.

24. The space between the axon of one neuron and the dendrites of another neuron is the synapse.

25. REM sleep is active, irregular sleep that includes rapid eye movements and is associated with brain wave activity that resembles wakefulness.

26.   _Myelin_ is a waxy substance that covers the axon of some neurons and facilitates transmission of neural impulses.

27.   Women experience _menopause_ when their menstrual periods end sometime during mid-life.

28.   The ability of an organ system to respond to a request for excess output is known as its _reserve capacity_

29.   The testes secrete a male hormone called _testosterone_ .

30.   According to the _orthogenetic principle_, growth proceeds from being global and undifferentiated to being increasingly specific, differentiated, and integrated.

31.   Children use their _gross motor skills_ when they run or otherwise make movements that involve large muscle groups.

32.   According to the _dynamic system approach_, children use sensory feedback to their movements to develop more sophisticated behavior patterns.

33.   The speed with which people can respond to a task is their _reaction time_ .

34.   Prejudice against older adults, or _ageism_, can result from the negative stereotypes that people hold.

35.   Some women take _HRT_ to reduce the symptoms associated with menopause.

36.   Some older adults experience _osteoarthritis_, a joint problem that results from gradual deterioration of the protective cartilage surrounding bones.

37.   Before a new motor skill emerges in its full form, infants often engage in _rhythmic stereotypes_ or repetitive movements of individual components that makeup the skill.

38.   A boy's first ejaculation is referred to as _semenarche_ .

MULTIPLE CHOICE SELF TEST

For each multiple choice question, read all alternatives and then select the best answer.

1.   Which structure is considered the "master gland" of the endocrine system?
      a.   thyroid gland
      b.   hypothalamus
      c.   adrenal gland
      d.   pituitary gland

2. Plasticity ensures that the brain
    a.   can recover from any sort of damage.
    b.   receives the maximum benefits from stimulation throughout the life span.
    c.   is not influenced by adverse environments.
    d.   is responsive to individual experiences.

3. Lateralization is a process by which
    a.   one hemisphere takes over for the other's functions after brain damage has occurred.
    b.   specialization of the functions of the left and right hemisphere occurs.
    c.   neurons in the brain develop rapidly.
    d.   neurons are covered by a myelin sheath.

4. As the body ages from childhood to adulthood, the brain
    a.   develops more neurons.
    b.   begins to form a myelin sheath around many neurons.
    c.   grows longer dendrites that may form new connections with other neurons.
    d.   releases large quantities of neurotransmitters.

5. The primitive reflexes
    a.   are essential to survival.
    b.   disappear sometime during infancy.
    c.   include rooting, sucking, and swallowing.
    d.   protect the infant from various adverse conditions.

6. The cephalocaudal principle predicts that
    a.   growth of the brain and spinal cord will be the last to occur.
    b.   growth will proceed from bones and cartilage to internal organs.
    c.   growth will proceed from head to tail.
    d.   growth will proceed from the midline to the extremities.

7. Based on the cephalocaudal principle of growth, infants typically can _____ before they can _____.
    a.   stand; roll over
    b.   roll over; control their arms or hands
    c.   walk backward; walk up steps
    d.   sit; walk

8. Research on infant states suggests that
    a.   there is large variability in amount of time infants spend in different states.
    b.   infants are remarkably similar in the amount of time spent in different states.
    c.   increased age brings an increase in the number of behavioral states that infants can experience.
    d.   neurological health can be predicted by the amount of time spent in different states.

9.	The developmental norm for grasping small objects is _____ months of age, and the developmental norm for standing alone is _____ months of age.
	a.	6, 18
	b.	2, 6
	c.	4, 11
	d.	12, 8

10.	According to the dynamic systems approach
	a.	motor movements unfold according to a strict genetic plan.
	b.	children adjust their movements in response to sensory feedback.
	c.	children learn to walk by watching the movements of those around them.
	d.	motor movements are correlated with mental capabilities.

11.	Which of the following hormone(s) trigger the adolescent growth spurt?
	a.	progesterone
	b.	androgens
	c.	activating hormones
	d.	thyroxine

12.	Regarding the timing of maturation
	a.	Sheila, who matures early, is likely to be more popular than Mary, who matures late.
	b.	Bill, who matures late, is likely to be more academically skilled than Mark, who matures early.
	c.	Tom, who matures early, is likely to be confident and poised relative to Steve, who matures late.
	d.	Mike, who matures "on time" is likely to be viewed most favorably by his parents and teachers, relative to other boys in his class who mature early or late.

13.	The secular trend refers to
	a.	earlier maturation and decreased body size from generation to generation.
	b.	later maturation and decreased body size from generation to generation.
	c.	historical changes in life expectancy from generation to generation.
	d.	earlier maturation and increased body size from generation to generation.

14.	The apparent decline of physical performance of females by the end of adolescence
	a.	is a myth not supported by any data.
	b.	results largely from socialization differences between males and females.
	c.	results from an overall decline in the proportion of muscle mass relative to fat.
	d.	is similar to the decline that occurs in males.

15. Menopause is a time when
    a. women no longer ovulate or menstruate.
    b. most women experience mood swings for extended periods of time.
    c. women continue to ovulate but do not menstruate.
    d. women experience an increase in hormone levels.

CRITIAL THINKING QUESTIONS

By answering the following questions, you will strengthen your understanding of the material in this chapter. These questions require higher level thinking skills such as integration and application of concepts. Sample answers are provided for three of the questions. These illustrate one possibility, but there are other answers you could provide that might be just as good. For the other questions, you can check yourself by referring to the text (a hint is provided), or by asking a peer or your instructor to review your answer.

1. Suppose you are in charge of writing a newsletter for adults who are approaching retirement age. In one issue of the newsletter, you want to write an informative article on physical changes that these adults might experience as they age. What would this article say?
    [Sample answer provided]

2. What are the psychological implications of the timing of puberty?
    [Sample answer provided]

3. What changes occur in the nervous system early in life and late in life?
    [Sample answer provided]

4. Write an article for parents with a newborn infant. What changes in motor skills can they anticipate as their child goes through infancy, childhood, and adolescence?
    [Hint: There is information about this throughout the chapter, but especially in the sections on "The Infant," "The Child," and "The Adolescent." You will need to integrate material from several subsections of these three sections.]

5. What evidence is there that lateralization takes place at an early age, yet still allows for plasticity in brain function across the life-span?
    [Hint: Review the material in the section "The nervous system," especially the subsection on brain development.]

ANSWERS

Summary and Guided Review (Fill-in the blank)

1. catch-up growth
2. hormones
3. pituitary
4. growth
5. thyroid
6. testosterone
7. androgens
8. estrogen
9. adrenal
10. neurons
11. synapse
12. myelin
13. plasticity
14. lateralization
15. risk-taking
16. plasticity
17. cephalocaudal
18. proximodistal
19. orthogenetic
20. reflexes
21. primitive
22. 70%
23. REM
24. developmental norm
25. gross motor
26. fine motor
27. seven
28. twelve
29. pincer grasp
30. proximodistal
31. maturation
32. rate
33. dynamic systems
34. rhythmic stereotypies
35. reaction times
36. growth spurt
37. menarche
38. semenarche
39. genetic
40. secular trend
41. males
42. males
43. 40's
44. osteoporosis
45. osteoarthritis
46. reserve capacity
47. ageism
48. premenstrual syndrome
49. menopause
50. hot flashes
51. hormone replacement therapy
52. andropause
53. slower
54. disuse

Review of Key Terms

1. androgens
2. reflexes
3. fine motor skills
4. pituitary gland
5. cephalocaudal principle
6. plasticity
7. lateralization
8. adolescent growth spurt
9. andropause
10. secular trend
11. osteoporosis
12. premenstrual syndrome (PMS)
13. growth hormone
14. catch-up growth
15. hot flashes
16. endocrine gland
17. estrogen
18. proximodistal principle
19. pincer grasp
20. puberty
21. neuron
22. developmental norm
23. menarche
24. synapse
25. REM sleep
26. myelin
27. menopause
28. reserve capacity
29. testosterone
30. orthogenetic principle

31.	gross motor skills	35.	hormone replacement therapy (HRT)
32.	dynamic systems approach	36.	osteoarthritis
33.	reaction time	37.	rhythmic stereotypies
34.	ageism	38.	semenarche

Multiple Choice Self Test

1.	D (p. 113)	6.	C (p. 118)	11.	B (p. 131)
2.	D (p. 115)	7.	D (pp. 118-119)	12.	C (p. 133)
3.	B (p. 115)	8.	A (pp. 119-120)	13.	D (p. 132)
4.	C (p. 116)	9.	C (pp. 119-121)	14.	B (pp. 134-135)
5.	B (pp. 119-121)	10.	B (p. 126)	15.	A (p. 137)

Critical Thinking Questions

1. *Worried about a few physical changes as you approach retirement? Well, it's not as bad as you may have heard. Sure, you have a few wrinkles, some gray hair, and a little extra weight around the middle. It will probably take you longer to do the things you sped through as a young adult. For women, menopause may mean hot flashes and vaginal dryness, making intercourse more painful. Old age may also bring a loss of bone mass, or osteoporosis, which can lead to fractures and seriously erode quality of life. Unfortunately, statistics indicate that a majority of older adults have some sort of chronic impairment, such as arthritis. Despite this, a majority of older adults report that their health is actually quite good, suggesting that they take impairments in stride or find ways to work around them.*

The good news is that if you take care of yourself and remain healthy and active, you can look forward to a satisfying old age. Older adults who are disease free perform just as well on many physical tasks as younger adults. Many older adults perform tasks more slowly because they are out of shape; continuing to exercise may reduce this disadvantage of aging. In many ways, the saying, "use it or lose it," applies to the physical functioning of older adults.

2. *The psychological effects of the timing of puberty are different for boys and girls. In general, boys who mature earlier than their peers experience some advantages. They are rated as more socially competent and, self-assured, and are more popular among their peers. Along with these positive outcomes, though, are a few negative ones. Early maturing boys are more likely to get involved in substance abuse earlier than other boys. Early maturation for boys may be largely advantageous because it makes them look more mature, whether or not they really are. Late maturing boys experience several disadvantages. They are more anxious and less self-assured than other boys. They score somewhat lower on achievement tests and are more likely to experience behavior problems.*

For girls, the pattern is different. Early maturing girls may experience several disadvantages. They are likely to feel awkward if they are one of the only girls in their peer group to develop breasts or other observable signs of puberty. While boys going through puberty might welcome the increase in size, deepening of their voices, and sexual maturity, girls going through puberty often don't feel the same way about getting larger and becoming sexually mature. In addition, parents and society seem to be more uncomfortable with girls' emerging sexuality than with their boys' emerging sexuality. This may help explain why girls who mature early experience some problems with self-esteem. Another problem for early-maturing girls is that they tend to socialize with older peers, which exposes them to dating, drinking, and sex at an earlier age than their on-time peers.

  Girls who mature late may experience some anxiety, wondering when they will start to develop and catch up to their peers. But for the most part, there are no significant disadvantages for late-maturing girls, like there are for late-maturing boys.

  In sum, early-maturing girls and late-maturing boys experience more problems than other adolescents. But the influence of the timing of puberty also depends on other individual characteristics, such as personality, and how the individual interprets the events of puberty.

3. *Early in life, the nervous system changes in significant ways. The process of myelination is occurring rapidly during infancy and then tapers off throughout childhood and adolescence. Myelination enables neurons to send and receive messages more efficiently. The young brain is also responsive to the individual's experiences and can develop in a variety of ways, showing plasticity. The greatest period of plasticity is infancy, when the brain is vulnerable to damage, but also is more capable of recovering from damage than it will be later in life. The young brain is becoming increasingly organized with areas specialized for specific functions. Lateralization of the brain also occurs early in life. This means that the two hemispheres of the brain do not develop identically, but develop in different ways to specialize in different functions. Once it reaches maturity, it is more difficult for an area of the brain that is dedicated to one function to pick up another function.*

  At the other end of the age spectrum, there is some gradual and mild degeneration within the nervous system. Neurons are lost and there is reduced functioning of many of the remaining neurons. The protective myelin covering many neurons begins to deteriorate, leading to a general slowing of the older nervous system. In addition, there are often decreases in levels of some neurotransmitters, which can lead to a variety of problems depending on the type of neurotransmitter. There is still some plasticity in the older brain, though, especially for individuals who remain active and mentally involved.

CHAPTER SIX

PERCEPTION

OVERVIEW

You should take note of the point at the beginning of this chapter: sensation and perception are at the very heart of human functioning. Without sensation and perception, there would be no meaningful cognitive activity or social interactions, no enjoyable walks through the neighborhood, and no ability to appreciate music or food. The centrality of sensation and perception makes it important to understand changes in these processes across the life span.

Many significant changes in perceptual processes occur during infancy, with few changes during childhood, adolescence, and early adulthood. During middle and older adulthood, there are again some notable changes in perceptual processes. Thus, there is weighty coverage of vision, hearing, taste, smell, touch, temperature, and pain in the sections on "The Infant" and "The Adult." Additionally, the section on infants discusses several clever methods of assessing infants' perceptual abilities. The section on children concentrates on the development of attentional processes, which are so important to perception.

LEARNING OBJECTIVES

After reading and studying the material in this chapter, you should be able to answer the following questions.

1.   What are the views of empiricists and nativists on the nature/nurture issue as it relates to sensation and perception?

2.   How are perceptual abilities of infants assessed?

3.   What are the infants' visual capabilities? What sorts of things do infants prefer to look at?

4.   What are the auditory capabilities of infants? What do we know about infants' abilities to perceive speech?

5.   What are the taste and smell capabilities of infants? To what extent are infants sensitive to touch, temperature, and pain?

6.   To what extent can infants integrate their sensory experiences? What is an example of cross-modal perception?

7.   What role do early experiences play in development of perceptions? What factors contribute to normal visual perception?

8.   What changes occur in attention from infancy to adulthood?

9.   What changes occur in visual capabilities and visual perception during adulthood?

10.   What changes in auditory capabilities and speech perception occur during adulthood?

11.   What changes occur in taste and smell, and in sensitivity to touch, temperature, and pain during adulthood?

CHAPTER SUMMARY AND GUIDED REVIEW

The following summary provides an overview of the main points contained in this chapter of the text. Fill-in the blanks with terms that appropriately complete the sentence. Scattered throughout the summary are questions in parentheses. These are meant to encourage you to think actively as you are reading and connect this summary to the more detailed information provided in the text. You can answer these questions as you are filling in the blanks or you can complete all the blanks, then go back and reread the entire summary, addressing the questions in order to provide more depth of understanding.

The process by which sensory receptors detect stimuli and transmit it to the brain is called
(1) _Sensation_. The process of interpreting this information is called
(2) _perception_. These processes are at the center of human understanding.

ISSUES OF NATURE AND NURTURE

One issue concerning perceptual development is whether infants are born with knowledge or need to acquire all knowledge through their senses. The (3) _empiricists_ took the latter position and believed that infants began life as blank slates. This position represents the (4) _nurture_ side of the nature/nurture issue. The (5) _nativists_ argued that infants are born with knowledge, which represents the (6) _nature_ side of the nature/nurture issue.

THE INFANT

Assessing Perceptual Abilities

Infants' perceptual capabilities are often assessed with a technique called
(7) _habituation_, which measures decreased responding to a stimulus that has been presented repeatedly. (***Can you explain the rationale of this approach?***) Another technique is to present two stimuli to infants and measure their (8) _preferential looking_ which shows that they can discriminate the two stimuli. Sometimes, researchers use (9) _evoked potentials_ when they measure electrical activity of the brain in response to stimulation. In some instances, infants can be operantly conditioning to respond in a particular way when a particular stimulus is presented; their response to a second stimulus can then be measured to determine whether they perceive the stimuli to be similar or different.

Vision

A newborn's ability to perceive visual detail, or their (10) _visual acuity_, is poor. This may result from problems with (11) _visual accommodation_, which refers to the changing shape of the lens of the eye to bring objects at varying distances into focus. Young infants can visually detect differences in stimuli and prefer to look at (12) _patterned_ stimuli such as faces. (***Is the apparent preference for faces really a preference for faces? Why or why not?***) Young infants tend to be attracted to patterns that have (13) _contour_ or light-dark transitions, stimuli that move, and stimuli that are moderately complex. In general, we can conclude that infants prefer to look at (14) _what they can see well_ (fill-in this blank with a phrase).

At around 2 months of age, infants begin to visually explore the entire field of a figure or form, rather than just an exterior border of the figure. They also begin to prefer (15) _normal_ faces over scrambled facial features. This might suggest that infants are beginning to form (16) _mental representation_ for familiar objects.

Another aspect of visual perception is perception of three-dimensional space or (17) _depth perception_. Infants develop (18) _size consistency_, which is the tendency to perceive an object as its same size despite changes in the retinal image of the object as its distance from the eyes changes. Depth perception has been assessed using an apparatus called the (19) _visual cliff_, which has an apparent drop-off. Early research showed that infants of crawling age perceived depth, demonstrated by their avoidance of the drop-off. A major limitation of this assessment technique was that infants needed to be able to be crawling.

(*How has depth perception been assessed in younger infants?*)

An important perceptual task for infants is learning to distinguish one object from another. To organize the world of objects, infants use (20) common motion as a cue to establish the boundaries of objects. In addition, infants seem to be equipped with organized systems of knowledge, called (21) intuitive theories, that help them understand their world.

Hearing

Newborns' auditory capabilities are well developed. Infants are able to discriminate basic speech sounds, or (22) phonemes, early in life. In fact, unlike adults, infants can discriminate speech sounds of languages not spoken in the home. Familiarity with voices begins to develop prenatally, and newborns are able to recognize their mothers' voices. (*Can you describe how this has been studied?*) Infants can also discriminate between rhythmic music and nonrhythmic noise soon after birth.

Taste and Smell

The sense of taste and the sense of smell, also called (23) olfaction, are well developed at birth. Infants show distinct taste preferences and those who are breast-fed can recognize their mothers on the basis of smell. (*How does experience influence taste?*)

Touch, Temperature, and Pain

Newborns are sensitive to tactile stimulation and may respond with reflexes if touched in certain areas. Newborns are also sensitive to temperature and to pain. The intensity of a painful experience can be communicated by the quality of an infant's (24) cries. Research suggests that infants learn from experience to anticipate pain with certain stimuli.

Integrating Sensory Information

Putting together information from different senses can help an infant make sense of the world. Some senses seem to be integrated earlier than other senses. For example, touch and vision, as well as vision and hearing, seem to be linked very early.

The ability to recognize through one sense modality an object that is familiar through another sense modality is called (25) cross-modal perception (*Can you provide an example of this?*) Cross-modal perception of all forms does not reliably occur until 4-7 months of age.

Influences on Early Perceptual Development

The presence of such significant early perceptual capabilities suggests that (26) nature plays a role in perceptual development. Early experiences are also necessary for normal development. Infants need to be exposed to a variety of (27) patterned stimulation for neurons in the visual areas of the brain to develop normally. Infants also need to be exposed to movement in their environment, especially if they are not able to move. Infants actively seek and explore their environments, which means that they typically expose themselves to appropriate sensory experiences. (*What three phases of exploratory behavior do infants go through?*) Finally, the way we perceive and interpret sensory experiences varies across cultures. (*What are some examples of these variations?*)

THE CHILD
The Development of Attention

Although much of sensory and perceptual development is complete by the end of infancy, children need to develop better (28) ____attention____, the selective focusing of perception and cognition on some particular aspect of the environment. Attention span increases during childhood and attention becomes more (29) ____selective____. (**What evidence is there to support this conclusion?**) In addition, visual search becomes more (30) ____systematic____ or exhaustive during childhood.

THE ADOLESCENT

Attention span continues to increase during adolescence as those parts of the brain involved in attention become fully myelinated. Adolescents also become more efficient at ignoring (31) ____irrelevant____ information so that they can focus their attention more effectively. Adolescents tend to use more efficient strategies for scanning visual displays.

THE ADULT

Sensory and perceptual capabilities gradually decline with age. There are increases in (32) ____sensory thresholds____ which means that a higher level of stimulation is needed for sensory detection as we age. Older people may also have trouble processing sensory information.

Vision

A number of changes occur within the eye as we age. Older people tend to be less sensitive to dim light, and the process of adjusting to low light levels, (33) ____dark adaptation____, does not function as well for older people. Many adults experience a loss of near vision starting in their 40's from a condition called (34) ____presbyopia____ caused by thickening of the lens. The ability to clearly see details, known as (35) ____visual acuity____, normally decreases with age. Significant decreases, however, are usually associated with pathological conditions. One such condition is (36) ____cataracts____, in which the lens of the eye becomes opaque and limits the amount of light entering the eye. Blurry vision and loss of vision from the center of the visual field are symptoms of age-related (37) ____macular degeneration____. Loss of peripheral vision can result from (38) ____retinitis pigmentous____, a group of disorders that involve deterioration of the cells of the retina. Vision loss may also occur from (39) ____glaucoma____ in which there is increased fluid pressure in the eye, which can eventually lead to blindness. (**What are some implications of these changes in visual capabilities?**)

Research shows that older adults perform worse on visual search tasks than younger adults, particularly when there are numerous distractions. Older adults have the greatest difficulties processing visual information in situations that are (40) ____novel____ and (41) ____complex____, but have few problems with familiar or simple tasks.

Hearing

Hearing problems are often associated with aging. One common problem is decreased sensitivity to high-frequency sounds, a condition called (42) ____presbycusis____. Older adults seem to have more trouble with speech perception than younger adults, especially under poor listening conditions, such as a great deal of (43) ____background noise____. As with visual perception, older adults perform better on auditory tasks that are familiar or meaningful to them.

Taste and Smell

Sensory thresholds for some tastes increase with age. Taste for (44) _____sweet_____ substances does not seem to change markedly across the life span. Sensitivity to odors and the ability to discriminate between them are highest from childhood to middle adulthood and then decline in old age. Decreases in taste and smell can affect recognition of different foods, although losses in the sense of (45) _____smell_____ seem to contribute more to problems of food recognition.

Touch, Temperature, and Pain

Sensitivity to touch and changes in temperature decrease with age. Sensitivity to pain seems to both increase and decrease in older adults. Older adults are less likely to report mild forms of pain, but were likely to report stronger forms of pain stimulation as being particularly strong.

The Adult in Perspective

The most serious age changes in perception occur with vision and hearing. Most older adults suffer some losses, although overall levels are fairly good.

REVIEW OF KEY TERMS

Below is a list of terms and concepts from this chapter. Use these to complete the following sentence definitions. You might also want to try writing definitions in your own words and then checking your definitions with those in the text.

age-related macular degeneration
attention
cataracts
cochlear implant
contour
cross-modal perception
dark adaptation
empiricist
glaucoma
habituation
intuitive theories
nativist
olfaction

perception
phoneme
presbycusis
presbyopia
retinitis pigmentosa (RP)
selective attention
sensation
sensory threshold
size constancy
visual accommodation
visual acuity
visual cliff

1. A group of hereditary disorders called retinitis pigmentosa (RP) involve the gradual deterioration of the cells of the retina.

2. The process of visual accommodation produces changes in the shape of the lens to bring objects at varying distances into focus.

3. Someone who believes that infants enter the world with knowledge that permits them to perceive meaningful patterns in the world is a(n) _nativist_.

4. The tendency to perceive an object as its same size despite changes in the retinal image of the object as its distance from the eyes changes is called _size constancy_

5. The detection of stimuli by the sensory receptors and the transmission of this information to the brain is the process of _sensation_.

6. Sense of smell, which is mediated by receptors in the nasal passage, is also called _olfaction_.

7. The _visual cliff_ is an apparatus with an apparent drop-off that is used to assess early depth perception.

8. The point at which a minimum level of stimulation can be detected by a sensory system is its _sensory threshold_

9. Decreased responding to a stimulus that has been presented repeatedly is _habituation_.

10. The basic unit of speech is a _phoneme_.

11. The process of _perception_ involves the interpretation of sensory input.

12. The ability to recognize through one sensory modality an object that is familiar through another is called _cross-modal perception_

13. _Contour_ refers to the dark and light boundaries or transitions of a perceptual pattern.

14. A _cochlear implant_ is a device that permits amplification of sound by directly stimulating the auditory nerve with electrical impulses.

15. The process of _attention_ selectively focuses perception and cognition on some aspect of the environment.

16. The sharpness of the visual system, or its ability to perceive detail, is _visual acuity_.

17. The process of adjusting to lowered levels of light is called _dark adaptation_

18. Vision loss may occur in _age-related_ when cells in the retina that are responsible for central vision are damaged. _macular degeneration_

19. A decreased ability to focus on objects that are close to the eye occurs in the condition of presbyopia.

20. Focusing perception or cognition on something specific is known as attention.

21. Opaque or cloudy areas in the lens of the eye that decrease the amount of light reaching the retina result in cataracts.

22. A person who believes that infants enter the world with no knowledge of the world, and learn everything through their senses is a(n) empiricist.

23. Increased fluid pressure in eye is a symptom of glaucoma.

24. Problems in hearing that result from aging, such as decreased sensitivity to high-frequency sounds, are called presbycusis.

25. The ability to deliberately focus on one thing while ignoring other things is selective adaptation

MULTIPLE CHOICE SELF TEST

For each multiple choice question, read all alternatives and then select the best answer.

1. Sensation refers to _____ of stimuli while perception refers to _____ of this information.
   a. detection; interpretation
   b. sense; the value
   c. interpretation; detection
   d. recognition; the use

2. Nativists argue that a child
   a. is born knowing nothing and learns through interaction with the environment.
   b. is born with knowledge and is very similar to an adult in terms of perceptual ability.
   c. is influenced intellectually by genetics, maturation and the environment.
   d. learns mainly through cultural experiences.

3. Suppose you repeatedly present a stimulus until an infant loses interest in it. This technique is known as
   a. visual accommodation.
   b. color discrimination.
   c. visual acuity.
   d. habituation.

4. Which of the following is TRUE about young infants' visual capabilities?
    a. Infants are not able to perceive color until sometime during the second half of the first year.
    b. Infants as young as two months can detect details of a patterned stimulus as well as adults.
    c. Infants are fairly good at detecting differences in brightness levels of stimuli.
    d. Infants' visual systems are at their peak performance.

5. Newborns appear to have a preference for viewing human faces. This probably reflects
    a. an innate ability to recognize faces.
    b. a preference for patterned stimuli with contour and some complexity.
    c. the fact that infants will learn to look at what they have been reinforced for in the past.
    d. the fact that infants can focus only on faces.

6. At around 2 or 3 months of age, infants prefer to look at "normal" faces as opposed to faces that have been distorted in some way. This suggests that infants
    a. cannot really detect a difference between them.
    b. have organized their perceptions according to Gestalt principles.
    c. prefer the simplest form or pattern.
    d. are developing mental representations of what a normal face looks like.

7. Very young infants are most visually attracted to a
    a. highly complex stimulus.
    b. moderately complex stimulus.
    c. colorful stimulus.
    d. black and white stimulus.

8. The visual cliff is an apparatus used to determine
    a. depth perception.
    b. size constancy.
    c. visual acuity.
    d. visual accommodation.

9. Two-month-olds tested on the visual cliff typically show a slower heart rate on the deep side than on the shallow side of the cliff. This suggests that two-month-olds
    a. are afraid of falling off the apparent cliff.
    b. detect a difference between the two sides of the visual cliff.
    c. perceive size constancy.
    d. have learned to avoid potential drop-offs.

10. Normal hearing in young infants is different from normal hearing in adults because infants
    a. are better able to hear soft sounds and whispers.
    b. have more difficulty discriminating between speech sounds.
    c. are unable to localize sound.
    d. can distinguish between all speech sounds, including those not used in the language of adults around them.

11. The point at which a dim light can still be detected is termed
    a. dark adaptation.
    b. sensory threshold.
    c. visual accommodation.
    d. visual acuity.

12. An infant who sucks on an object and then recognizes this object visually is showing evidence of
    a. selective attention.
    b. habituation.
    c. cross-modal perception.
    d. recognition of the object's distinctive features.

13. Research findings with animals suggest that, in order for normal perceptual development to occur, infants
    a. must be able to actively move through their environment.
    b. must be able to watch movement in the environment.
    c. must be exposed to patterned stimulation.
    d. Both B and C

14. Most age related hearing problems originate in the
    a. hearing center of the brain.
    b. auditory nerves and receptors.
    c. structures of the middle ear.
    d. outer ear membrane.

15. When speaking to people who are hard of hearing, the speaker should
    a. elevate the voice—shout if necessary.
    b. talk directly into the person's ear so they can hear better.
    c. repeat what she has just said instead of rewording the misunderstood statement.
    d. make sure the hearing impaired person can see him/her.

CRITICAL THINKING QUESTIONS

By answering the following questions, you will strengthen your understanding of the material in this chapter. These questions require higher level thinking skills such as integration and application of concepts. Sample answers are provided for three of the questions. These illustrate one possibility, but there are other answers you could provide that might be just as good. For the other questions, you can check yourself by referring to the text (a hint is provided), or by asking a peer or your instructor to review your answer.

1. In light of their sensory and perceptual abilities, what do young infants know about the people and world around them?
    [Sample answer provided.]

2. How can researchers measure an infant's perceptual abilities?
    [Sample answer provided.]

3. What sensory and perceptual changes can an older adult expect? What implications do these changes have with respect to an older adult's lifestyle?
    [Sample answer provided.]

4. Discuss the likely outcomes for an infant born with congenital cataracts that preclude any sort of visual stimulation.
    [Hint: Review the section in the text on "Influences on Early Perceptual Development."]

5. Based on what you know from this chapter about perceptual capabilities and preferences, what recommendations would you make for designing an infant's nursery? What recommendations would you make for an older adult's living quarters?
    [Hint: Think of the applications of the material in the sections that cover infants' sensory capabilities, particularly their vision and hearing. Likewise, consider the applications of the material covered in "The Adult."]

ANSWERS

Chapter Summary and Guided Review (Fill-in the blank)

1.	sensation	10.	visual acuity
2.	perception	11.	visual accommodation
3.	empiricists	12.	patterned
4.	nurture	13.	contour
5.	nativists	14.	what they can see well
6.	nature	15.	normal
7.	habituation	16.	mental representations (or schemata)
8.	preferential looking	17.	depth
9.	evoked potentials	18.	size constancy

19.	visual cliff	33.	dark adaptation
20.	common motion	34.	presbyopia
21.	intuitive theories	35.	visual acuity
22.	phonemes	36.	cataracts
23.	olfaction	37.	macular degeneration
24.	cries	38.	retinitis pigmentosa (RP)
25.	cross-modal perception	39.	glaucoma
26.	nature	40.	novel
27.	patterned	41.	complex
28.	attention	42.	presbycusis
29.	selective	43.	background noise
30.	systematic (or detailed)	44.	sweet
31.	irrelevant	45.	smell
32.	sensory thresholds		

Review of Key Terms

1.	retinitis pigmentosa	14.	cochlear implant
2.	visual accommodation	15.	attention
3.	nativist	16.	visual acuity
4.	size constancy	17.	dark adaptation
5.	sensation	18.	age-related macular degeneration
6.	olfaction	19.	presbyopia
7.	visual cliff	20.	attention
8.	sensory threshold	21.	cataracts
9.	habituation	22.	empiricist
10.	phoneme	23.	glaucoma
11.	perception	24.	presbycusis
12.	cross-modal perception	25.	selective attention
13.	contour		

Multiple Choice Self Test

1.	A (p. 144)	6.	D (pp. 147-48)	11.	B (p. 161)
2.	B (p. 144)	7.	B (pp. 146-47)	12.	C (p. 156)
3.	D (p. 145)	8.	A (p. 149)	13.	D (p. 157)
4.	C (p. 146)	9.	B (p. 149)	14.	B (p. 164)
5.	B (pp. 147-48)	10.	D (p. 152)	15.	D (pp. 165-66)

Critical Thinking Questions

1.   *Infants actually know a lot more than previously thought. They can recognize their mother's voice, and if they are breast-fed, they can recognize her by smell. They can see people and objects that are close to them, particularly if what they are looking at has sharp light-dark contrasts or bold patterns. This means that infants can see their parents' faces fairly well when parents are interacting with them. Infants seem to like looking at human faces more than other patterned stimuli, but this seems to be because the features of faces are interesting. Show them a picture of a scrambled face, and they will look at it almost as long as they look at a "normal"*

face. Objects in the environment that move are interesting to infants, as long as the movement is not too fast. Finally, infants like to look at things that are somewhat, but not overly, complex. As they mature, they prefer increasing complexity. The bottom line is that infants like to look at things that they can see well.

2.   *Testing infants is challenging because they can't communicate in the same ways as children and adults do. Researchers have used habituation and preferential looking tasks to learn a great deal about what infants know about the world around them. In habituation, the infant is exposed repeatedly to a stimulus (e.g., a picture or a sound). At first, they are interested and pay attention to the stimulus, but eventually, they get bored with the same stimulus being presented over and over, and they look away. The researcher then switches to a different stimulus. If the infant detects that this new stimulus is different from the old one, they will once again pay attention. Researchers can vary characteristics of the stimuli and measure how long it takes infants to become bored or for their attention to be recaptured. Preferential looking is similar, except that researchers present two stimuli at the same time and measure how long the infant looks at each one. If the infant does not detect any difference between the two stimuli, then there shouldn't be any difference in looking times. But if the infant detects a difference, he will presumably look longer at the one that he finds more interesting. A few researchers also measure electrical activity of the infant's brain while they are exposed to a stimulus. By noting differences in the pattern of electrical activity of the brain, researchers can infer what was detected and what the infant's preferences are. Finally, researchers have taken advantage of the fact that infants can learn through operant conditioning. They condition the infant to perform a simple action (e.g., sucking on a pacifier or turning their head) when they detect a particular stimulus. Then the research presents a second stimulus and measures whether the infant performs the action (suggesting that they do not detect a difference between the two stimuli) or not (suggesting that that they DO detect a difference).*

3.   *Most, but not all, adults can expect some sensory and perceptual declines as they get older. Sensory thresholds increase, which means that sensory stimulation needs to be stronger (e.g., noises need to be louder and odors need to be stronger) in order for them to be detected. Even when sensations are detected, the older adult may have more trouble processing the information or integrating it. Thus, it may be more difficult for the older adult to make sense of their world. In practical terms, a majority of older adults have vision problems and wear corrective lenses. Many of them have hearing problems and could benefit from hearing aids. Their taste buds aren't as sensitive as they once were, so they often end up putting more salt or seasonings on their food. Their sense of smell is also diminished, so they may use more perfume and don't potentially harmful smells as well as when they were younger. These changes make it more challenging for adults to get out; it limits their driving ability. Social interactions are more difficult when hearing and vision are diminished. Older adults with uncorrected problems may become socially isolated because they are increasingly uncomfortable in social situations.*

CHAPTER SEVEN

COGNITION

OVERVIEW

     This chapter covers two major views on cognitive development. First up is Piaget's constructivist theory, which views intelligence as a basic life function that helps us adapt to our environment. To master this theory, you will need to understand *what* develops, as well as *how* this development occurs in the Piagetian perspective. "What" develops are the cognitive schemes or structures and this growth is reflected in children's progression through Piaget's four stages of development: sensorimotor, preoperations, concrete operations, and formal operations. The "how" of development occurs through the processes of organization and adaptation, and is motivated by cognitive disequilibrium.

     In addition to the *what* and *how*, you need to have some sense of how the theory has fared in light of the decades of research that have been conducted on children's thinking. Piaget's theory stops short of being a life span theory; Piaget did not propose any new stages beyond formal operations in adolescence. As discussed in the chapter, though, other researchers have looked at cognitive changes during adulthood.

     The second perspective covered in this chapter comes from Vygotsky, who viewed cognitive development as a product of social interactions and the child's sociocultural context. Vygotsky believed that children learn problem solving skills from knowledgeable partners who guide them to more advanced levels of skill in the child's zone of proximal development. The textbook provides a discussion of Vygotsky's contributions and how they differ from Piaget's.

LEARNING OBJECTIVES

After reading and studying the material in this chapter, you should be able to answer the following questions.

1.   How do organization, adaptation, and disequilibrium guide development?

2.   What are the major achievements of the sensorimotor stage?

3.   What are the characteristics and limitations of preoperational thought?

4.	What are the major characteristics and limitations of concrete operational thought?

5.	What are the main features of formal operational thought?

6.	In what ways might adult thought be more advanced than adolescent thought?

7.	What are the limitations and challenges to Piaget's theory of cognitive development?

8.	What is the main theme of Vygotsky's theory of cognitive development?

9.	How does social interaction contribute to cognitive development according to Vygotsky's theory?

10.	In what ways are Vygotsky and Piaget similar and different in their ideas about cognition?

CHAPTER SUMMARY AND GUIDED REVIEW

The following summary provides an overview of the main points contained in this chapter of the text. Fill-in the blanks with terms that appropriately complete the sentence. Scattered throughout the summary are questions in parentheses. These are meant to encourage you to think actively as you are reading and connect this summary to the more detailed information provided in the text. You can answer these questions as you are filling in the blanks or you can complete all the blanks, then go back and reread the entire summary, addressing the questions in order to provide more depth of understanding.

The activity of knowing and the process of acquiring knowledge and solving problems is called (1) ___cognition___ .

PIAGET'S CONSTRUCTIVIST APPROACH

Piaget's field of study, known as (2) _genetic epistemology_, examined how children come to know reality. Piaget was interested in the common mistakes that children of different ages made and believed that these responses reflected different stages of thinking. He used a question-and-answer technique called the (3) _clinical method_ to determine the process of children's thinking. This method allows for flexibility but is not standardized for all children.

What is Intelligence?

According to Piaget, intelligence is a basic life function that helps an organism adapt to its environment. Further, organisms are actively involved in their own development. As knowledge is gained, people form cognitive structures, or (4) ___schemes___ , which are organized patterns of action or thought that allow us to interpret our experiences. Infants' schemes are action-oriented, while preschool-age children develop symbolic schemes. Older children can manipulate symbols in their heads to solve problems.

How Does Intelligence Develop?

Schemes develop through two innate processes. One is (5) ___organization___ in which children combine existing schemes into more complex schemes. (*What is an example of this process?*) The second process is (6) ___adaptation___ , which refers to the process of adjusting to the demands of the environment. This adjustment occurs through (7) ___assimilation___ , by which new experiences are interpreted in terms of existing schemes, and through (8) ___accommodation___ , in which existing cognitive schemes are modified to account for new experiences. (*What are examples of each of these processes?*) When we encounter new experiences, the conflict between new information and old understanding creates (9) ___disequilibrium___ , which stimulates cognitive growth. Piaget believed that humans actively create their understanding of the world in a process called (10) ___constructivism___ .

Major cognitive changes are organized into four distinct stages. Thinking in each stage is qualitatively different from thinking in the other stages. Progress through the stages occurs in an (11) ___invariant___ sequence, or unchanging order for all children, although the *rate* of progress may vary from child to child.

THE INFANT

According to Piaget, infants are in the (12) ___sensorimotor___ stage, which has six substages and is dominated by behavioral schemes.

Substages of the Sensorimotor Stage

Through six substages of sensorimotor development, infants gradually switch from relying on innate reflexes to using mental symbols to guide future behavior. (*Can you trace the development of a behavior, such as play, through the sensorimotor substages?*)

The Development of Object Permanence

One of the important achievements of the sensorimotor stage is (13) *object permanence*, or the understanding that objects continue to exist even though not directly experienced. Infants in substage four (8-12 months) will search for a concealed object if they watched while it was hidden, but if the object is then hidden in a new location, infants in this substage typically make the (14) *A not B* error. Not until substage six (18-24 months) are infants capable of mental representation and following invisible displacements of objects. Recent research suggests that infants have a rudimentary understanding of object permanence earlier than Piaget claimed. (***Why is object permanence an important concept for infants to develop?***)

The Emergence of Symbols

Piaget referred to the ability to use one thing to represent objects or experiences as the (15) *symbolic capacity*. As children get a little older, some may use this ability to invent (16) *imaginary companions*. (***What else can infants do once they have acquired this ability?***)

THE CHILD

The Preoperational Stage

According to Piaget, preschool-age children are in the preoperational stage of cognitive development where children use symbolic reasoning but not logical reasoning. They typically focus on the most obvious features of a task, or what has (17) *perceptual salience*. Children in this stage lack (18) *of conservation*, the understanding that certain properties of a substance or object remain the same despite superficial changes in appearance. There are several reasons for this. They lack the cognitive operation called (19) *decentration*, which means they have trouble focusing on two or more dimensions of a problem at the same time. Instead, preoperational children engage in (20) *centration* where they focus on a single aspect of the problem when more are relevant. In addition, preoperational children lack (21) *reversibility* or the process of mentally reversing an action. Preoperational children also have trouble with (22) *transformational thought* or the processes of change from one state to another and so their thought is static. (***Try writing responses to one of the conservation problems that demonstrate each of these concepts from a preoperational child's perspective.***)

Piaget also believed that preoperational children were (23) *egocentrism* because of their tendency to view the world from their own perspective and their trouble recognizing other points of view. Preoperational children have difficulty relating subclasses of objects to the whole class of objects because they tend to center on the most perceptually salient feature of the task, and so they have trouble solving (24) *class inclusion* problems.

Piaget seems to have underestimated what the preschool age child can do. Recent research suggests that they understand simple conservation concepts and classification systems, and they are not as egocentric as Piaget claimed. Nonetheless, preschool children rely more on their perceptions to solve tasks than older children do.

The Concrete Operations Stage

School-age children (roughly 7 to 11 years) are in Piaget's third stage of cognitive development—concrete operations. They have mastered the logical operations that were absent from preoperational thought. (***What are these mental operations?***) This allows concrete operational children to solve conservation tasks, although they don't solve all types at the same time, which Piaget described as (25) horizontal decalage. They can also mentally order items along a quantifiable dimension, an operation called (26) _seriation_, and have mastered (27) transitivity, a cognitive operation that allows children to recognize the relationships among elements in a series. (***What are examples of problems that children can solve by applying each of these operations?***) Finally, concrete operational children can solve (28) class inclusion problems because they understand that subclasses are included in a whole class.

THE ADOLESCENT
The Formal Operations Stage

According to Piaget, adolescents are entering the stage of formal operations. Like concrete operational children, adolescents can reason logically about objects. In addition, they can apply their mental actions to ideas, extending their reasoning to non-concrete, or (29) abstract concepts. This facilitates (30) hypothetical reasoning.

Formal operational thinkers also use systematic problem-solving strategies, rather than trial-and-error approaches often used by children in earlier stages. One type of reasoning that formal operational thinkers might use is (31) hypothetical-deductive, where individuals reason from general ideas to specific implications of these ideas. They are also increasingly able to (32) decontextualize or separate prior knowledge from current task demands.

Implications of Formal Thought

Mastery of formal operational thought takes place over several years and is often quite slow. There are several implications of formal operational thought. On the positive side, formal operational thought may be related to achieving a sense of identity and to advances in moral reasoning. On the other hand, formal operational thought may lead to a period of confusion or rebellion because of all the questions about life that formal operational thinkers can generate. Specifically, formal operational adolescents may experience (33) adolescent egocentrism where they have trouble separating their own thoughts and emotions from those of others. According to Elkind, this emerges in two forms. One is the (34) imaginary audience, which involves confusing your own thoughts with those of a hypothetical audience. (***Can you provide an example of this phenomenon?***) A second form is the (35) personal fable, which is a tendency to think that your thoughts or feelings are unique and that others cannot possibly experience the same thoughts or feelings.

THE ADULT

Piaget believed that formal operational thought was mastered by most 15-18 year olds, however more recent research suggests otherwise.

Limitations in Adult Cognitive Performance

Many adults do not reason at the formal operational level. Although average intelligence contributes to formal operational thought, formal education is an important factor as well. (***Can you explain why this is the case?***) Further, we tend to apply formal operational thought to areas with which we have some expertise and knowledge.

Growth Beyond Formal Operations?

Despite the fact that formal operational thought is not completely mastered by all adults, some researchers believe that Piaget did not go far enough with cognitive development and have proposed growth beyond formal operations, that is, (36) postformal thought. One suggestion is that adults are more likely than adolescents to use (37) relativistic thinking thinking, which means that they believe that knowledge depends on the subjective perspective of the person with the knowledge. (*What does Perry's work with college students indicate about changes in thought throughout college?*). Adults may also be better able to uncover and resolve contradictions between ideas, and to think about entire systems of ideas.

Aging and Cognitive Skills

Cross-sectional studies with older adults suggest that they perform poorly on concrete and formal operational tasks. Older adults may approach tasks using different styles of thinking that are useful in everyday life, but not on laboratory-type tests.

PIAGET IN PERSPECTIVE

Piaget's Contributions

Piaget's contributions to developmental psychology are enormous. His theory has stimulated a tremendous amount of research and his insights about development—such as active involvement in one's own development and sequencing of cognitive development—continue to guide our understanding of children's thinking.

Challenges to Piaget

Piaget's contributions must be viewed in the context of various challenges to the theory. One criticism of Piaget is that he (38) underestimating the cognitive abilities of young children. Piaget has also been criticized for blurring the distinction between competence and (39) performance. Some researchers do not believe that development is best characterized by a series of broad, coherent (40) stages or qualitative changes in thinking. Piaget has also been criticized for describing development but not really (41) explain development. Other researchers have criticized Piaget for not giving enough attention to the role of (42) social influences on cognitive development.

VYGOTSKY'S SOCIOCULTURAL PERSPECTIVE

Vygotsky developed a theory of cognitive development that emphasizes the sociocultural context of development and the influence of social interactions.

Culture and Thought

Culture and historical context shape what people know and how they think.

Social Interaction and Thought

Social interactions that foster cognitive growth typically take place in what Vygotsky called the zone of (43) proximal development. This is the difference between what learners can do (44) independently and what they can do with assistance. Vygotsky believed that children learned through (45) guided participation as they interacted with more skilled thinkers or problem solvers.

The Tools of Thought

According to Vygotsky, the primary means of passing on successful problem solving strategies is through (46) _____language_____. Vygotsky noted that young children often talked to themselves when working on a problem and he believed this (47) _private speech_ guided the child's thoughts and behaviors. Through social interactions, (48) _____social_____ speech is transformed into (49) _____private_____ speech, and eventually this becomes (50)_____inner_____ speech. (***How is this different from Piaget's view of early speech and thought?***)

Evaluation of Vygotsky

Vygotsky has been criticized for placing too much emphasis on (51) _social interaction_ (recall that Piaget was criticized for *not enough* emphasis on this). Unlike Piaget, Vygotsky believed that different social and historical contexts create differences in cognitive development. Vygotsky thought that (52) _____adults_____ were more important to children's cognitive development. This is different from Piaget's view because Piaget believed that (53) _____peers_____ were especially important to children's learning.

REVIEW OF KEY TERMS

Below is a list of terms and concepts from this chapter. Use these to complete the following sentence definitions. You might also want to try writing definitions in your own words and then checking your definitions with those in the text.

A- not-B error
accommodation
adaptation
adolescent egocentrism
assimilation
centration
class inclusion
clinical method
cognition
conservation
decentration
decontextualize
egocentrism
genetic epistemology
guided participation
horizontal décalage
hypothetical-deductive reasoning
imaginary audience

imaginary companions
object permanence
organization
perceptual salience
personal fable
postformal thought
private speech
relativistic thinking
reversibility
scheme (schema)
seriation
static thought
symbolic capacity
transductive reasoning
transformational thought
transitivity
zone of proximal development

1. _Egocentrism_ is the tendency to view the world from one's own perspective and to have trouble recognizing other points of view.

2. _Guided participation_ is a method of learning through interaction with others who provide aid and support.

3. According to Piaget, the inborn tendency to combine existing schemes into new and more complex schemes is _organization_.

4. Understanding that objects continue to exist even when those objects are no longer directly experienced is called _object permanence_

5. Adolescents sometimes create an _imaginary audience_ when they confuse their own thoughts with the thoughts of a hypothetical audience.

6. In Piaget's theory, _adaptation_ is an inborn tendency to adjust to the demands of the environment.

7. The _A-not-B error_ is often made by 8 to 12 month old infants who successfully find an object hidden at one location and then continue to search at this hiding location after watching the object being hidden at a second location.

8. Cognitive development that may emerge after formal operations is referred to as _postformal thought_

9. The process of interpreting new experiences in terms of existing cognitive structures is called _assimilation_.

10. _Transformational thought_ is the ability to understand changes from one state to another.

11. The _zone of proximal development_ is the difference between what one can do independently and what one can do with assistance.

12. Preschoolers often show _perceptual salience_ when they focus on the most obvious features of a task.

13. The process of mentally "undoing" an action is called _reversibility_.

14. _Private_ speech is not directed toward another person but helps direct the speaker's thoughts and behaviors.

15. Children in Piaget's preoperational stage have trouble with conservation tasks because they have _static thought_, or a focus on endpoints of the problem rather than on the transformation that occurred.

16.   _Accommodation_ is the process of modifying existing cognitive structures in order to understand or adapt to new experiences.

17.   Piaget used the _clinical method_, an interview technique in which a child's response to each question determines the next question.

18.   _Hypothetical-deductive_ reasoning occurs when specific implications are derived from general ideas or hypotheses, and are then systematically tested.

19.   Children in the preoperational stage often draw faulty cause-effect conclusions by incorrectly connecting two things simply because they occur close together, a limit to their thinking called _transductive reasoning_

20.   A _scheme_ is an organized pattern of thought or action used to interpret our experiences.

21.   Teens may exhibit _adolescent egocentrism_ when they fail to differentiate their own thoughts and feelings from those of other people.

22.   The ability to use images, words, or gestures to represent objects and experiences emerges with the development of _symbolic capacity_.

23.   A cognitive operation called _seriation_ allows children to mentally order items along a quantifiable dimension.

24.   The _personal fable_ refers to the tendency to think that you and your thoughts and feelings are unique.

25.   _Transitivity_ is a cognitive operation that allows children to recognize the relationship among elements in a series.

26.   Understanding that certain properties of a substance or object remain the same despite superficial changes in appearance is called _conservation_.

27.   The tendency to focus on a single aspect of problem when more aspects are relevant is called _centration_.

28.   _Relativistic thinking_ is an understanding that knowledge depends on the subjective perspective of the person with the knowledge.

29.   _Class inclusion_ is the understanding that subclasses are included in a whole class.

30.   The ability to focus on two or more dimensions of a problem at one time is called _decentration_.

31.   Piaget called the study of how we come to know reality _genetic epistemology_

32.   The term _horizontal decala_ represents Piaget's recognition that different cognitive skills related to the same stage of cognitive development may emerge at different times.

33.   The activity of knowing and the processes through which knowledge is acquired is called _cognition_ .

34.   The ability to separate prior knowledge and beliefs from the demands of the current task is called _decontextualize_ .

35.   Some children in the preoperational stage may invent an _imaginary companion_ using their capacity for symbolic thought.

MULTIPLE CHOICE SELF TEST

For each multiple choice question, read all alternatives and then select the best answer.

1.   An example of accommodation is
        a.   believing that all four-legged animals with fur are dogs.
        b.   realizing that a cat fits into a different category than a dog.
        c.   the confusion that a child experiences when new events challenge old schemas.
        d.   a child who sees a cat and refers to it as a dog.

2.   Which of the following statements best characterizes Piaget's position on the nature-nurture issue?
        a.   The environment is primarily responsible for providing children with cognitive skills.
        b.   Innate mechanisms are primarily responsible for determining intelligence.
        c.   Ideas are not innate or imposed by others, but are constructed from experiences.
        d.   Some cognitive skills result from innate characteristics while others are influenced only by environmental experiences.

3.   Throughout the sensorimotor stage, infants change from
        a.   focusing on symbols to using simple mental operations.
        b.   an egocentric perspective to one that considers other viewpoints.
        c.   relying on reflexes for understanding their world to mentally planning how to solve simple problems.
        d.   focusing on sensory information to focusing on motoric information for gaining knowledge about their world.

4.   Which of the following is an example of object permanence?
        a.   visually tracking a moving object
        b.   searching for a shoe under the bed because this seems like a likely hiding place
        c.   searching for a toy where the child just watched it being hidden
        d.   using goal directed behavior to systematically check all possible hiding locations
                for a toy

5.   Which of the following responses to a conservation problem indicates that the child has
        reversibility of thought?
        a.   The amount of water in the two cups is the same because even though one is
                taller, the other one is wider.
        b.   The amount of water in the two cups looks about the same, so I'd say they were
                equal.
        c.   I didn't see you spill any water, so the amounts are the same.
        d.   If you'd pour the water back into the original container, you'd see it has the same
                amount of water as the other container.

6.   Research on Piaget's description of preoperational thought has found that
        a.   when task demands are reduced, young children can successfully solve some
                problems at a more sophisticated level.
        b.   when task demands are reduced, it has little impact on performance because
                children do not yet have the cognitive capabilities to solve the problem.
        c.   Piaget was correct in his description of <u>when</u> certain abilities emerged, but was
                not always accurate in his description of what underlying thought was required for
                these abilities.
        d.   Piaget overestimated what most preschool-age children can do.

7.   Formal operational children are different from concrete operational children in that
        a.   formal operational children can deal with possibilities.
        b.   formal operational children focus on realities.
        c.   concrete operational children systematically test all possible solutions to a
                problem.
        d.   concrete operational children are more likely to be egocentric.

8.   Piaget has been criticized by modern developmentalists who suggest that
        a.   Piaget was somewhat pessimistic concerning the timing of cognitive abilities in
                adolescents.
        b.   Piaget was overly optimistic concerning the abilities of infants and young
                children.
        c.   development is a gradual process rather than a stagelike process.
        d.   development is stagelike but stages follow a different pattern than what Piaget
                suggested.

9.	Research by Perry with college students suggests that their thinking progresses from
	a.	assuming that truth is absolute to understanding that truth is relative.
	b.	uncertainty about the "correctness" of answers to absolute certainty about the correctness.
	c.	considering all possible options to selecting a single answer.
	d.	being able to think logically about ideas to thinking logically about multiple sets of ideas.

10.	Research with older adults solving Piagetian tasks shows that
	a.	nearly all are reasoning at the formal operational level.
	b.	older adults perform worse than younger adults on many concrete operational tasks.
	c.	older adults perform similarly to younger adults on all Piagetian tasks.
	d.	older adults are more egocentric than younger adults and tend to use transductive reasoning.

11.	Which of the following is NOT a valid criticism of Piaget's theory?
	a.	He underestimated what infants and young children understand.
	b.	He claimed that development progressed through a few universal stages.
	c.	He did not give as much attention to social influences as some believe he should have.
	d.	He did not do a very good job of describing development.

12.	In comparing Piaget's perspective to Vygotsky's perspective, which of the following is TRUE?
	a.	Piaget believed that knowledge was constructed through independent exploration of the world while Vygotsky believed that social interactions were needed for development of more advanced thinking.
	b.	Both believed that language development was independent of cognitive development.
	c.	Vygotsky believed that private speech was not a developmentally important phenomenon, while Piaget used it as evidence of egocentrism.
	d.	Piaget and Vygotsky both proposed that children progress through major stages in reaching mature cognitive understanding of the world.

13.	Vygotsky used the term zone of proximal development to refer to the
	a.	influence that thought and language have on one another.
	b.	child's approximate level of cognitive skill on a particular task.
	c.	difference between what someone can do independently and what they can do with another person's help.
	d.	point at which the child progresses from one level of understanding to another.

14. Vygotsky would be MOST likely to agree with which one of the following statements?
    a. Knowledge depends on one's culture and social experiences.
    b. Interaction with the physical environment is critically important to development.
    c. Cognitive development precedes language development.
    d. Children's cognitive development progresses in a universal fashion.

15. Which of the following is the best example of Vygotsky's idea of <u>guided participation</u>?
    a. A child asks a friend to participate in a new game.
    b. A child works through a new puzzle with the help of a parent.
    c. A child uses a new word to request something from a parent.
    d. A child volunteers to help set the dinner table.

COMPARE THE MAIN IDEAS OF PIAGET AND VYGOTSKY

This exercise will help you compare Piaget's views on cognitive development with those of Vygotsky. Use Table 7.3 in the text to check your answers.

	PIAGET	VYGOTSKY
1. Is cognitive development universal or context specific?		
2. What sorts of activities lead to cognitive growth?		
3. Is knowledge best constructed individually or with others?		
4. How do cognitive development and language relate to one another?		
5. Are peers or adults more important in the development of cognition?		
6. What is the relationship between learning and development?		

CRITICAL THINKING QUESTIONS

By answering the following questions, you will strengthen your understanding of the material in this chapter. These questions require higher level thinking skills such as integration and application of concepts. Sample answers are provided for three of the questions. These illustrate one possibility, but there are other answers you could provide that might be just as good. For the other questions, you can check yourself by referring to the text (a hint is provided), or by asking a peer or your instructor to review your answer.

1. Apply Piaget's description of cognitive development to a social issue such as divorce, birth of a new sibling, or adoption. What would a child's understanding of one these events be in each of Piaget's four stages of cognitive development?
    [Sample answer provided.]

2. When you consider the preschool-aged child in light of Piaget's description of the preoperational stage and modern research findings, how would you characterize the cognitive abilities of the preschool-aged child?
    [Sample answer provided.]

3. Suppose you need to design a program to teach 6-year-old children a new academic skill. How would you approach this from Piaget's perspective? How would you approach this from Vygotsky's perspective? How would the two programs be similar or different?
    [Sample answer provided.]

4. Piaget's theory has stimulated a tremendous amount of research on cognitive development over the past 30 years. Considering what we have learned from this research, how would Piaget's theory need to be updated to account for the findings that have emerged since the theory was developed?
    [Hint: Read the "Challenges to Piaget" section in the text, as well as the research on Piaget's theory that was discussed in sections on "The Infant," "The Child," "The Adolescent," and "The Adult."]

5. Some researchers have demonstrated that Piagetian skills such as conservation can be taught. What are the implications of this for the principles of Piaget's theory?
    [Hint: Read "Did Piaget underestimate the preschool child?" and "Challenges to Piaget."]

ANSWERS

Chapter Summary and Guided Review (Fill-in the blank)
1. cognition   3.   clinical method
2. genetic epistemology   4.   schemes

5. organization
6. adaptation
7. assimilation
8. accommodation
9. disequilibrium
10. constructivism
11. invariant
12. sensorimotor
13. object permanence
14. A-, not-B error
15. symbolic capacity
16. imaginary companions
17. perceptual salience
18. conservation
19. decentration
20. centration
21. reversibility
22. transformations
23. egocentric
24. class inclusion
25. horizontal decalage
26. seriation
27. transitivity
28. class inclusion
29. abstract

30. hypothetical
31. hypothetical-deductive
32. decontextualize
33. adolescent egocentrism
34. imaginary audience
35. personal fable
36. postformal
37. relativistic
38. underestimated
39. performance
40. stages
41. explaining
42. social
43. proximal
44. independently
45. guided participation
46. language
47. private speech
48. social
49. private
50. inner
51. social interaction
52. adults
53. peers (other children)

Review of Key Terms

1. egocentrism
2. guided participation
3. organization
4. object permanence
5. imaginary audience
6. adaptation
7. A, not-B, error
8. postformal thought
9. assimilation
10. transformational thought
11. zone of proximal development
12. perceptual salience
13. reversibility
14. private
15. static thought
16. accommodation
17. clinical method
18. hypothetical-deductive

19. transductive reasoning
20. scheme
21. adolescent egocentrism
22. symbolic capacity
23. seriation
24. personal fable
25. transitivity
26. conservation
27. centration
28. relativistic thinking
29. class inclusion
30. decentration
31. genetic epistemology
32. horizontal décalage
33. cognition
34. decontextualize
35. imaginary companion

1.	B (p. 173)	6.	A (p. 181)	11.	D (p. 192)
2.	C (pp. 172-73)	7.	A (p. 183)	12.	A (p. 192)
3.	C (p. 177)	8.	C (p. 192)	13.	C (p. 193)
4.	C (p. 175)	9.	A (p. 190)	14.	A (p. 193)
5.	D (p. 179)	10.	B (p.190)	15.	B (p. 194)

Critical Thinking Questions

1. *Considering adoption, children in the sensorimotor stage most likely would not understand the concept because they are just experiencing the beginning of thought at the end of this stage.*

A preoperational child might be able to tell people, "I'm adopted," but they wouldn't really understand what this meant. For one thing, they have static thought and focus on end results. They would only know that they ended up with the people they call Mom and Dad, but not really grasp the process that led to this. In addition, preoperational children exhibit centration, which allows them to focus on only a single aspect of a problem. They might be able to focus on where babies come from, but not integrate this with other concepts that occur with adoption. Another difficulty for the preoperational child is class inclusion. This child would have trouble understanding that adoption is one "classification" of ways a parent can "get" a child, but that most children are not gotten this way. Also, children in preoperations are egocentric, so they would have trouble understanding the perspective of other people involved (e.g., the mother who gave them up for adoption). Finally, preoperational children can't understand that they are the children of their biological mother and their adoptive mother; they center on one or the other.

The concrete operational child would be better able to comprehend adoption because of their increased powers of logical reasoning. For instance, concrete operational children can decenter, so they can focus on more than one aspect of the problem. They would also understand that adoption is one of several ways that children end up in a particular family. Not until formal operations, though, would adolescents gain a better understanding of why they were adopted. They could consider all the abstract issues that go into adoption decisions and reason about possibilities (e.g., what might have happened if they had not been adopted). On the negative side, formal operational children could devise hypothetical reasons for why their biological parents did not want to raise them and this might create some anguish. They may also be interested in knowing more about their biological parents, as this information might allow them to systematically test various theories they have constructed about their circumstances.

2. *Preschool-aged children are able to use the symbolic capacity that they achieved at the end of the sensorimotor period to expand their language as well as their play. They can, for example, engage in pretend play by using one thing to represent something else. They begin to internalize more of their cognition—i.e., they no longer have to act motorically on sensory information in order to learn about the world around them.*

Preschoolers are limited in their ability to think logically. Young children are often fooled by the surface appearance of something and aren't advanced enough cognitively to delve beneath the surface. When tested with the original tasks used by Piaget, preschoolers often appear far less capable than concrete-operational older children. But when tasks are simplified, *or training is provided, preschoolers demonstrate a greater understanding. There is a difference between preschool-aged children and elementary school-aged children, but the gap is not as wide as Piaget claimed. Preschool-aged children do tend to be egocentric, as Piaget claimed, but there are times and situations when this is not the case. Similarly, there are times and situations when older children (and even adults) <u>are</u> egocentric.*

In sum, preschoolers have some accurate intuitions about the world, but lack the ability to systematically test these intuitions. They are more bound by their perceptions than older children.

3.   *Piaget's program would be organized to encourage children to interact with their physical environment. He believed that children needed opportunities to explore objects in order to discover properties of these objects as well as elementary principles about the world in general. Thus, interactions between the individual and physical objects would be a key feature of the Piagetian program. The individual has to construct her own understanding of the world; it can't come from someone else. Piaget would expect that all the children in the program would proceed through his four universal stages of cognitive development. He would also argue that children can't be rushed to learn something before they are cognitively ready. They can only assimilate and accommodate information at their own pace. Development can't be speeded up.*

Vygotsky's program would be organized to encourage social interactions among children and especially between a child and a more knowledgeable peer. He believed that children learned a great deal through interactions with others. Vygotsky used the term zone of proximal development to highlight the gap between what a learner can do independently and what she can do or understand with the guidance and support of a more skilled partner. This suggests that children can be led to learn something earlier than they might otherwise have learned on their own. Vygotsky would not believe that all the children would progress through the same stages. Depending on their cultural background and the sorts of social interactions they had, they might follow quite different paths of cognitive development.

CHAPTER EIGHT

MEMORY AND INFORMATION PROCESSING

OVERVIEW

This chapter focuses on memory processes and uses the information processing model to describe how information is moved in and out of the memory stores. You will learn that young children and older adults have trouble with some learning and memory tasks. To understand these difficulties with memory, four hypotheses are explored. These involve changes in: 1) basic capacities, 2) memory strategies, 3) metamemory, and 4) knowledge base. These provide a useful way to organize much of the research on developmental changes in memory and information processing.

The chapter also considers the intriguing question of why we cannot remember much, if anything, from our infancy and early childhood years. You will learn when autobiographical memories begin and how such memories are stored. You will also learn how time and experience can alter our memories, something that has significant implications for eyewitness testimony.

LEARNING OBJECTIVES

After reading and studying the material in this chapter, you should be able to answer the following questions.

1.   What is the general orientation of the information-processing model to cognition? What are the specific components of the model?

2.   How do researchers assess infant memory? What information can infants typically remember? What are the limitations of infants' memory?

3.   What are four major hypotheses about why memory improves with age? Which of these hypotheses is (are) supported by research?

4.   When do autobiographical memories begin and what possible explanations can account for childhood amnesia?

5.   How do scripts influence memory?

6.   How do problem solving capacities change during childhood?

7.   What developments occur in the information processing abilities of adolescents?

8.   In what ways do memory and cognition change during adulthood? What are the strengths and weaknesses of older adults' abilities? What factors help explain the declines in abilities during older adulthood?

9.   How are problem solving skills influenced by aging?

CHAPTER SUMMARY AND GUIDED REVIEW

The following summary provides an overview of the main points contained in this chapter of the text. Fill-in the blanks with terms that appropriately complete the sentence.   Scattered throughout the summary are questions in parentheses. These are meant to encourage you to think actively as you are reading and connect this summary to the more detailed information provided in the text. You can answer these questions as you are filling in the blanks or you can complete all the blanks, then go back and reread the entire summary, addressing the questions in order to provide more depth of understanding.

THE INFORMATION PROCESSING APPROACH
Information processing theorists attempt to understand human learning and remembering by comparing these processes to the workings of a (1) __computer__.

The Memory Systems
A popular information-processing model proposes that information coming into the information-processing system (i.e., the person) is held briefly in a (2) __sensory register__. If the person pays attention to this information, it will be moved into (3) __short-term memory__ also called working memory. Information to be remembered for any length of time must somehow be moved into (4) __long-term__ memory.
In order to remember something, it must first get into the system by being (5) __encoded__. Then it goes into (6) __storage__, which is when it is held in long-term memory. When the information is needed, it must be taken out or

(7) _retrieved_ from long-term memory. Retrieval of information by reproducing it without cues uses (8) _recall_, which is more difficult than indicating whether or not the information has been previously experienced, which uses (9) _recognition_ memory. Between these two forms of retrieval is (10) _cued_ recall where some sort of hint is given.

Implicit and Explicit Memory

Some memory tasks require deliberate attempts to remember something; they involve (11) _explicit memory_. In contrast, others involve (12) _implicit memory_ which occurs automatically and without conscious effort. Age differences are small on tasks of (13) _implicit memory_ memory and larger on (14) _explicit memory_ memory tasks that require deliberate processing.

Problem Solving

Using the information-processing system to achieve a goal or make a decision is (15) _problem solving_. To be able to do this, the information-processing system includes a number of executive (16) _control processes_ to monitor, plan, and interpret information.

THE INFANT
Memory

Researchers use various techniques to assess infant memory. Infants show memory when they (17) _imitate_ or repeat an action performed by a model. Or assessment might be done by repeatedly presenting them with a stimulus until they no longer respond to it, a process called (18) _habituation_. To test long-term memory, some researchers have relied on (19) _operant conditioning_ to train an infant to respond to a stimulus. (**_Can you explain how this can be used to demonstrate infant memory?_**) Infants will likely have trouble with retrieval of information unless they are provided with sufficient (20) _cues_ to aid retrieval. Evidence of pure recall memory comes when infants show (21) _deferred_ imitation and also when they can solve object permanence tasks.

Problem Solving

By 9 months, there is some evidence of simple problem-solving skills.

THE CHILD
Explaining Memory Development

Although the basic memory and information processing skills are present during infancy, memory clearly improves during childhood. There are four main hypotheses about why this improvement occurs.

Do basic capacities change? One possibility is that basic capacities change. For example, some neo-Piagetian theorists propose that working memory space increases during childhood. Research shows that total capacity increases somewhat, but more importantly, children become more efficient and faster at using the space they have as many processes become (22) _automatized_ and require little effort.

Do memory strategies change? Another possibility for the improvement in learning and memory is that memory strategies improve with age. Although young children can deliberately

metamemory: knowledge of memory & to monitoring &
regulating memory processes
ex: what memory strategies or more/less effective

remember when they are highly motivated, their memory strategies are not always very effective.
One strategy is to use (23) __rehearsal__, or repeating the items to be remembered.
Another strategy is (24) __organization__, or classifying items to be remembered into
meaningful groups. A third strategy is to use (25) __elaboration__, or creating
meaningful links between the items to be remembered. Rehearsal typically develops first,
followed by use of organization and finally by spontaneous use of elaboration in adolescence.

Strategies emerge gradually. At first, children cannot use or benefit from a strategy even
if taught to use one, which is the (26) __mediation__ phase of strategy use. In the next
phase, children show (27) __production__ when they use strategies they are taught but
do not produce them on their own. In a phase called (28) __utilization__, children
can produce the strategy but their performance does not benefit from it. Effective strategy use
occurs when children can produce and benefit from a strategy. Even when effective memory
strategies are used, appropriate (29) __retrieval__ strategies must also be employed
for successful recall.

Does knowledge about memory change? A third explanation for the improvement in
learning and memory is that knowledge about memory and other cognitive processes changes
with age. Knowledge of memory and memory processes is called (30) __metamemory__
and does improve with age. (*Can you provide evidence that shows growth in this skill?*) These
improvements are associated with increases in memory, although the relationship depends on the
nature of the task.

Does knowledge of the world change? A fourth possibility is that increased knowledge
of the world in general, or (31) __knowledge base__, leads to improvements in memory.
There is research evidence that children who have an extensive knowledge base in a particular
area can outperform adults who are novices in the same area.

Autobiographical Memory

Memories for events that have happened to you personally form the collection of
(32) __autobiographical memory__ Although infants and toddlers show evidence of memory, older
children and adults exhibit (33) __childhood amnesia__ for their early experiences. Research
shows that we have few, if any, memories of events prior to age (34) __2 to 3__.
Prior to this, there may not be enough space in working memory to hold multiple pieces of
information about an event and lack of (35) __language__ may also reduce what can
be stored. Infants and toddlers may also lack a sense of self that they can use to organize
memories of things that happened to them. Another possibility comes from
(36) __fuzzy-trace__ theory, which predicts that verbatim and general accounts of an
event are stored separately.

Children construct (37) __scripts__ of routine daily activities and use these
when retelling events. Memories for an event change over time and change with the introduction
of new information, indicating that memory is a (38) __reconstruction__ and not an exact
replication. Reporting events that you have witnessed is a form of (39) __eyewitness memory__
(*What factors affect the accuracy of this recall?*)

metacognition: knowledge of human mind & of the range
of cognitive processes
ex: understanding that your better at learning math
than biology

Problem Solving

Problem solving capacities also change during childhood. Siegler uses a (40) rule assessment approach to determine what information children take in and what rules they generate to solve a problem. Siegler's research shows that 3-year-olds guess; that is, they use no strategies. By age 4 or 5, most children are rule governed, but the type of rule used changes with age and children have trouble integrating multiple pieces of information. Siegler believes that problem solving skills develop, not as a series of stages, but as (41) overlapping waves where children have a variety of strategies available at any given time and gradually choose the ones most effective for the task at hand.

THE ADOLESCENT

During adolescence, some new learning and memory strategies, such as elaboration, emerge. Adolescents' use of strategies is more deliberate, selective, and spontaneous than younger children's. Adolescents know more in general, so their (42) knowledge bases expand, and they also show improvements in their understanding of their learning and memory processes, or their (43) metacognition .

THE ADULT
Developing Expertise

During adulthood, developing expertise in a field facilitates memory and problem solving within this field. (***In what ways can this affect memory and problem solving?***) Experts have more extensive and organized knowledge bases than novices. Expertise, though, is (44) domain specific because expertise in one area does not improve memory in other areas.

Learning, Memory, and Aging

Self-reports suggest that memory declines with age. Declines in memory are slight and usually do not occur until one's 60's or 70's. Also, since much of the research in this area has used (45) cross-sectional designs, the apparent declines could be due to other factors related to cohort differences. Not all adults experience memory problems and not all tasks create memory difficulties for older adults. Older adults tend to have trouble with (46) timed tasks because they are slower than younger adults to learn and retrieve information. They also have trouble on tasks that are (47) unfamiliar or have little relevance to them. Tasks requiring rarely used skills and tasks requiring (48) recall memory rather than recognition memory are also problematic for older adults. Finally, older adults show more trouble with (49) explicit memory tasks that require effortful learning.

Possible explanations for the learning and memory declines observed in older adults are basically the same as those considered for young children's performance. Unlike young children, older adults know much about the world, so they do not have deficient (50) knowledge base Metamemory problems also do not seem to contribute greatly to memory declines in older adults. Older adults do not always spontaneously use effective strategies. They also need to devote more space than younger adults to short-term or (51) working memory, which leaves less space to devote to other purposes. (***What might account for declines in short-term memory capacity?***)

Sensory losses experienced by many older adults can also impede memory performance.

In addition, there are many (52) ___contextual___ factors associated with the specific learner and task that influence memory. For instance, the declines in memory observed for older adults compared to younger adults may be due to generational or (53) ___cohort___ differences. Older adults tend to be less educated and may not be as motivated to perform as younger adults.

Problem Solving and Aging

Older adults also seem to perform more poorly than young adults on problem solving tasks. On a twenty-questions task, being able to rule out multiple items by asking (54) ___constraint-seeking___ questions is most efficient. Older children and young adults use this strategy, but older adults do not unless the task is altered to make it more familiar to them. Older adults perform better on problems involving everyday problems than on unfamiliar or laboratory tasks.

REVIEW OF KEY TERMS

Below is a list of terms and concepts from this chapter. Use these to complete the following sentence definitions. You might also want to try writing definitions in your own words and then checking your definitions with those in the text.

autobiographical memories
childhood amnesia
constraint-seeking questions
cued recall memory
deferred imitation
elaboration
encoding
executive control processes
explicit memory
eyewitness memory
fuzzy trace theory
implicit memory
information-processing approach
knowledge base
long-term memory
mediation deficiency
metacognition

metamemory
method of loci
mild cognitive impairment (MCI)
organization (as memory strategy)
problem solving
production deficiency
recall memory
recognition memory
rehearsal
retrieval
rule assessment approach
scripts
sensory register
short-term memory
storage
utilization deficiency
working memory

1. Reporting events that you have seen is the essence of _____.

2. The memory strategy of ___eyewitness memory___ involves repeating items to be remembered.

3. According to ___fuzzy trace theory___, verbatim and general accounts of an event are stored separately in memory.

4. ___Implicit memory___ is memory that occurs unintentionally.

5. An older adult with ___MCI___ has some memory loss, but it is not the pathological memory loss associated with disease.

6. ___Retrieval___ is the act of getting information out of long-term memory when it is needed.

7. ___Organization___ is a memory strategy that involves classifying items to be remembered into meaningful groups.

8. Memory that requires individuals to indicate whether they have previously experienced a stimulus is ___recognition memory___

9. We often construct ___scripts___ of familiar events and then use these mental representations to guide future behavior in similar settings.

10. Sometimes, children can produce a strategy but do not benefit from it because of task demands; this is known as ___utilization deficiency___

11. ___Short-term memory___ is a memory store that temporarily stores a limited amount of information and allows active use of this information.

12. Our ___autobiographical memories___ consists of everyday events that we have experienced.

13. The memory strategy of ___elaboration___ involves creating meaningful links between the items to be remembered.

14. ___long-term memory___ is a memory store that is relatively permanent and holds our knowledge of the world and our past experiences.

15. Knowledge of our own memory and memory processes is called ___metamemory___

16. Creating a mental map of space and using this image as a memory device is the ___method of loci___

17. ___Sensory register___ is the process of getting information into the information-processing system, and processing it.

18. ___Recall___ is a type of memory that requires individuals to reproduce a previously encountered stimulus without cues.

19. Our lack of memory for the first few years of life is called ___Childhood amnesia___

20. Holding information in long-term memory is referred to as ___storage___.

21. Using the information-processing system to achieve a goal or make a decision is known as ___problem solving___

22. A person's _knowledge base_ is their knowledge of a content area.

23. _executive control processes_ are the information processing tools that plan and monitor problem solving and decision making.

24. _Explicit_ memory is intentional and deliberate.

25. The _information processing_ approach to cognition uses a computer analogy and emphasizes mental processes involved in attention, perception, memory, and decision making.

26. _Metacognition_ refers to knowledge about the mind and cognitive processes that might be used.

27. Children exhibit a _production deficiency_ when they use strategies they are taught, but do not produce the strategies on their own.

28. _constraint seeking questions_ is a problem solving strategy that rules out several possible solutions rather than just one.

29. The _sensory register_ holds a very brief, but literal image or record of stimuli.

30. The _rule assessment approach_ is an analysis of problem solving ability that determines what information is encoded and what rules are generated by the problem solver.

31. Providing a hint to facilitate retrieval is _cued recall_ .

32. Short-term memory is also referred to as _working memory_.

33. Infants show _deffered imitation_ when they can reproduce an action they have previously seen at some later time.

34. Children who do not use or benefit from a strategy even when they are taught to use it show a _mediation deficiency_

MULTIPLE CHOICE SELF TEST

For each multiple choice question, read all alternatives and then select the best answer.

1. In the information-processing model, the "hardware" would be _____ and the "software" would be _____.
   a. the short-term and long-term memory stores; strategies for storing and recalling information
   b. memory; the short-term and long-term memory stores
   c. the sensory receptors; the central nervous system
   d. the central nervous system; sensory receptors

2.	Tim is introduced to a professional colleague at a meeting, but has no idea what the person's name is immediately after it was spoken! It is most likely that the name:
	a.	never made it past Tim's sensory register.
	b.	is stuck in Tim's short-term memory.
	c.	is lost in Tim's long-term memory.
	d.	could be cued to recall later on if Tim would relax a bit.

3.	Taking an essay exam is an example of _____, while taking a multiple choice exam uses _____ memory.
	a.	long term memory; short term
	b.	recall; reconstruction
	c.	recall; recognition
	d.	recognition; long term memory

4.	Memory that is deliberate and effortful is _____, and memory that is unconscious or effortless is _____.
	a.	implicit; explicit
	b.	recall; recognition
	c.	explicit; implicit
	d.	cued recall; automatized

5.	Habituation is sometimes used to assess infant's memory. Habituation occurs when an infant
	a.	stops responding to a repeatedly presented stimulus.
	b.	is conditioned to respond to a familiar stimulus.
	c.	learns to respond to a desired stimulus.
	d.	turns in the direction of a novel stimulus.

6.	At age 8, Jill can remember more than her 3-year-old brother, Harry. This is MOST LIKELY because:
	a.	Jill is smarter than Harry.
	b.	Jill has a larger sensory register than Harry.
	c.	Jill has a much better understanding of the strengths and weaknesses of her memory system than Harry.
	d.	Jill makes more efficient use of her working memory than Harry does.

7.	Bob knows that he remembers the material in biology better when he takes notes from a chapter he is reading, than when he simply highlights passages in the text. His knowledge of this BEST illustrates
	a.	chunking.
	b.	elaboration.
	c.	metamemory.
	d.	organization.

8. Memory strategies tend to develop in order, with _____ appearing first, followed by _____ , and then _____ .
    a. organization; elaboration; rehearsal
    b. organization; rehearsal; elaboration
    c. rehearsal; elaboration; organization
    ⓓ rehearsal; organization; elaboration

9. Most children and adults cannot remember much about their lives prior to about age 3. This is because
    a. early experiences are unimportant.
    ⓑ they store verbatim rather than general accounts of events, leading to greater loss of information.
    c. they are not using the proper strategies to retrieve this information from long-term memory.
    d. they have no ability to store memories prior to age three.

10. Siegler's research regarding the rule assessment approach to problem solving (with the balance beam problem) shows that
    a. most children master the correct rule by age 8.
    b. even the youngest children, age 3, use logical rules to solve the problem.
    c. children master a single rule, applying it to all tasks, before moving on to another rule.
    ⓓ children progress from guessing to trying several rules to selection of correct rules.

11. One difference between the memory strategy use of preadolescents and adolescents is that adolescents
    a. randomly select a strategy.
    b. use fewer strategies to remember important information.
    c. remember more irrelevant information than younger children.
    ⓓ are better able to distinguish the more relevant points from the irrelevant points.

12. Which of the following statements accurately describes memory performance of adults?
    a. Memory systematically declines throughout adulthood.
    ⓑ Memory declines may in older adulthood but they are typically small.
    c. Memory does not change from adolescence through middle adulthood, but after this, memory declines quite rapidly.
    d. Older adults experience no memory declines because they use more memory strategies than younger adults.

13. Research on expertise shows that
    a. experts do not know any more than nonexperts but are able to organize their knowledge more effectively.
    b. it depends on domain-specific knowledge and strategies.
    c. experts spend more time thinking through all possible options on a problem before selecting the correct one.
    d. expertise generalizes from one area to another, so experts tend to be good on multiple tasks.

14. Among adults, problem-solving skills
    a. tend to improve steadily across the life-span.
    b. decline rapidly during middle age.
    c. frequently depend on the meaningfulness of the problem at hand.
    d. decline more rapidly in women than in men.

15. Some older adults develop a mild cognitive impairment and demonstrate:
    a. substantial memory loss and signs of dementia.
    b. an inability to store new memories.
    c. lack of interest in the world around them.
    d. memory loss beyond what is considered normal, but not the pathological loss associated with disease.

CRITICAL THINKING QUESTIONS

By answering the following questions, you will strengthen your understanding of the material in this chapter. These questions require higher level thinking skills such as integration and application of concepts. Sample answers are provided for three of the questions. These illustrate one possibility, but there are other answers you could provide that might be just as good. For the other questions, you can check yourself by referring to the text (a hint is provided), or by asking a peer or your instructor to review your answer.

1. What practical suggestions regarding the memory and problem solving skills of older adults would be helpful to someone who works with older adults?
   [Sample answer provided.]

2. In what ways are the memory and problem solving skills of young children and older adults similar?
   [Sample answer provided.]

3. What factors might explain the childhood amnesia that prevents most of us from recalling events of our infancy and early childhood?
   [Sample answer provided.]

4.   As children's eyewitness testimony in court proceedings has increased, we have seen more research on children's reliability as witnesses. Based on what you know about memory development from this chapter, what conclusions and suggestions can you make regarding the use of children as witnesses?
[Hint: Review the section on "The Child," with attention to strengths and weaknesses of children's memory.]

5.   What advice would you give elementary and secondary school aged students to improve their memory and learning skills?
[Hint: Review the section "The Child" and "The Adolescent."]

ANSWERS

Chapter Summary and Guided Review (Fill-in the blank)

1.	computer	28.	utilization deficiency
2.	sensory register	29.	retrieval
3.	short-term memory	30.	metamemory
4.	long-term	31.	knowledge base
5.	encoded	32.	autobiographical memory
6.	storage	33.	childhood amnesia
7.	retrieved	34.	2 to 3
8.	recall	35.	language
9.	recognition	36.	fuzzy trace
10.	cued	37.	scripts
11.	explicit memory	38.	reconstruction
12.	implicit memory	39.	eyewitness memory
13.	implicit	40.	rule assessment
14.	explicit	41.	overlapping waves
15.	problem solving	42.	knowledge bases
16.	control processes	43.	metacognition
17.	imitate	44.	domain specific
18.	habituation	45.	cross-sectional
19.	operant conditioning	46.	timed
20.	cues	47.	unfamiliar
21.	deferred	48.	recall
22.	automatized	49.	explicit
23.	rehearsal	50.	knowledge bases
24.	organization	51.	working
25.	elaboration	52.	contextual
26.	mediation deficiency	53.	cohort
27.	production deficiency	54.	constraint-seeking

Review of Key Terms

1.	eyewitness memory	4.	implicit memory
2.	rehearsal	5.	mild cognitive impairment (MCI)
3.	fuzzy trace theory	6.	retrieval

7.	organization	21.	problem solving
8.	recognition memory	22.	knowledge base
9.	scripts	23.	executive control processes
10.	utilization deficiency	24.	explicit
11.	short-term memory	25.	information-processing
12.	autobiographical memories	26.	metacognition
13.	elaboration	27.	constraint-seeking questions
14.	long-term memory	28.	production deficiency
15.	metamemory	29.	sensory register
16.	method of loci	30.	rule assessment approach
17.	encoding	31.	cued recall memory
18.	recall memory	32.	working memory
19.	childhood amnesia	33.	deferred imitation
20.	storage	34.	mediation deficiency

Multiple Choice Self Test

1.	A (p. 200)	6.	D (p. 205)	11.	D (p. 213)
2.	A (p. 201)	7.	C (p. 207)	12.	B (p. 216)
3.	C (p. 201)	8.	D (p. 206)	13.	B (p. 214)
4.	C (p. 201)	9.	B (p. 209)	14.	C (p. 222)
5.	A (p. 203)	10.	D (p. 211)	15.	D (pp. 216-217)

Critical Thinking Questions

1.   *It's true that older adults have some trouble with memory and problem solving relative to younger adults. Still, like everyone, they have strengths and weaknesses, and the trick is to maximize their strengths and minimize their weaknesses. To help them perform better, avoid timed tasks. Older adults are slower to learn and retrieve information and may need more time to accomplish these tasks than their younger counterparts. They also do poorly when given novel words to remember or unfamiliar tasks to solve. But they do just fine if the material and tasks are familiar to them. Indeed, given their life experiences, older adults have a more extensive knowledge base than other age groups. Another disadvantage for older adults is that they are often tested in situations that are common for young adults who are working or going to school, but not for people who have been retired or away from school for many years. By testing older adults in situations that they typically experience, where they can use well-practiced skills, they perform better. Like all age groups, older adults are better on recognition tasks than recall tasks, so we can optimize their performance by testing them with a recognition format. Similarly, we can optimize performance by structuring learning situations as implicit rather than explicit. It's also important to consider sensory changes that older adults might experience—visual and auditory declines can tax the information processing system leading to memory trouble. Correcting vision and hearing problems can help memory problems in some cases. Fortunately, research shows that older adults can benefit from memory training (you can teach an old dog new tricks), and significant problems with memory and problem solving are unusual.*

2.   *The memory and problem solving abilities of young children and older adults have some common features, but also some important differences. Like young children, older adults may not spontaneously use strategies. And both young children and older adults need to devote more*

space in working memory to carrying out basic mental operations such as recognizing stimuli. This leaves less space for other purposes, such as thinking about or rehearsing material. Both young children and older adults do relatively well when learning and remembering can take place automatically (i.e., when mental effort is not required), but struggle when they need to exert more mental effort. The problem with working memory is probably due to slower functioning of the nervous system both early and late in life.

Although the question asks for similarities and not differences between young children and older adults, there are two differences worth noting. Older adults have a much larger knowledge base than younger children, and they also know more about how their memory works (metamemory). These advantages may allow older adults to compensate for their slow working memory and their lack of spontaneous strategy use so that they end up outperforming young children on many memory tasks.

3.　　*Most people have trouble remembering anything that happened to them before the age of 2 or 3 years. This is called childhood amnesia. One explanation for this is that infants and toddlers may not have enough space in working memory to hold all the pieces of information about an event that would be needed to recall the event. Another possibility is that their language limitations constrain what infants and toddlers can store and later recall about an event. Thus, perhaps language is needed to store memories in some kind of linguistic code that can be retrieved later on. A third explanation is that memories from this early period of life are no longer useful in light of the new developmental tasks that children face. Finally, the fuzzy-trace theory suggests that verbatim and general accounts of an event are stored separately. Verbatim information is problematic and likely to be lost over long periods of time, but general accounts (e.g., remembering the "gist" of an event) remain viable for longer periods of time. Young children seem to store more verbatim information about events and gradually move to storing the more efficient general information as they get a little older.*

CHAPTER NINE

INTELLIGENCE AND CREATIVITY

OVERVIEW

The chapter opens by considering the meaning of intelligence: is it one ability or many? If it consists of multiple abilities, what are these abilities? As with other chapters, there are sections devoted to each of the major age groups—infants, children, adolescents, and adults—where developmental changes in intelligence are discussed. In particular, the stability and continuity of IQ scores are considered, as are the potential uses of IQ scores.

Genetic and environmental factors that influence IQ scores are discussed in this chapter. Recall that genetic influences on intelligence were discussed earlier in the text (Chapter 3 on Genetics), and it might be useful for you to review the evidence for genetic contributions that was presented in the earlier chapter. The section in this chapter focuses on environmental factors, including the home, social class, and culture.

A discussion of the extremes of intelligence—mental retardation and giftedness—is also included in this chapter. Finally, creativity is discussed, including its definition and measurement, and whether or not we can identify developmental changes in creativity.

LEARNING OBJECTIVES

After reading and studying the material in this chapter, you should be able to answer the following questions.

1.   What is the psychometric approach to intelligence and how have different psychometric theorists defined intelligence?

2.   What are the traditional measures of intelligence and what are some of the advantages and disadvantages of these approaches? What are some alternatives to these traditional measures of intelligence?

3.   How is infant intelligence measured? To what extent is infant intelligence related to later intelligence?

4.   Are IQ scores stable during childhood? What factors contribute to gains and losses in IQ scores?

5.   How well do IQ scores predict school achievement? To what extent is IQ related to occupational success?

6.   How do IQ and mental abilities change with age? What factors predict declines in intellectual abilities in older adults?

7.   To what extent does wisdom exist in older adults?

8.   What evidence shows genetic influence on IQ scores? What other factors influence IQ scores?

9.   How are mental retardation and giftedness defined? What are the outcomes for individuals who are mentally retarded or gifted?

10.   What is creativity? How does it change across the life span?

CHAPTER SUMMARY AND GUIDED REVIEW

The following summary provides an overview of the main points contained in this chapter of the text. Fill-in the blanks with terms that appropriately complete the sentence. Scattered throughout the summary are questions in parentheses. These are meant to encourage you to think actively as you are reading and connect this summary to the more detailed information provided in the text. You can answer these questions as you are filling in the blanks or you can complete all the blanks, then go back and reread the entire summary, addressing the questions in order to provide more depth of understanding.

WHAT IS INTELLIGENCE?
The Psychometric Approach
        The psychometric approach views intelligence as a trait or set of traits that vary among people and can be measured. Early views of intelligence were influenced by Spearman who concluded that a (1)_____ factor contributed to performance on many different tasks. Somewhat later, Thurstone identified seven distinct (2) _____ mental abilities. Cattell and Horn proposed a still popular idea that intelligence consists of two major dimensions. The ability to solve novel problems is (3) _____ intelligence and the ability to use knowledge acquired through experiences is (4)_____ intelligence.

Gardner's Theory of Multiple Intelligences
        More recently, Gardner proposed that there are multiple intelligences, including at least eight distinct abilities. (***Can you give examples or list the different abilities?***) Evidence that someone can be good in one ability but poor in another ability comes from individuals with (5) _____.

Sternberg's Triarchic Theory
        Sternberg's triarchic theory emphasizes three aspects of intelligent behavior. According to the (6) _____ subtheory of the model, intelligent behavior depends on the sociocultural context in which it is displayed and so can be expected to vary from one culture or subculture to another. The (7) _____ subtheory predicts that intelligent behavior will be affected by the experience that one has with a situation or task. The intelligent response to a task the first time it is encountered may differ from what is considered intelligent after many encounters with the same task. The increased efficiency that comes with familiarity and practice with a task reflects (8) _____. Administering an intelligence test to two groups of people that has items familiar to one group but not to the other introduces (9) _____ and makes it unfair to compare performances of the two groups. The third aspect of Sternberg's triarchic model is the (10) _____ subtheory and includes the strategies, or (11) _____ components of intelligence. Sternberg has expanded his triarchic theory of intelligence to include the idea that intelligence involves the ability to do well in life, something he calls (12) _____.

THE INFANT
Developmental Quotients
        Infant achievement is typically measured with the (13) _____ Scales of Infant Development. This test includes a motor scale and a mental scale, which are used to assign a (14) _____. A third component of the test is an infant behavioral record. Bayley scores can be used to chart developmental progress and low scores may indicate mental retardation.

Infant Intelligence and Later Intelligence
        Scores on the Bayley do not accurately predict later IQ, possibly because the infant tests and IQ tests measure qualitatively different abilities. Another possibility is that intelligence during infancy is highly influenced by universal (15) _____ processes. Starting around the age of two, these forces lessen and individual differences become more

apparent. Recent research suggests that later IQ may be better predicted by performance on some measures of infant (16) _____, such as speed of habituation and preference for novelty. (*Why might this be a better predictor?*)

THE CHILD
How Stable are IQ Scores during Childhood?

Starting at age 4, there is a fairly strong relationship between IQ scores obtained at different times throughout childhood. However, although group scores are fairly stable, scores of individual children can fluctuate quite substantially. (*What do these findings suggest?*)

Causes of Gain and Loss

One reason for fluctuating IQ scores is an unstable environment. The (17) _____ hypothesis suggests that intellectual development of children from impoverished environments is diminished and this effect builds over time so that children's intelligence actually seems to decline. (*Is there any research support for this hypothesis?*)

THE ADOLESCENT
Continuity between Childhood and Adulthood

Intelligence continues to grow during early adolescence, but levels off in late adolescence. This may be related to basic brain changes. Individual performance on IQ tests tends to be more stable at this age and predicts adult IQ performance quite well.

IQ and School Achievement

IQ scores are often used to predict school achievement and they are fairly good at doing this. Prediction is more accurate for high school grades than for college grades. (*Why is this the case?*)

THE ADULT
IQ and Occupational Success

In adults, there is a relationship between IQ scores and occupational status. Specifically, the more prestigious jobs are filled with people who, overall, have higher IQs than people in less prestigious jobs. IQ scores are also related to measures of actual job performance.

IQ and Health

Correlational research shows that people who score higher on IQ tests are often healthier and live longer than people who score lower. One possible explanation for this connection is (18) _____ because people who are smarter may have better jobs. In addition, people who are smarter may be better at monitoring health and applying treatments.

Changes in IQ with Age

Cross-sectional research on intelligence across the life span indicates that IQ scores rise slowly until age 44 and decline thereafter. Longitudinal research has also shown some decline in IQ in old age. However, sequential studies of changes in intelligence show that some gains in intelligence are made throughout middle adulthood, and declines, if they occur, typically occur only late in life. (***Do you remember how sequential designs eliminate the weaknesses inherent to cross-sectional and longitudinal designs?***) Sequential designs are able to illustrate generational or (19) _____ effects on intelligence. This research also indicates that (20) _____ intelligence declines earlier and more sharply than (21) _____ intelligence. On the Wechsler adult test, IQ scores on the (22) _____ scale decline earlier than IQ scores on the (23) _____ scale. In addition, performance on (24) _____ tests declines in old age and may reflect a general slowing of the adult's information processing ability. However, declines in intellectual performance are not universal.

Predictors of Decline
    For individuals who do experience a decline in intellectual performance, poor (25) _____ is often the culprit. People tend to experience a (26) _____ a few years before they die. Another factor contributing to declining intellectual performance is lack of a (27) _____ lifestyle.

Potential for Wisdom
    A person who has exceptional insight about life is often considered to have wisdom. In general, wisdom is not common among older adults. Research indicates that (28) _____ is more relevant than age to the development of wisdom. (***What qualities are thought to indicate wisdom?***) Certain cognitive styles seem to foster wisdom, as does a supportive social environment.

FACTORS THAT INFLUENCE IQ SCORES
Genes
    Differences in IQ scores across the life span are influenced by genetic factors, as evidenced by the results of twin studies and adoption studies. (***What pattern of results would demonstrate a genetic influence on IQ scores?***)

Home Environment
    Research shows that at least ten environmental factors are associated with low IQ scores. These include being a member of a minority group and receiving little positive affection from one's mother. (***What are other risk factors for low IQ?***) An instrument for measuring the amount and type of intellectual stimulation in a child's home is the (29) _____. Scores on this inventory predict children's cognitive functioning fairly well. In particular, (30) _____ involvement with the child, provision of appropriate (31) _____ materials, and opportunities for various types of stimulation were strongly related to the child's cognitive functioning. Research suggests that the best predictor of a child's IQ at age two is (32) _____. Later, quality of home environment significantly predicts IQ.

Social Class
    IQ scores are affected by the socioeconomic status of the child's family, such that children who come from disadvantaged backgrounds score lower than children from middle-class homes. According to the (33) _____, average IQ scores have increased around the world. (***What factors might account for this phenomenon?***) Children from impoverished backgrounds who are adopted into advantaged homes show improvements in IQ.

Race and Ethnicity

A great deal of controversy has surrounded the finding that children of different racial and ethnic backgrounds score lower on IQ tests than white Euro-American children. There are several possible reasons for this. One is (34) _____ in testing because the tests are more appropriate for children from white, middle-class backgrounds. In an attempt to eliminate or reduce this possibility, (35) _____ IQ tests have been developed. Differences between racial and ethnic groups are still apparent on these tests.

Another possibility is that minority children are not as highly (36) _____ in testing situations as white, middle-class children. Related to this, research shows that African American children perform poorly when they believe that tests may be measuring qualities associated with negative stereotypes of African Americans.

A third possibility is that there are (37) _____ differences between ethnic and racial groups that contribute to observed differences on IQ tests. There are, in fact, genetic differences (38) _____ groups, but these differences do not translate into differences (39) _____ groups.

A fourth explanation for average group differences is environmental variation. Support for this explanation comes from the finding that the IQ scores of black children increase when these children are adopted into white, middle-class homes. This suggests that children, regardless of their racial background, do better when they grow up in intellectually (40) _____ environments, with responsive parents and exposure to the culture of the test.

THE EXTREMES OF INTELLIGENCE

Mental Retardation

Individuals who are diagnosed with mental retardation show below average intellectual functioning and impairments in (41) _____. (***What are the different levels of mental retardation?***) Retardation that is due to some identifiable biological cause is termed (42) _____ retardation and usually accounts for the more severe and profound cases of retardation. (***What are examples of this type of mental retardation?***) Retardation that is due to a combination of low genetic potential and poor environment is (43) _____ retardation and usually results in mild retardation.

Giftedness

Individuals who have high IQ scores or show special abilities are considered gifted. Terman's longitudinal study of gifted children dispelled a number of myths about gifted individuals. In short, gifted individuals are not the social misfits or weaklings that many people believed them to be. As adults, children from Terman's study were generally healthy, happy, and productive.

WHAT IS CREATIVITY?

Individuals who can produce novel responses or works are considered to be high in creativity. This involves (44) _____ thinking, or the ability to come up with a variety of ideas or solutions to a problem. Creativity is often measured by the total number of different ideas that one can generate in response to a problem, or (45) _____. IQ tests typically measure (46) _____ thinking, which involves coming up with the one "correct" answer to a problem.

Creativity in Childhood and Adolescence

Children who are creative tend to show more freedom, originality, humor, violence, and playfulness, and engage in more pretend play than children who are not creative. Creativity seems to be related to a child's (47) _____. Performance on tests of creativity tends to increase throughout childhood and adolescence. Individuals who have creative talent are likely to achieve accomplishments if they are highly (48) _____ and grow up in a nurturing environment.

Creative Achievement in Adulthood

Creative output seems to increase throughout early adulthood and declines only in older adulthood. This pattern varies, though, depending on the field of work. According to one theory, people may have a certain limit on their creative potential. Creativity involves generating the ideas, or (49) _____, and executing the ideas to produce creative output, which is (50) _____. Individuals may generate ideas at different rates, accounting for differences in creativity across different fields as well as differences related to age.

REVIEW OF KEY TERMS

Below is a list of terms and concepts from this chapter. Use these to complete the following sentence definitions. You might also want to try writing definitions in your own words and then checking your definitions with those in the text.

automatization
componential subtheory
contextual subtheory
convergent thinking
creativity
crystallized intelligence
cultural-familial retardation
culture bias
cumulative-deficit hypothesis
developmental quotient (DQ)
divergent thinking
dynamic assessment
experiental subtheory
fluid intelligence
Flynn effect
giftedness

HOME inventory
ideational fluency
intelligence quotient (IQ)
mental age (MA)
mental retardation
normal distribution
organic retardation
psychometric approach
savant syndrome
stereotype threat
successful intelligence
terminal drop
test norms
triarchic theory of intelligence
wisdom

1. The increase in average IQ scores that has occurred over the course of the 20th century is termed the _____.

2. _____ allows us to use our minds to solve novel problems.

3. _____ is retardation that is caused be some combination of low genetic potential and a poor environment.

4. The _____ provides an index of an infant's performance on developmental tasks relative to other infants the same age.

5. The rapid decline in intellectual abilities that often occurs within a few years before dying is called the _____.

6. The _____ is a theoretical perspective that views intelligence as a trait or set of traits on which people differ and these differences can be measured.

7. Intelligence tests typically measure _____, or thinking that produces a single answer to question or problem.

8. _____ is the ability to use knowledge acquired through specific learning and life experiences.

9. The ability to produce novel responses or words is referred to as _____.

10. The _____ proposes that impoverished environments inhibit intellectual growth, and these negative effects accumulate over time.

11. On an intelligence test, the _____ is level of age-graded problems that a child can solve.

12. Sternberg's _____ is an information-processing theory that emphasizes the context, experience, and information-processing components of intelligent behavior.

13. _____ are standards of typical performance on a test as reflected by average scores and the range of scores around the average.

14. Creativity tests often measure _____, the type of thinking that produces a variety of solutions to a problem when there is no one right answer.

15. _____ refers to the total number of different ideas that one can generate when asked to think of all the possible solutions to a problem or question.

16. The process of _____ refers to the increased efficiency of information-processing that comes with familiarity and practice.

17. People with _____ either have high IQ scores or show special abilities in areas valued by society.

18. Retardation that is due to some identifiable biological cause associated with hereditary factors, diseases, or injuries is called _____.

19. The _____ of Sternberg's triarchic theory of intelligence focuses on the information processing components.

20. An index of a person's performance on an intelligence test relative to their chronological age is a(n) _____.

21. _____ is the notion that IQ tests favor children from certain cultural backgrounds, namely white middle-class backgrounds.

22. Some members of minority groups may experience _____ because they fear that others will assume they have the qualities associated with the negative stereotypes of their group.

23. Sternberg argues that people are intelligent to the extent that they have the ability to succeed in the life they choose for themselves, a concept he calls _____.

24. A person who has an extraordinary talent but who is otherwise mentally retarded is diagnosed with _____.

25. Individuals with _____ perform significantly below average on intelligence tests and show deficits in adaptive behavior skills during the developmental period.

26. The _____ is an instrument for measuring the amount and type of intellectual stimulation in a child's home environment.

27. _____ is a technique that evaluates how well children learn new material with instruction.

28. Some older adults are believed to show _____, or sound judgment and advice about important life issues.

29. The _____ is a bell-shaped distribution with most scores falling close to the average score.

30. The _____ of Sternberg's triarchic theory draws attention to the importance of the sociocultural context in which behavior occurs.

31. Responding to a task for the first time versus responding after much practice illustrates the _____ of Sternberg's triarchic theory.

MULTIPLE CHOICE SELF TEST

For each multiple choice question, read all alternatives and then select the best answer.

1. Which of the following is an example of crystallized intelligence?
    a.   remembering unrelated word pairs (e.g., dog-couch)
    b.   solving verbal analogies
    c.   realizing the relationship between geometric figures
    d.   solving word comprehension problems (e.g, what does "participate" mean?)

2. The _____ emphasizes the importance of context, experience, and information-processing components in defining intelligent behavior.
    a.   triarchic theory of intelligence
    b.   psychometric approach to intelligence
    c.   factor analysis approach
    d.   structure-of-intellect model

3. Sternberg's contextual component of intelligence suggests that intelligence
    a.   depends on expectations of particular cultures.
    b.   is consistent across different contexts.
    c.   varies with the amount of experience a person has.
    d.   consists of general and specific mental abilities.

4. Successful intelligence is characterized by:
    a.   getting a high score on an intelligence test such as the Stanford-Binet.
    b.   gaining knowledge at a faster rate than other individuals the same age.
    c.   demonstrating the abilities needed to succeed in one's chosen field, within a particular sociocultural context.
    d.   doing well in school.

5. The Bayley Scale of Infant Development is a useful indicator of
    a.   childhood intelligence.
    b.   whether or not the child is gifted.
    c.   a child's developmental progress through major milestones.
    d.   problem solving abilities that the child possesses.

6. Correlations between scores on infant intelligence tests and scores on later intelligence tests show that
    a.   infants who score high typically score high as children and adolescents.
    b.   infant intelligence scores can predict later intelligence for those who score around the mean of 100.
    c.   there is little relationship between infant intelligence and later intelligence.
    d.   infant intelligence scores can predict childhood intelligence but not adult intelligence.

7. Correlations of IQ measured during early and middle childhood with IQ measured during adolescence and young adulthood indicate that for individuals, IQ scores
   a. are quite stable.
   b. can fluctuate quite a bit.
   c. generally increase with age.
   d. generally decrease with age.

8. The cumulative-deficit hypothesis suggests that
   a. lack of intellectual stimulation produces an overall deficit in intelligence that is stable over time.
   b. lack of intellectual stimulation depresses intellectual growth more and more over time.
   c. lack of intellectual stimulation early in life is less damaging than lack of intellectual stimulation later in life.
   d. parents with low IQ scores will have children with low IQ scores.

9. The relationship between IQ and occupational status indicates that
   a. IQ scores are more likely to predict job preference than job performance.
   b. people with high IQ scores do not work in low status occupations.
   c. people with high IQ scores are more likely to work in high status occupations than people with low IQ scores.
   d. there is no relationship between these two factors.

10. A child's home environment
   a. is unrelated to their intelligence.
   b. can increase or decrease their intelligence depending on whether children have lots of toys and frequent visits from friends.
   c. can increase their intelligence when parents are involved with them and responsive to their needs.
   d. can decrease their intelligence if parents are overly responsive and spoil their children.

11. Which of the following describes how intellectual abilities change with age?
   a. Overall, intellectual abilities decline significantly with age.
   b. Crystallized intelligence declines with age more than fluid intelligence.
   c. Fluid intelligence declines with age more than crystallized intelligence.
   d. No decline in intelligence occurs with age.

12. Declines in intellectual performance among older adults may occur because of all of the following EXCEPT
   a. unstimulating life styles.
   b. slower response times.
   c. poor health.
   d. lack of sufficient knowledge base.

13. Research on ethnic and racial differences in IQ scores shows that differences
    a. do not really exist.
    b. result from genetic differences between racial groups.
    c. can be reduced with the appropriate environmental intervention.
    d. do exist but cannot be reduced or eliminated.

14. Mental retardation is defined by
    a. deficits in intelligence and difficulties with adaptive behavior, both evidenced during the developmental period.
    b. abnormal brain development.
    c. inability to function at grade-level in school.
    d. low scores on standardized intelligence tests that become increasingly poor over time.

15. With respect to creativity in adulthood,
    a. creative endeavors decrease throughout adulthood.
    b. creative endeavors increase in young adulthood and then usually peak and remain steady in middle adulthood.
    c. creative endeavors are at their peak during college years and early adulthood.
    d. creative endeavors decline significantly for older adults in all fields.

COMPARE THEORETICAL VIEWS ON INTELLIGENCE

Answer the three questions on the left for each theory or theorist. Use Table 9.6 on page 252 of the text to check yourself.

	PIAGET	VYGOTSKY	INFORMATION PROCESSING	PSYCHOMETRIC APPROACH
What is intelligence?				
What changes with age?				
What is of most interest?				

CRITICAL THINKING QUESTIONS

By answering the following questions, you will strengthen your understanding of the material in this chapter. These questions require higher level thinking skills such as integration and application of concepts. Sample answers are provided for three of the questions. These illustrate one possibility, but there are other answers you could provide that might be just as good. For the other questions, you can check yourself by referring to the text (a hint is provided), or by asking a peer or your instructor to review your answer.

1. In order to make the most accurate prediction about later IQ based on <u>infant</u> measures, what information or test would you want to have access to? Justify your answer.
   [Sample answer provided.]

2. How would you describe a smart infant, a smart child, a smart adolescent, and a smart adult?
   [Sample answer provided.]

3. How can we best define and identify a child who has mental retardation?
   [Sample answer provided.]

4. Discuss evidence that supports the conclusion that IQ scores are influenced by genetic factors. Discuss evidence that supports the conclusion that IQ scores are influenced by environmental factors.
   [Hint: Review the section in this chapter on "Factors that influence IQ scores." Also go back and review the section in Chapter Three on "Intellectual Abilities," which describes data that support genetic influences on intelligence.]

5. It has been noted that there may be culture bias in intelligence testing, resulting in certain groups of people scoring lower or higher than other groups of people. Another finding regarding intelligence tests is that they are relatively accurate at predicting academic success, job performance, and even health. What conclusions can be logically drawn from these two seemingly disparate findings?
   [Hint: You need to integrate your understanding of these two pieces of information. Review the sections of the chapter on "IQ and school achievement," "IQ and occupational success," and "Culture bias." Then consider how you could synthesize these findings to arrive at a logical conclusion.]

ANSWERS

Chapter Summary and Guided Review (Fill-in the blank)

1.	general	26.	terminal drop
2.	primary	27.	stimulating
3.	fluid	28.	expertise
4.	crystallized	29.	HOME inventory
5.	savant syndrome	30.	parental
6.	contextual	31.	play
7.	experiential	32.	mother's IQ
8.	automatization	33.	Flynn effect
9.	culture bias	34.	culture bias
10.	componential	35.	culture fair
11.	information processing	36.	motivated
12.	successful intelligence	37.	genetic
13.	Bayley	38.	within
14.	developmental quotient	39.	between
15.	maturational	40.	stimulating
16.	attention	41.	adaptive behavior
17.	cumulative-deficit	42.	organic
18.	socioeconomic	43.	cultural-familial
19.	cohort	44.	divergent
20.	fluid	45.	ideational fluency
21.	crystallized	46.	convergent
22.	performance	47.	home environment
23.	verbal	48.	motivated
24.	timed	49.	ideation
25.	hcalth	50.	elaboration

Review of Key Terms

1.	Flynn effect	17.	giftedness
2.	fluid intelligence	18.	organic retardation
3.	cultural/familial retardation	19.	componential subtheory
4.	developmental quotient (DQ)	20.	intelligence quotient (IQ)
5.	terminal drop	21.	culture bias
6.	psychometric approach	22.	stereotype threat
7.	convergent thinking	23.	successful intelligence
8.	crystallized intelligence	24.	savant syndrome
9.	creativity	25.	mental retardation
10.	cumulative-deficit hypothesis	26.	HOME inventory
11.	mental age (MA)	27.	dynamic assessment
12.	triarchic theory of intelligence	28.	wisdom
13.	test norms	29.	normal distribution
14.	divergent thinking	30.	contextual subtheory
15.	ideational fluency	31.	experiential subtheory
16.	automatization		

Multiple Choice Self Test

1.	D (p. 227)	6.	C (p. 232)	11.	C (pp. 237-239)
2.	A (p. 230)	7.	B (p. 233)	12.	D (pp. 238-239)
3.	A (pp. 230-231)	8.	B (p. 233)	13.	C (p. 244)
4.	C (p. 231)	9.	C (p. 236)	14.	A (p. 246)
5.	C (p. 232)	10.	C (pp. 241-242)	15.	B (p. 251)

Critical Thinking Questions

1.   *I would want to have access to a measure of infant attention, such as how quickly an infant becomes bored with a stimulus (speed of habituation) or the extent to which an infant prefers a novel stimulus rather than a familiar one (preference for novelty). These sorts of measures show how quickly an infant processes information. The faster they process information, the more quickly they learn, and the brighter they will be later on.*

The Bayley DQ scores don't correlate very well with later IQ scores, probably because the Bayley measures motor skills and behaviors. While these may be important measures during infancy of whether an infant is "on track," they are not important components of later intelligence. Intelligence tests focus on verbal and quantitative reasoning, not motor skills.

Another useful measure to collect during infancy might be scores on the HOME Inventory. This provides an estimate of how stimulating the home is, and is related to later performance on IQ tests. Infants and young children who grow up in homes that provide stimulation and interaction with parents typically score higher on measures of intelligence.

Finally, it might also help to know the IQ score of the infant's mother. Maternal IQ predicts infant's IQ, although it is less useful as children get older, suggesting that environmental factors begin to influence intelligence.

2.   *The simplest way to answer this question is to note that a smart person of any age is someone who can process lots of information quickly. Efficient information processing allows a person to take in more information than someone who doesn't process the same information as quickly. It also means they can solve problems more efficiently. This is why measures of information processing and attention during infancy correlate with later IQ scores more than scores on traditional infant tests like the Bayley Scales.*

3.   *The American Association on Mental Retardation diagnoses retardation using three criteria:*

- *Significantly below average intellectual functioning on a standard intelligence test such as Stanford-Binet. Significantly below average is normally interpreted as two standard deviations below the mean of 100, which would be a cut-off score of 68-70, depending which IQ test is used.*
- *Significant deficits in adaptive behaviors such as being able to take care of oneself. Thus, the person has trouble meeting age-appropriate standards of everyday functioning.*
- *Starting before the age of 18. Mental retardation is thought to be a problem originating during the developmental period. If the first two criteria are first observed after the age of 18, some disorder other than mental retardation would be diagnosed.*

CHAPTER TEN

LANGUAGE AND EDUCATION

OVERVIEW

This chapter begins by delving into language development, a complex skill learned though an informal educational system of parents and others. You will need to understand the various components of language that children need to master in order to learn language. You will also need to understand the developmental course of language. Finally, how do theorists account for the fact that children learn language with little formal instruction? The textbook covers the three major theoretical views on language development—learning theory, Chomsky's nativist perspective, and the social interactionist perspective—and also considers whether there is support for a critical period for language acquisition.

Next, the chapter addresses the formal educational system and achievement motivation. Even infants show evidence of motivation when they try to control or master their environments. Mastery motivation is enhanced by sensory stimulation and growing up in a responsive environment. Many young children attend some sort of preschool program, which can be beneficial to disadvantaged children. Children exhibit clear differences in levels of achievement motivation and you will learn about some of the factors that contribute to these differences. Children also enter the formal school system and must focus on the complex task of learning to read. You'll need to understand what it takes to master this skill and why some children experience difficulties.

Among adolescents, research reveals the discouraging finding that achievement motivation often declines as children move from elementary school to middle school and to high school. Science and math education become higher priorities as children move through school, and cross-cultural research illustrates some differences in this area between U.S. teens and teens in other cultures. Some teens integrate work with school, which seems to interfere with academic success when work hours are long and the job is menial.

Adults' motivation is influenced by their work and family contexts. Some adults struggle with problems associated with illiteracy and some adults seek continued educational opportunities.

LEARNING OBJECTIVES

After reading and studying the material in this chapter, you should be able to answer the following questions.

1.	What components of language must children master? What is the typical developmental course of language development?

2.	How do learning, nativist, and interactionist perspectives explain the acquisition of language? Which explanation is best supported by research?

3.	What factors influence mastery motivation of infants? How is this related to later achievement?

4.	What are the pros and cons of early education?

5.	What factors contribute to differences in levels of achievement motivation during childhood and what can be done to foster achievement motivation?

6.	What are the components of learning to read? Is there a most effective way of teaching reading? What distinguishes skilled and unskilled readers?

7.	How does school affect children? What factors characterize effective schools?

8.	What changes in achievement motivation occur during adolescence? What factors contribute to these changes?

9.	How does science and math education in the United States compare to science and math education in other countries?

10.	What are the pros and cons of integrating work with school during adolescence?

11.	How does achievement motivation change during adulthood?

12. How do literacy, illiteracy, and continued education affect adult's lives?

CHAPTER SUMMARY AND GUIDED REVIEW

The following summary provides an overview of the main points contained in this chapter of the text. Fill-in the blanks with terms that appropriately complete the sentence. Scattered throughout the summary are questions in parentheses. These are meant to encourage you to think actively as you are reading and connect this summary to the more detailed information provided in the text. You can answer these questions as you are filling in the blanks or you can complete all the blanks, then go back and reread the entire summary, addressing the questions in order to provide more depth of understanding.

MASTERING LANGUAGE
Mastering language is accomplished at a young age despite its complex nature.

What Must be Mastered
Language is a system of symbols that can be combined using agreed-on rules to produce messages. The sound system of language is its (1)_____. The meaning of language is its (2)_____ aspect. Children must come to understand that the symbols of a language represent things or ideas. The rules specifying how to combine symbols meaningfully make up the (3)_____ of language. Rules specifying how to use language appropriately in different contexts make up the (4)_____ of language. (***What is an example of this?***) Communication is also influenced by (5)_____ or variations in how words are spoken.

The Course of Language Development
Prelinguistic vocalizations begin at birth with several distinct cries. By the end of the first month, infants begin (6)_____, or repeating vowel-like sounds, and by 3 or 4 months of age, infants combine vowel and consonant sounds to produce (7)_____. These early utterances are the same across all cultures until about six months of age when experience begins to alter them. (***What evidence shows that experience has an impact on babbling?***) Infants can understand the meanings of many words before they can (8)_____ the words. Infants and caregivers often engage in (9)_____ by both looking at and attending to a common item.

At about one year, infants produce their first meaningful words, often called (10)_____ because when combined with gestures or intonation, these single words can convey the meaning of an entire sentence. The pace at which language develops escalates around 18 months of age during a (11)_____. Young children often err in their speech by using fairly specific words to refer to a general class of objects, which is a mistake called a(n) (12)_____. (***Can you provide an example of this?***) Young children may also err by using a general word too narrowly, which is an (13)_____. (***Can you provide an example?***)

Around 18 to 24 months, infants typically begin to combine two or more words into simple sentences called (14) _____ speech. These early sentences may be best described in terms of a (15) _____, which focuses on the semantic relations between words. The language of preschool-age children is developing rapidly with their ability to use symbols. Their understanding of grammatical rules is often evident in the mistakes they make. For example, children often over apply rules they have learned to cases that are irregular, an error called (16) _____. Chomsky proposed that language be described in terms of (17)_____, which consists of rules of syntax for transforming basic sentences into other forms. (*Can you provide an example of one of these rules?*)

Later Language Development

School-age children refine their pronunciation skills, and produce longer and more complex sentences. They can talk about events that have happened in the past or will happen in the future, which they are able to do as they acquire the ability to (18) _____. They also develop an ability to think about language and use language in ways not possible at younger ages, which shows increased (19) _____. There are also increases in vocabulary and improvements in use of pragmatics across most of the life span.

How Language Develops

There are several theoretical explanations of how children come to learn language. The (20) _____ perspective claims that children learn language the same way they learn everything else—through observation, imitation, and reinforcement. This perspective seems to best explain how children acquire the development (21) _____ and phonology of language, but not the development of the rules of (22) _____. (*What evidence supports this explanation of language acquisition?*)

The (23) _____perspective proposes that humans have an inborn mechanism, called a (24) _____, that allows children to infer the rules governing the speech they hear and then apply these rules to their own speech. (*What evidence supports this explanation of language acquisition?*) This theory may explain (25) _____ developments but has difficulty with other aspects of language acquisition. (*What are the two major problems with this perspective?*)

The (26) _____ perspective acknowledges that both the learning and nativist perspectives have some valuable aspects. Innate capacities and the language environment interact to influence language development. These theorists emphasize how the social interactions between infants and adults contribute to language and cognitive developments. Adults typically converse with infants using (27) _____ speech, a simplified speech that is spoken slowly and in a high-pitched voice. Adults may also respond to a child's vocalization by using (28)_____, or a more complete expression of what the child said. (*What other things do adults do to facilitate language development?*)

Children seem to learn language with apparent ease, while adults often have great difficulty learning a language. This suggests that there might be a (29) _____ for language acquisition. Research supports the idea of a sensitive period, but does not clearly show when this period ends.

THE INFANT
Mastery Motivation
Infants are thought to have mastery motivation, or the desire to successfully control their environment. Mastery motivation is influenced by the presence of appropriate sensory stimulation, an environment that is (30) _____, and a secure relationship with a caregiver. (***Can you describe how these factors influence mastery motivation?***)

Early Education
Many children attend preschool prior to entering kindergarten and first grade. Children in high-quality preschools are often ahead of children who do not attend preschool in (31) _____ skills, but are not significantly different in terms of intellectual skills, at least once they enter the formal school system. However, children who come from disadvantaged homes often benefit (32) _____ from having this experience. (***What general conclusions can be made about early education?***)

THE CHILD
Young children have developed internal standards of performance and can begin to appraise their performances.

Achievement Motivation
High achievers tend to attribute their successes to internal and stable factors such as (33) _____, and attribute their failures to (34) _____ factors, or to internal factors that they can change. Students with this pattern of attributions have a (35) _____, which means they thrive on challenges and will keep working on a problem because they believe their work will eventually pay off. Low achievers often attribute their failures to internal and stable causes, which may cause them to develop a (36) _____ orientation, or the belief that one cannot control the consequences of certain situations and so fail to act in these situations.

Young children are less likely to develop learned helplessness than older children. Younger children tend to adopt (37) _____ in achievement situations so that they can learn new things and improve their abilities. Older children tend to adopt (38) _____ to demonstrate what ability they have, but not really to improve it. Students who continue to focus on (39) _____ tend to do better in school. (***What can parents do to foster their child's achievement and mastery orientation? What can schools do to promote achievement?***)

Learning to Read
Learning to read is a complex perceptual task that begins when children understand the (40) _____ or the idea that letters in printed words represent the sounds in spoken words. Learning to read also depends on acquiring (41) _____, the understanding that words can be broken down into basic units of sound, or phonemes. The developmental precursors of reading are referred to as (42) _____ and can be fostered by repetitious storybook reading. Serious problems with reading might indicate (43) _____, which shows up in a variety of ways depending on the child. (***What distinguishes skilled from unskilled readers?***) Research suggests that the best approach

to teaching reading is based on (44) _____, or a code-oriented approach that teaches children letter-sound correspondence rules.

Effective Schools

Elementary and secondary schools help develop children's basic knowledge and academic skills. Some elementary and secondary schools are more effective than others. Factors that do <u>not</u> contribute to effective schooling include the amount of monetary support that a school receives, the average size of classes (within a range of 20 to 40 students), and grouping according to ability. Factors that <u>do</u> contribute to the effectiveness of a school include a strong emphasis on (45) _____ well-managed classrooms (both in terms of classroom activities and discipline problems), and teachers who can work with other teachers. In addition, student characteristics interact with school factors to affect student outcome, something called (46) _____. (***Can you explain how ability level interacts with program characteristics?***)

THE ADOLESCENT
Declining Levels of Achievement

Achievement motivation patterns change over the course of childhood and adolescence. Research suggests that children valued academic achievement more as they progress through school, but their expectations for (47) _____ drop, and they become more focused on (48) _____ rewards such as grades and less concerned about the intrinsic satisfaction associated with achieving greater competence. This trend may occur because of cognitive growth as egocentric thinking decreases. Children who receive (49) _____ at school for their failures may also experience a decline in achievement motivation. In addition, peer pressure and changes related to puberty may also influence the achievement motivation. Finally, declines in achievement motivation are more likely when there is a mismatch or (50) _____ between the adolescent and their school situation.

Science and Math Education

Secondary schools often take reading skills for granted and focus on content areas such as science and math. Cross-cultural research suggests that U.S. students do not do as well in these subjects as students in other countries. There are several possible reasons for this difference. For example, Asian students spend more time on academics and complete more (51) _____ than U.S. teens. In addition, Asian parents seem especially committed to the educational enterprise. (***What other factors might contribute to this pattern of findings?***)

Integrating Work and School

Many adolescents work during their high school years. Most of the research on working students suggests that the consequences are (52) _____, especially when work hours are long and tasks are menial. (***What factors can make the work experience for high school students a positive one?***)

Pathways to Adulthood

As they enter adolescence, the educational paths of many individuals are already determined. Intelligence, school aptitude, and achievement motivation are reasonably stable and influence whether an individual gets good grades. Grades, in turn, influence whether an individual graduates from high school and college, and level of education affects the sorts of occupations a person can hold.

THE ADULT

Achievement Motivation

Overall, level of achievement motivation remains fairly stable from childhood and adolescence to adulthood. Research with adults shows some changes in need for achievement, but younger and older men are more similar than different on this quality. Achievement motivation of women declines, at least as it pertains to (53) _____ motivation. Changes in motives during adulthood are influenced more by work and family contexts than by (54) _____.

Literacy

Literacy is the ability to use printed information to function in society and achieve goals. Few adults are completely illiterate, but many do not have (55) _____ literacy that would allow them to develop their full potential. Literacy programs have not been very successful. (***What factors contribute to the success/failure of these programs?***)

Continuing Education

An increasing number of adults seek continued educational experiences. These learners represent a very (56) _____ group of adults with various reasons for enrolling in post-secondary course work.

REVIEW OF KEY TERMS

Below is a list of terms and concepts from this chapter. Use these to complete the following sentence definitions. You might also want to try writing definitions in your own words and then checking your definitions with those in the text.

ability grouping
alphabetic principle
aptitude-treatment interaction (ATI)
babbling
child-directed speech
cooing
cooperative learning methods
decontextualized language
dyslexia
emergent literacy
expansion
functional grammar
goodness of fit

holophrases
inclusion
intonation
joint attention
language
language acquisition device (LAD)
learned helplessness orientation
learning goals
literacy
mastery motivation
mastery orientation
metalinguistic awareness
morphology

overextension
overregularization
performance goals
phonological awareness
phonology
pragmatics

semantics
syntax
telegraphic speech
transformational grammar
underextension
vocabulary spurt

1.   An important skill in learning to read is _____, or knowing that spoken words can be broken down into basic units.

2.   When two people (such as an infant and caregiver) look at the same object at the same time, they are engaged in _____.

3.   Some schools use _____ in which students are grouped and taught according to their competence level.

4.   The idea that letters in printed words represent the sounds in spoken words is the _____.

5.   Children who adopt _____ in achievement settings try to learn new things to improve their abilities.

6.   An infant's repetition of vowel-like sounds in association with positive affective states is called _____.

7.   Young children sometimes use a general word too narrowly, an error called a(n) _____.

8.   The _____ is an inborn mechanism for acquiring language that allows children to infer rules governing others' speech and then use these rules to produce their own speech.

9.   Language that is not confined to the immediate conversational context is _____.

10. During the _____ there is a dramatic increase in language acquisition.

11. Children with _____ have serious trouble learning to read despite normal intellectual ability.

12. _____ is a form of simplified speech used by adults when speaking to young children.

13. The rules of syntax specifying how to transform basic sentences into other forms are called _____.

14. Children use _____ when they construct two or three word sentences that contain only critical content words.

15. The motive to successfully interact with one's environment is called _____.

16. The process of _____ is intended to fully integrate students with disabilities into the regular classroom.

17. The analysis of early language in terms of the semantic relations between words is called the _____ of language.

18. Children who adopt a _____ in achievement settings try to prove their ability rather than improving it.

19. The _____ of language refers to the relationship between words or symbols and what they represent or mean.

20. Developmental precursors of reading skills in young children are called _____.

21. Knowledge of language as a system is _____.

22. _____ is the system of rules specifying how to combine words to form sentences.

23. _____ consists of a system of symbols that can be combined according to agreed-on rules to create messages.

24. _____ involve working together in teams to produce a group effort rather than competing individually.

25. Children are _____ when they repeat consonant-vowel combinations.

26. Single words that, when combined with gestures or intonation, convey the meaning of an entire sentences are called _____.

27. _____ are the rules specifying how language is to be used appropriately in different social contexts.

28. _____ is the system of speech sounds of a language.

29. Children sometimes over-apply grammatical rules to irregular nouns and verbs, an error known as _____.

30. _____ refers to the notion that student characteristics and school environment interact to affect student outcome.

31. An attribution style called _____ credits successes to internal and stable causes and failures to internal causes that can be changed.

32. Variations in pitch, loudness, and timing of words or sentences are components of _____.

33. Individuals with an attribution style with a _____ believe that they cannot control the consequences of certain situations, and as a result, they give up trying to succeed in these situations.

34. The rules for forming words are the _____ of language.

35. Young children have a tendency to use fairly specific words to refer to a general class of objects or events, an error known as _____.

36. Parents often use _____ when they provide comments that are more complete follow-up expressions of a thought expressed by a child.

37. The ability to use printed information to function in society and achieve goals is _____.

38. The extent to which an individual and their unique characteristics mesh with their environment is _____.

MULTIPLE CHOICE SELF TEST

For each multiple choice question, read all alternatives and then select the best answer.

1. Phonology refers to the _____ of language, while semantics refers to the _____ of language.
    a. sound system; meaning
    b. rules for forming sentences; meaning
    c. meaning; rules for how to use language
    d. rules for combining sounds; rules for forming sentences

2. Calling all four-legged animals "doggie" is an example of
    a. overregularization.
    b. underextension.
    c. overextension.
    d. telegraphic speech.

3. Learning theorists argue that language is acquired through
   a. biologically programmed learning capacities.
   b. imitation of others' language and reinforcement for recognizable speech.
   c. cognitive understanding of speech sounds and their relationship to real objects and actions.
   d. a device that allows children to sift through language and generate rules that govern the language.

4. Johan speaks with simple two- and three-word sentences, such as "Kitty gone." This indicates that Johan has developed
   a. overregularized speech.
   b. holophrastic speech.
   c. telegraphic speech.
   d. organizational speech.

5. When getting ready for bed, Rachel says that she is going to "go brush my tooths." This is an example of
   a. overregularization.
   b. underextension.
   c. overextension.
   d. holophrastic speech.

6. Which of the following claims does Chomsky make about language acquisition?
   a. Infants have an inborn knowledge of all aspects of language and automatically begin using language.
   b. Infants have an inborn mechanism for sifting through the language they hear and eventually generate rules for that language.
   c. Infants are able to listen to the language around them and imitate the sounds they hear.
   d. Infants must be exposed to language in the first two years of life in order for language to develop.

7. A child with mastery orientation toward learning might say which of the following?
   a. I did well on that test because it was easy.
   b. I did well on that test because the teacher likes me.
   c. I did well on that test because I knew the material.
   d. I did well on that test because I wanted to earn the money Dad promised me for getting an "A."

8. Children with a learned helplessness orientation
   a. have high expectations for success and get upset when they cannot achieve these high standards.
   b. work hard to achieve only small gains in performance.
   c. have low expectations for success and give up easily.
   d. believe that external factors are responsible for their failures.

9. Research indicates that
    a. infants do not have sense of motivation.
    b. from a very early age, infants are motivated to control their environments.
    c. infants can develop mastery motivation if they are externally rewarded for all their efforts.
    d. infants who are insecurely attached to their parents will not develop any mastery motivation.

10. Young children are often more confident than older children about their chances for success because younger children
    a. adopt learning goals.
    b. adopt performance goals.
    c. are given easier tasks than older children.
    d. attribute outcomes to external factors while older children attribute outcomes to internal factors.

11. Compared to skilled readers, unskilled readers tend to
    a. emphasize the meaning of a sentence rather than the pronunciation of individual words.
    b. systematically focus on all syllables in a word.
    c. skip over words or parts of words.
    d. be less motivated to learn to read.

12. One factor that contributes significantly to school effectiveness is
    a. a comfortable setting where the emphasis is on academics.
    b. average class size.
    c. level of monetary support that the school receives.
    e. strict guidelines and adherence to rules.

13. Achievement motivation declines during adolescence for all of the following reasons EXCEPT
    a. cognitive advances that allow adolescents to understand their strengths and weaknesses.
    b. pressure from peers to be popular or athletic.
    c. increasingly receiving positive feedback based on quality of their accomplishments rather than effort.
    d. having teachers who use cooperative learning styles.

14. Research on adolescents and work indicates that
    a. working while in high school is beneficial for most adolescents.
    b. there are more potential disadvantages than advantages to working while in high school.
    c. work contributes to improvements in social-emotional development, but does not influence cognitive development.
    d. work is associated with higher levels of achievement and self-esteem.

15. Cross-cultural research on science and math education indicates that
    a. United States' teens perform higher than teens in most other nations.
    b. Teens in the U.S. spend more time studying science and math subjects in school but do not perform as well on standardized tests compared to teens in other .nations.
    c. Teens in the U.S. spend less time on academics during school hours than teens in some other nations and score about in the middle compared to other nations.
    d. Parents of U.S. teens have high expectations for their children and push them to succeed in science and math more so than parents of teens from other nations.

COMPARE LEARNING AND PERFORMANCE GOALS

Answer the following set of questions for learning and performance goals. Use Table 10.4 on page 268 of the text to check your answers.

	LEARNING GOALS	PERFORMANCE GOALS
What is the child's view of ability?		
What is the child's focus in the classroom?		
How does the child explain successes and failures?		
Who regulates the child's learning?		
What is the child's reaction to successes and failures?		

CRITICAL THINKING QUESTIONS

By answering the following questions, you will strengthen your understanding of the material in this chapter. These questions require higher level thinking skills such as integration and application of concepts. Sample answers are provided for three of the questions. These illustrate one possibility, but there are other answers you could provide that might be just as good. For the other questions, you can check yourself by referring to the text (a hint is provided), or by asking a peer or your instructor to review your answer.

1. Based on research described in the text, what recommendations would you make regarding adolescents and work?
   [Sample answer provided.]

2. How could you prevent the drop in achievement motivation that often occurs as children move through school?
   [Sample answer provided.]

3. Trace the course of language development through infancy and early childhood and note factors that might influence the path of early language development.
   [Sample answer provided.]

4. Consider how deafness affects the language development of children. Questions to think about include: Do you need to hear speech to develop speech? More generally, do you need to be exposed to a language (spoken or unspoken) in order to develop a language? What is the relationship between thought and language? Is language an important basis for thought (Is it a <u>necessary</u> basis for thought)?
   [Hint: Read the Exploration box, "Language Acquisition among Deaf Children" on pages 264-65 of the text. You might also review the section in Chapter 7 that covers Piaget's and Vygotsky's views on the thought-language connection.]

5. What factors are likely to increase or decrease our achievement motivation as we move through childhood and adolescence?
   [Hint: Review the sections in the text on "Achievement Motivation" and "Declining Achievement Motivation."]

ANSWERS

Chapter Summary and Guided Review (Fill-in the blank)

1.	phonology	5.	intonation
2.	semantic	6.	cooing
3.	syntax (or grammar)	7.	babbling
4.	pragmatics	8.	produce (or express)

9. joint attention
10. holophrases
11. vocabulary spurt
12. overextension
13. underextension
14. telegraphic
15. functional grammar
16. overregularization
17. transformational grammar
18. decontextualize language
19. metalinguistic awareness
20. learning
21. semantics
22. syntax
23. nativist
24. language acquisition device
25. syntactic
26. interactionist
27. child-directed
28. expansion
29. critical period
30. responsive
31. social
32. cognitively

33. ability
34. external
35. mastery orientation
36. learned helplessness
37. learning goals
38. performance goals
39. learning goals
40. alphabetic principle
41. phonological awareness
42. emergent literacy
43. dyslexia
44 phonics
45. academics
46. aptitude-treatment interaction
47. success
48 external
49. negative feedback
50. poor fit
51. homework
52. negative
53. career-related
54. age
55. functional
56. diverse (or heterogeneous)

Review of Key Terms
1. phonological awareness
2. joint attention
3. ability grouping
4. alphabetic principle
5. learning goals
6. cooing
7. underextension
8. language acquisition device
9. decontextualized language
10. vocabulary spurt
11. dyslexia
12. child-directed speech
13. transformational grammar
14. telegraphic speech
15. mastery motivation
16. inclusion
17. functional grammar
18. performance goal
19. semantics

20. emergent literacy
21. metalinguistic awareness
22. syntax
23. language
24. cooperative learning methods
25. babbling
26. holophrases
27. pragmatics
28. phonology
29. overregularization
30. aptitude-treatment interaction
31. mastery orientation
32. intonation
33. learned helplessness orientation
34. morphology
35. overextension
36. expansion
37. literacy
38. goodness of fit

Multiple Choice Self Test

1.	A (p. 255)	6.	B (p. 261)	11.	C (p. 271)
2.	C (p. 257)	7.	C (p. 268)	12.	A (p. 274)
3.	B (p. 260)	8.	C (p. 268)	13.	D (p. 276)
4.	C (p. 258)	9.	B (p. 265)	14.	B (p. 279)
5.	A (p. 259)	10.	A (p. 268)	15.	C (p. 278)

Critical Thinking Questions

1.   *Overall, I would have to recommend NOT working, or working a limited number of hours. Research shows that adolescents who work 20 or more hours a week while going to high school get lower grades than those who do not work at all or work less than 10 hours. The ones who work a lot also tend to be disengaged in school; they cut class and do not spend as much time on homework. Further, the more teenagers work, the less control their parents have in their lives, which may contribute to higher rates of delinquency and alcohol and drug use. Some of the problems with school and parents started before the teens started working, but increased once they started working.*

Not all work experiences for teenagers are negative. Work that teaches teenagers valuable skills and allows for some advancement can be valuable. Unfortunately, most teenagers get jobs that are menial and repetitive and provide little opportunity for decision making.

2.   *Research shows that achievement motivation is high throughout elementary school, but then declines, usually starting with the entry to middle or junior high school. Several factors contribute to the decrease in achievement motivation including family characteristics, cognitive growth, negative feedback, and peer pressures. Some of the variables that contribute to lowered levels of achievement motivation cannot be changed, nor would we want to change all of them. For example, advances in cognitive development may bring the realization that you are not very good at something, leading to a decline in motivation. There is also not a lot we can do to change the family characteristics of children. Children who come from a small, caring family with a stable parent who uses consistent discipline will be advantaged when it comes to school achievement, whereas children who come from unstable families will be at-risk academically.*

But there are several factors that can be addressed. When children are in the early grades of school, teachers often praise them for effort and not for the end-product. Thus, if a child spends a lot of time drawing a picture, he may receive praise for his effort even if the picture looks terrible. As children get into the later grades, effort is no longer rewarded. Grades are awarded on the basis of measurable end-products. Students end up moving from learning goals in elementary school (i.e., working on something because they want to try to improve their understanding of it) to performance goals when they move to middle school (i.e., working on something in order earn an external reward such as a good grade). Students can benefit if teachers and schools can keep the focus on learning goals throughout middle and high school.

The peer group that a student belongs to can also make a difference in achievement motivation. Peers become increasingly influential as children enter middle and high school. Most children want to feel accepted and liked by their peers. They might downplay their intelligence if they believe that being smart will detract from how their peers perceive them. This may be especially true for students from minority groups.

Finally, there is also evidence that experiencing puberty during the transition from elementary to middle or junior high school might affect achievement motivation more than if puberty is experienced either earlier or later than the school transition. This could have implications for when schools have children switch from the smaller, friendlier elementary school to the larger and often stricter middle school.

3.   *Infants can communicate even before they begin to use a language system. Their earliest form of communication is crying, which can be used to convey hunger, pain, fatigue, and other basic states. Around 6 weeks of age, infants begin to coo, or repeat vowel-like sounds. They add consonant sounds at around 3-4 months of age and are babbling between 4 and 6 months. Up until about 6 months, the babbling from babies all over the world sounds about the same. But from this point on, experience begins to show as babbling begins to more closely resemble the language that infants are hearing around them. During the second half of the first year, infants can understand many words that they hear even though they can't yet produce the words. At around 1 year, infants begin to produce recognizable words and often use these to convey fairly complex ideas (holophrases). At around 18 months, they experience a vocabulary spurt when their vocabulary increases substantially. The next stage in language acquisition is combining words into simple sentences called telegraphic speech. Children often make mistakes as they are acquiring language, but these mistakes are often "smart" because they show that children are mastering the rules of language but have just not learned all the exceptions to the rules. For example, they might say, "the dog goed out" because they know the rule of adding "ed" to the end of verbs but haven't learned that "go" is an exception requiring "went." By the age of 5 and with no formal instruction, children have acquired adult-like speech.*

CHAPTER ELEVEN

SELF AND PERSONALITY

OVERVIEW

How do perceptions of ourselves develop and change over the life span? How do personalities emerge and change? This chapter addresses these sorts of questions about self-concepts and personality. A sense of self emerges during infancy and becomes more established during childhood. Children think of themselves and others in fairly concrete terms, whereas adolescents and adults think more abstractly.

The beginnings of personality are evident in an infant's temperament. You will learn that some aspects of personality are fairly stable from childhood on, but other aspects change in response to changes in a person's social environment. This chapter also covers Erikson's theory of psychosocial development. Erikson believed that personality evolved over the entire life span as people are confronted with different crises that can be resolved in positive or negative ways. Erikson's eight stages are introduced at the beginning of the chapter and then elaborated throughout the chapter.

LEARNING OBJECTIVES

After reading and studying the material in this chapter, you should be able to answer the following questions.

1.   What is personality and how do psychoanalytic, trait, and social learning theories explain personality development?

2.   How does self-concept emerge during infancy and how does it change across the life span?

3.   How has infant temperament been categorized? How do these temperament styles interact with caregiver characteristics? How does temperament relate to later personality?

4.   What changes occur in the development of children's and adolescent's self-esteem? What factors influence self-esteem?

5.   What factors influence the development of identity during adolescencc?

6.   How do adolescents make vocational choices? How does work affect adolescents?

7.   How does personality change during adulthood? Why do people change or remain the same?

8.   What is the focus of each of Erikson's psychosocial stages? What factors can influence how each crisis is resolved?

9.   How do career paths change during adulthood? How does Levinson's theory conceptualize family and work roles?

10.   How are older adults influenced by retirement?

CHAPTER SUMMARY AND GUIDED REVIEW

The following summary provides an overview of the main points contained in this chapter of the text. Fill-in the blanks with terms that appropriately complete the sentence. Scattered throughout the summary are questions in parentheses. These are meant to encourage you to think actively as you are reading and connect this summary to the more detailed information provided in the text. You can answer these questions as you are filling in the blanks or you can complete all the blanks, then go back and reread the entire summary, addressing the questions in order to provide more depth of understanding.

CONCEPTUALIZING THE SELF

An organized set of attributes, motives, values, and behaviors unique to an individual is that person's (1) _personality_. Personalities are often described in terms of (2) _traits_ that are thought to be relatively consistent across situations and times. Your perception of your traits and attributes is your (3) _self-concept_ and your overall evaluation of the characteristics that make up your self-concept is (4) _self-esteem_.

PERSPECTIVES ON PERSONALITY DEVELOPMENT

Psychoanalytic Theory

According to Freud, personality forms in infancy and early childhood and changes very little after this. Erikson believed that personality continued to grow and change across the life span. Erikson also stressed (5) _social_ influences more so than Freud did. (*In what other ways are Freud and Erikson different?*)

Trait Theory

According to the psychometric approach, personality is a set of traits that can be measured. Statistical procedures have been used to identify distinct groups of personality traits. Research suggests that personality can be described in terms of the (6) _Big Five_ dimensions of neuroticism, extraversion, openness to experience, agreeableness, and conscientiousness. All of these traits are influenced to some extent by (7) _genetic_ factors, although culture also has some influence.

Social Learning Theory

Social learning theories propose that personality is strongly influenced by (8) _environmental_ factors and can change when these factors change. (*How are stage theory views of personality different from non-stage theory views of personality?*)

THE INFANT

The Emerging Self

Infants begin to differentiate themselves from the world around them when they realize they can make things happen. They demonstrate an understanding of different views when they engage in (9) _joint attention_ with caregivers. One of the first signs that infants recognize themselves as distinct individuals is when they recognize themselves in a mirror. (*When does this understanding emerge?*) Infants begin to form a (10) _categorical_ self and classify themselves along dimensions such as age and gender. The ability to recognize self depends in part on (11) _cognitive_ development and also on social experiences. Our understanding of self is also influenced by social interactions and reflects how others people respond to us, a concept known as the (12) _looking-glass_ self. (*Can you describe how other people might affect our self-concept and self-esteem?*)

Temperament

Temperament is the tendency to respond in predictable ways to events. Researchers such as Buss and Plomin have focused on three dimensions of temperament that are partly influenced by genetic factors. These are emotionality, activity, and (13) _sociability_. In addition, Kagan has studied (14) _behavioral inhibition_, or the tendency to be shy and restrained with unfamiliar people or situations. Again, there seems to be a genetic influence on this characteristic as well as stability across time. (**What is the evidence showing a genetic influence?**)

Another way of classifying infant temperament is using categories that are based on behavioral dimensions such as mood, regularity of habits, and adaptability. In Thomas and Chess's original research, about 40% of the infants were classified as having an (15) _easy_ temperament, meaning that they had regular habits, were typically happy and content, and were adaptable to new experiences. About 10% of the infants were considered to have a (16) _difficult_ temperament because they were active, irritable, did not have regular habits, and responded negatively to new experiences. About 15% of the infants were (17) _slow-to-warm-up_ and were inactive, somewhat moody, and had somewhat regular habits. Whether or not infant temperament persists into childhood and adulthood may depend on (18) _goodness of fit_ between the individual and environment. (**Can you describe how this might lead to change or to consistency of temperamental characteristics?**)

THE CHILD
Elaborating on a Sense of Self
Preschool children's self-concepts tend to be physical and (19) _concrete_. School-age children can describe their inner traits and begin to compare their abilities to those of companions. This leads to (20) _social comparison_ where children evaluate themselves relative to others.

Self-esteem is also developing during childhood. Preschools can distinguish between their competencies and their inadequacies. By the middle of elementary school, children have well-defined feelings about themselves and are able to distinguish between their competencies in different areas, indicating that self-esteem is (21) _multidimensional_. Evaluations of self become more realistic around age eight. Children develop an (22) _ideal self_ based on what they think they *should* be like.

In general, some children have higher self-esteem than others because they are more competent and they receive more positive feedback from others. High self-esteem is fostered by parents who are warm and democratic. (**How does feedback from others contribute to the development of high or low self-esteem?**)

The Personality Takes Form
A number of important personality dimensions do not stabilize until childhood, although some aspects of early temperament do carry over to later personality. By age three, some predictions about later personality can be made based on observations of temperament.

THE ADOLESCENT
Self-Conceptions
The self-concepts of adolescents become more psychological and (23) _abstract_, and they are more self-aware than younger children. Adolescents' descriptions of themselves are also more differentiated and more coherent or (24) _integrated_ than those of younger children.

Self-Esteem

For a small group of adolescents, there is a drop in self-esteem, particularly among girls with multiple stressors. Most adolescents, though, leave adolescence with self-esteem that is about the same as when they entered adolescence.

Forging a Sense of Identity

Erikson believed that adolescents are faced with the important psychosocial task of identity versus (25) role confusion. Some cultures support an extended (26) moratorium period to allow adolescents to experiment with various identities. There are several developmental trends in achieving a sense of identity. Adolescents who have not experienced a crisis of identity and have not made a commitment to an identity are in the (27) diffusion status, while adolescents who have not experienced a crisis but have made a commitment fall into the (28) foreclosure status. Adolescents who have faced a crisis (or are currently facing one) but have not yet made a commitment fall into the (29) moratorium status. Adolescents who have faced a crisis about who they are and what they believe in, and who have made a commitment, have achieved (30) identity achievement status. (*What gender differences exist in identity formation?*)

Identity formation is a lengthy process and occurs at different rates for different domains. It is influenced by cognitive development and by relationships with parents. (*What kinds of parent-adolescent relationships are associated with each of the identity statuses?*) It is also affected by experiences outside the home and the broader cultural context. (*How do each of these factors influence identity formation?*)

Vocational Identity and Choice

Choosing a career is an important part of identity formation. According to Ginzberg's theory, vocational choice begins in the (31) fantasy stage when children choose largely whimsical vocations. This is followed by the (32) tentative stage during which adolescents consider their interests, abilities, and values when thinking of careers. Finally, young adults enter the (33) realistic stage and narrow their choices based on available opportunities. Vocational choice is really a matter of finding a good fit between your personality and an occupation.

THE ADULT
Self-Conceptions

Self-esteem and descriptions of self are fairly stable throughout adulthood; self-esteem decreases somewhat in old age. Older adults' evaluations of their ideal selves are closer to their evaluation of their real selves than those of younger adults. Individuals also change their (34) standards of evaluation over time, as well as their comparison group. Culture influences self-concept. In (35) individualistic cultures, individuals put their personal goals ahead of group goals. In (36) collectivist cultures, individuals give greater priority to personal goals. (*What does cross-cultural research show about how these different orientations affect self-concept and self-esteem?*)

Continuity and Discontinuity in Personality

In addressing whether personality is stable across adulthood, two questions arise. One question is whether an individual's (37) _ranking_ within a group on some personality trait remains the same, which is the stability of individual differences. A second question is whether there is stability in the (38) _average_ levels of some personality trait within a group. Longitudinal research has focused on five major dimensions of personality. With respect to the first question, individual rankings on these dimensions of personality are fairly stable across time. (*Can you provide a concrete example of what this means for a specific individual?*) With respect to the second question, cross-sectional research suggests that older adults have different personalities than younger adults. However, these results may reflect (39) _cohort_ or generational effects, suggesting that the (40) _historical_ context in which people develop affects their personalities.

Personality does show some growth from adolescence to middle adulthood, but there is little systematic change in personality from middle adulthood to later adulthood. The personalities of some people remain stable, while those of other people change across the life span. Personalities may remain stable because of the influence of (41) _genetic_ factors or because childhood experiences continue to impact on personality throughout the life span. It is also possible that personalities remain stable because (42) _environment_ remain stable. Changes in the environment might explain why some personalities change, and maturation and aging might also contribute to change. Change may also occur when there is a poor fit between the person and his/her environment.

Eriksonian Psychosocial Growth

According to Erikson, infants confront the conflict of (43) _trust vs. mistrust_. Toddlers must achieve a sense of (44) _autonomy_ or risk feeling shame and doubt. Preschool children and kindergartners struggle with the conflict of (45) _initiative vs. guilt_ and school-age children must master (46) _industry_ or possibly develop feelings of inferiority. As already noted, adolescents face the task of developing an identity. Young adults face the psychosocial task of (47) _intimacy_ versus isolation. Research supports Erikson's claim that individuals' must achieve a sense of (48) _identity_ before being able to develop true intimacy. (*How might the relationship between identity and intimacy differ for men and women?*) Middle-age adults are concerned with the psychosocial crisis of (49) _generativity vs. stagnation_ as they work to produce something lasting and important for future generations. Finally, older adults face the psychosocial conflict of (50) _integrity_ versus despair. Elderly adults may engage in a process of (51) _life review_ where they reflect on unresolved issues in order to come to terms with their lives.

Midlife Crisis?

According to Levinson's theory, adults construct and reconstruct a (52) _life structure_ that describes the pattern of their life. During middle age, many adults experience a (53) _midlife crisis_ when they question their entire life structure. Research suggests that this is more a self-evaluation than a crisis.

Vocational Development and Adjustment

Young adults explore a number of careers before settling into one that is a good fit. As they change, or the job changes, they reevaluate the fit. Vocational development is influenced by personality as well as one's (54) _gender_. (*Explain how these variables influence vocational development.*) In turn, vocational experiences influence our personality and adjustment.

Despite age-related physical and cognitive declines, older adults remain good workers because they use a strategy of (55) selective optimization w/ compensation. (***How do the three processes that make-up this strategy help older adults cope?***)

Workers go through several phases as they adjust to retirement. Initially, the freedom of retirement creates a (56) honeymoon _____ phase, which may then give way to the (57) disenchantment _____ phase as the novelty of being retired wears off. Eventually, they move on to the (58) reorientation _____ of constructing a satisfying lifestyle post-retirement.

Personality and Successful Aging

The text presents two general theories about successful aging. One is the (59) __activity_____ theory, which suggests that adults will be satisfied with their lives if they can continue to maintain their preexisting activity levels. The other theory of aging holds that successful aging requires (60) disengagement _____ of the aging individual from society and vice versa. (***Does one of these theories more accurately portray successful aging? Why?***)

REVIEW OF KEY TERMS

Below is a list of terms and concepts from this chapter. Use these to complete the following sentence definitions. You might also want to try writing definitions in your own words and then checking your definitions with those in the text.

activity	industry versus inferiority
activity theory	initiative versus guilt
autonomy versus shame and doubt	integrity versus despair
behavioral inhibition	intimacy versus isolation
Big-fish-small-pond effect	joint attention
Big Five	life review
categorical self	life structure
collectivist culture	looking-glass self
difficult temperament	midlife crisis
diffusion status	moratorium period
disengagement theory	moratorium status
easy temperament	personality
emotionality	selective optimization with compensation
ethnic identity	self-concept
foreclosure status	self-recognition
generativity versus stagnation	self-esteem
goodness of fit	slow-to-warm-up temperament
ideal self	social comparison
identity	sociability
identity achievement status	temperament
identity versus role confusion	trust versus mistrust
individualistic culture	

1.   The process of _____ takes into account how one compares to others, and uses that information to judge one's self.

2.   An identity status called _____ is when a person has not experienced a crisis and has not reached a commitment.

3.   Having a clear sense of who you are, where you are heading, and where you fit into society refers to having a(n) _____.

4.   The psychosocial conflict of _____ occurs when a young child tries to accept more grown-up responsibilities that she/he may not be able to handle.

5.   A(n) _____ is achieved when a person has experienced a crisis and has made a commitment to certain goals.

6.   The psychosocial conflict of _____ usually occurs during elementary school when children need to acquire important academic and social skills.

7.   Classification of one's self along dimensions such as age and sex shows development of a(n) _____ .

8.   A person's _____ is reflected in his/her tendency to respond in predictable ways to events.

9.   _____ is an identity status in which a person has not experienced a crisis but has made a commitment.

10.   Your understanding of yourself, including unique attributes or traits, is your _____.

11.   A _____ is the process of reflecting on unresolved conflicts of the past in order to come to terms with your self and derive new meaning from the past.

12.   The psychosocial conflict of _____ faces young adults who must develop strong friendships and intimate relationships.

13.   _____ is the first psychosocial conflict in which infants must develop a basic sense of trust.

14.   Your feelings about the characteristics that make up your self constitute your _____.

15.   Adolescents experience the psychosocial conflict of _____ when they must develop a sense of who they are socially, sexually, and professionally.

16. The _____ refers to the fact that our understanding of self is a reflection of how other people view us and respond to us.

17. Older adults face the psychosocial conflict of _____ during which they must assess their life and find it meaningful.

18. _____ is an identity status in which a person is currently experiencing a crisis or actively addressing identity issues and has not yet made a commitment.

19. _____ is defined as an organized combination of attributes, motives, values, and behaviors that is unique to each individual.

20. The psychosocial conflict of _____ involves being productive in one's work and with one's family.

21. The major dimensions of personality are collectively referred to as the _____.

22. During the psychosocial conflict of _____, toddlers must learn some independence.

23. The concept of _____ conveys the idea that the overall pattern of a person's life reflects their priorities and relationships with other people and with society.

24. The degree to which a child's temperament is compatible with the expectations and demands of his/her environment is reflected in the _____ between child and environment.

25. Adults experience a _____ when they question their life structure and raise concerns about the direction of their lives.

26. Infants who are generally content, adaptable to new experiences, keep regular habits, and tolerant of frustrations or discomforts are classified with a(n) _____.

27. A dimension of temperament that reflects the degree to which a baby is sluggish is _____.

28. Infants who are inactive, moody, moderately regular in their habits, and take some time to adapt to new situations are classified with a(n) _____.

29. _____ is the tendency to be very shy or restrained in unfamiliar settings.

30. A dimension of temperament that reflects how reactive babies are to events is _____.

31. _____ refers to a sense of personal identification with the values and traditions of a particular ethnic group.

32. Infants who are active, irritable, irregular in their habits, not very adaptable to new situations, and easily frustrated are classified with a(n) _____.

33. Society provides a _____ for most adolescents so that they can experiment with different roles in order to find their identity.

34. The ability to recognize one's self in a mirror or photo is _____.

35. The degree to which one is interested in and responsive to people is reflected in the personality trait of _____.

36. According to _____, aging adults will find their lives satisfying to the extent that they are able to maintain their existing levels of activity.

37. In a(n) _____, people place greater emphasis on group identity and goals than on personal identity and goals.

38. A strategy called _____ involves focusing on important skills, practicing these skills, and finding ways to get around the need for other skills.

39. According to _____, successful aging involves a mutual withdrawal of the aging person from society and society from the aging individual.

40. In a(n) _____, people emphasize personal goals rather than group goals, and socialize children to be independent.

41. When two people look at the same object at the same time, they are engaged in _____.

42. Our _____ is composed of expectations of what we think we "should" be like.

43. Self-concept is likely to be higher when students are in smaller groups of similar-ability students than larger groups or groups with higher achieving students, a phenomenon known as the _____.

For each multiple choice question, read all alternatives and then select the best answer.

1. Self-esteem refers to a person's
    a. cognitive understanding of self.
    b. perception of his or her abilities and traits.
    c. overall evaluation of his or her worth as a person.
    d. knowledge of who they are.

2. According to Erik Erikson, personality
    a. develops in the first five or six years after birth and changes little after this.
    b. develops and changes throughout the life span.
    c. development is complete in adolescence once a sense of identity has been achieved.
    d. is formed in childhood and only changes later in life under extreme environmental conditions.

3. Someone who adheres to social learning theory would believe that
    a. personality develops through a series of systematic stages that are similar for all people.
    b. personality is shaped by the environment during childhood, but once it is formed, changes very little in response to environmental changes.
    c. some aspects of personality are determined only by genetic factors while other are determined only by environmental factors.
    d. personality traits are only consistent across the life span if the person's environment remains the same.

4. Infants with a spot of rouge on their noses who recognize themselves in a mirror will
    a. reach for the nose of their mirror image.
    b. reach for their own nose.
    c. look behind the mirror.
    d. begin to cry indicating that they are confused.

5. Research on behavioral inhibition suggests that
    a. whether one is inhibited as a toddler determines whether one will be shy as an adult.
    b. inhibited toddlers are more likely to turn out to be shy children than uninhibited toddlers.
    c. inhibited toddlers were securely attached as infants.
    d. inhibited children show the same patterns of physiological arousal to events as uninhibited children.

6. An infant who is classified as "slow-to-warm-up"
   a. follows a somewhat regular schedule, is inactive, and somewhat moody.
   b. follows a somewhat regular schedule, is active, and tolerates frustrations fairly well.
   c. follows a regular schedule, appears content, and is adaptable to new experiences.
   d. docs not follow a regular schedule, is inactive, and reacts very negatively to new experiences.

7. When Harter's self-perception scale was administered to children in third through ninth grades, it was found that
   a. only the oldest children had well-defined self-concepts.
   b. children typically did not distinguish between their competencies in different areas.
   c. children showed a "halo effect" by evaluating themselves high in all areas.
   d. children's ratings of themselves were consistent with how others rated them.

8. Adolescents who have experienced a crisis involving identity but have not resolved the crisis or made a commitment are classified in Marcia's _____ status.
   a. diffusion
   b. moratorium
   c. foreclosure
   d. identity achievement

9. An adolescent who says "My parents taught me that abortion is wrong and so I just would not consider having an abortion or voting for someone who supports abortion." This statement reflects which identity status?
   a. diffusion
   b. moratorium
   c. foreclosure
   d. identity achievement

10. Vocational choices
   a. are stable across an individual's life span.
   b. become increasingly realistic across adolescence.
   c. are usually not related to one's ability.
   d. are influenced very little by environmental opportunities.

11. Longitudinal research on the major dimensions of personality suggests that they
   a. are relatively consistent over time in adults.
   b. change considerably over time in adults.
   c. are strongly correlated with infant temperament.
   d. cannot be reliably measured in adults.

12. Findings from cross-sectional research that, as a group, adult personalities change systematically over time, may reflect
    a. the fact that personality is affected by the historical context in which it develops.
    b. changes in the way personality has been measured over the years.
    c. the fact that personality begins to disintegrate as we age.
    d. the fact that people grow more similar as they get older.

13. Compared to adults who do not achieve a firm sense of identity, those adults who <u>do</u> achieve a sense of identity are
    a. equally likely to form genuine intimacy with another person.
    b. more likely to form genuine intimacy with another person.
    c. less likely to form intimate relationships because they feel very good about themselves as individuals.
    d. more likely to form many pseudo intimate relationships but no intimate relationships.

14. According to Levinson's theory of adult development, men
    a. typically settle into their final career choice in early adulthood.
    b. follow career paths that are similar to women's paths.
    c. question their career and family choices very little.
    d. experience a midlife crisis and question their life structure.

15. The theory that successful aging requires a gradual withdrawal from society is
    a. Levinson's theory.
    b. disengagement theory.
    c. withdrawal theory.
    d. activity adjustment theory.

REVIEW THE FOUR IDENTITY STATUSES

For this exercise, consider the area of career identity. For each of the four identity statuses, note whether or not a crisis has been experienced (Yes or No) and whether or not a commitment has been made (Yes or No). Also provide an example related to career identity for each type of status. Check your answers by referring to Table 11.3 on page 301 of the text.

TYPE OF IDENTITY STATUS	CRISIS?	COMMITMENT?	EXAMPLE
Diffusion			
Moratorium			
Foreclosure			
Identity Achievement			

CRITICAL THINKING QUESTIONS

By answering the following questions, you will strengthen your understanding of the material in this chapter. These questions require higher level thinking skills such as integration and application of concepts. Sample answers are provided for three of the questions. These illustrate one possibility, but there are other answers you could provide that might be just as good. For the other questions, you can check yourself by referring to the text (a hint is provided), or by asking a peer or your instructor to review your answer.

1. Taking into consideration everything you have read about personality, how would you summarize the findings on stability of personality characteristics across the life span? [Sample answer provided.]

2. Discuss evidence on the genetic and environmental influences on personality. [Sample answer provided.]

3. How does self-esteem change across the life span, and what factors influence self-esteem in positive or negative directions? [Sample answer provided.]

4. To what extent is personality continuous and/or discontinuous in adulthood? [Hint: Review the section on "Continuity and discontinuity in personality."]

5. Based on research, what could you tell parents who are concerned about their infant's or toddler's temperament (perhaps it is a difficult temperament, or the infant is inhibited)? [Hint: Review the section of the chapter on "Temperament," paying particular attention to the discussion of "Goodness of Fit."]

ANSWERS

Chapter Summary and Guided Review (Fill-in the blank)

1. personality
2. traits
3. self-concept
4. self-esteem
5. social
6. Big Five
7. genetic
8. environmental
9. joint attention
10. categorical
11. cognitive
12. looking-glass
13. sociability
14. behavioral inhibition
15. easy
16. difficult
17. slow-to-warm-up
18. goodness of fit
19. concrete
20. social comparison
21. multidimensional
22. ideal self
23. abstract
24. integrated
25. role confusion
26. moratorium
27. diffusion
28. foreclosure
29. moratorium
30. identity achievement
31. fantasy stage

32. tentative stage
33. realistic stage
34. standards
35. individualistic
36. collectivist
37. ranking
38. average
39. cohort
40. historical
41. hereditary (or genetic)
42. environments
43. trust vs. mistrust
44. autonomy
45. initiative vs. guilt
46. industry
47. intimacy
48. identity
49. generativity vs. stagnation
50. integrity
51. life review
52. life structure
53. midlife crisis
54. gender
55. selective optimization with compensation
56. honeymoon
57. disenchantment
58. reorientation
59. activity
60. disengagement

Review of Key Terms

1. social comparison
2. diffusion
3. identity
4. initiative versus guilt
5. identity achievement status
6. industry versus inferiority
7. categorical self
8. temperament
9. foreclosure status

10. self-concept
11. life review
12. intimacy versus isolation
13. trust versus mistrust
14. self-esteem
15. identity versus role confusion
16. looking-glass self
17. integrity versus despair
18. moratorium status

19.	personality	32.	difficult temperament
20.	generativity versus stagnation	33.	moratorium period
21.	Big Five	34.	self-recognition
22.	autonomy versus shame and doubt	35.	sociability
23.	life structure	36.	activity theory
24.	goodness of fit	37.	collectivist culture
25.	midlife crisis	38.	selection optimization with compensation
26.	easy temperament	39.	disengagement theory
27.	activity	40.	individualistic culture
28.	slow-to-warm-up temperament	41.	joint attention
29.	behavioral inhibition	42.	ideal self
30.	emotionality	43.	big-fish-small-pond effect
31.	ethnic identity		

Multiple Choice Self Test

1.	C (p. 287)	6.	A (p. 293)	11.	A (pp. 308-310)
2.	B (p. 287)	7.	D (pp. 294-295)	12.	A (pp. 309-11)
3.	D (pp. 289-290)	8.	B (pp. 300-01)	13.	B (p. 312)
4.	B (p. 290)	9.	C (pp. 300-01)	14.	D (p. 315)
5.	B (p. 292)	10.	B (p. 304)	15.	B (p. 317)

Critical Thinking Questions

1.   *The beginnings of personality emerge during infancy with temperament characteristics. Some of these characteristics persist beyond infancy if there is "goodness of fit" between the child's characteristics and the demands of the environment. Social experiences shape temperament into what we think of as a child's personality. Components of this personality tend to persist over time if the traits are valued by society and are consistent with gender roles expectations. In terms of the "Big Five" personality traits, there is a good deal of stability in these throughout adulthood. Thus, a young adult who is extraverted is likely to be extraverted as an older adult. An older adult who is not very open to new experiences was probably not very open as a younger adult. Correlations, though, between scores on personality measures are not perfect, indicating that there is some change over time. In particular, research shows that personalities are still forming throughout adolescence and early adulthood, and become more established sometime during one's thirties.*

2.   *Personality is often conceptualized in terms of the Big Five characteristics of openness, conscientiousness, extraversion, agreeableness, and neuroticism. All five characteristics seem to be influenced by genetic factors; identical twins score more similarly to one another on these traits than do other less genetically related pairs of individuals. These traits are also consistent over a person's lifespan, which suggests either a genetic basis or a consistent environment. The Big Five traits appear to be universal; they characterize personality differences across cultures that are very different in terms of parenting, values, and language. Some personality characteristics seem more influenced by genetic factors; others are more open to influence from the environment.*

3.	*Self-esteem emerges sometime during childhood when children begin to compare themselves to others and evaluate their worth. By age 9 or 10, children can distinguish between at least five different dimensions of self worth and have well-defined feelings about whether they are good or bad on these dimensions. Accuracy of their evaluations increases throughout elementary school. Self-esteem is influenced by how competent children are; those who are more competent usually recognize this and feel better about themselves. Self-esteem is also influenced by the kind of feedback children receive from parents and others; those who receive more positive feedback feel better about themselves than children who receive negative feedback. Self-esteem tends to drop as children enter adolescence, partly because they have a more realistic understanding of their abilities and where they fit with others. Adolescents who are the "big fish in a little pond" tend to feel better about themselves than adolescents who are the little fish in a big pond. After the drop in adolescence, self-esteem gradually increases throughout adulthood, reaching a peak about the time that adults retire. There is then a slight decline in self-esteem in old age. But most adults retain their level of self-esteem even in old age. They tend to be more realistic than when they were young. They also change their goals and standards as they age so that what might have been a failure at age 30 is not perceived as a failure at age 75. Finally, they compare themselves to other old people rather than to younger adults, which also helps preserve their self-esteem.*

CHAPTER TWELVE

GENDER ROLES AND SEXUALITY

OVERVIEW

Most students find this chapter particularly interesting, perhaps because gender issues are so central to our lives. The first and largest part of this chapter is devoted to the discussion of gender roles across the life span. This includes a description of several theoretical explanations of how gender role behaviors are acquired: Money and Ehrhardt's biosocial theory, Freud's psychoanalytic theory, social learning theory, and the cognitive theories. Pay particular attention to how these theories can be integrated to best explain gender typing, and to the evidence that supports the theories.

The second part of the chapter covers developmental issues related to sexuality. This includes expressions of sexuality during infancy and childhood, with discussions of children's knowledge about sex, their sexual behavior, and the sexual abuse of children. This section also covers the sexual orientation, behavior and morality of adolescents, and changes in sexuality during adulthood.

LEARNING OBJECTIVES

After reading and studying the material in this chapter, you should be able to answer the following questions.

1. What are gender norms and stereotypes? How do they play out in the behaviors of men and women?

2. What actual psychological differences exist between males and females?

3. How does Eagly's social role hypothesis explain gender stereotypes?

4   How do gender role stereotypes influence infants' behavior and treatment?

5.	How do children acquire gender role stereotypes? In what ways do children exhibit gender-typed behavior?

6.	What theoretical explanations account for gender-typed behaviors? How well supported are these theories?

7.	How do gender roles change throughout adulthood?

8.	What is androgyny? To what extent is it useful?

9.	How are infants affected by their sex? What do we know about infant sexuality?

10.	What do children know about sex and reproduction? How does sexual behavior change during childhood?

11.	What factors contribute to the development of sexual orientation? What are adolescents' sexual attitudes and behavior today?

12.	What changes occur in sexual activity during adulthood?

The following summary provides an overview of the main points contained in this chapter of the text. Fill-in the blanks with terms that appropriately complete the sentence. Scattered throughout the summary are questions in parentheses. These are meant to encourage you to think actively as you are reading and connect this summary to the more detailed information provided in the text. You can answer these questions as you are filling in the blanks or you can complete all the blanks, then go back and reread the entire summary, addressing the questions in order to provide more depth of understanding.

MALE AND FEMALE

Males and females differ in a number of ways. They differ genetically because they have different (1)_____, which trigger release of different levels of (2) _____. Males and females also differ because societies expect them to adopt different patterns of behavior, or (3) _____, specifying how they should act as males or females. Gender-role (4) _____ are society's expectations of what males and females should be like, and these create gender-role (5) _____, or overgeneralizations about what males and females are like. Children learn their biological sex and acquire the behaviors and values that society considers appropriate for members of that sex through a process of (6) _____.

Gender Norms and Stereotypes

Girls in our society have traditionally been encouraged to adopt traits such as nurturance and kindness that emphasize (7) _____, or connectedness to others. Boys have been encouraged to adopt traits such as dominance, independence, assertiveness, and competitiveness that are indicative of the masculine gender role or (8) _____. Stereotypes about women's and men's roles continue to exist, although women describe themselves as having more masculine traits than they did in the past.

Are There Gender Differences?

Research reveals some differences between males and females, although these are often small and inconsistent. Most research shows that, on average, females have greater (9) _____ ability than males. Beginning in adolescence, males outperform females on some tests of (10) _____ ability and on measures of (11) _____ reasoning such as the mental rotation task. As early as two years of age, males tend to behave more (12) _____ than females. (***What other gender differences have been supported by more recent research?***) Findings of psychological sex differences are based on averages for males and females and do not apply to all individuals. Many differences that we think exist between males and females are based on (13) _____. In addition, Eagly's (14) _____ hypothesis suggests that the roles played by men and women in society help create our stereotypes about gender.

THE INFANT
Differential Treatment
Our society begins to treat males and females differently at birth. Adults interact differently and interpret reactions differently when they believe they are interacting with a male infant rather than a female infant.

Early Learning
By age 2 ½ to 3, children show that they have acquired (15) _____ because they can state whether they are male or female. Even before this time, children are beginning to act in ways that society finds gender appropriate.

THE CHILD
At about the same time that young children acquire gender identity, they begin to learn gender (16) _____, or society's ideas about what males and females are like. They also acquire gender-typed behaviors.

Acquiring Gender Stereotypes
Children as young as 2½ years already hold stereotypical beliefs about boys' and girls' activities. Children around 6 or 7 years believe that these stereotypes are absolute while older children are more flexible in their thinking about gender-role stereotypes. (*Why is there this developmental difference in thinking about gender-role stereotypes?*) Young children also express positive feelings about gender-stereotypic occupations and negative feelings about gender counter-stereotypic ones.

Gender-Typed Behavior
Young children prefer toys that society deems gender-appropriate and they develop a preference for same-sex playmates, with increased (17) _____ into separate groups of boys and girls during elementary school. Boys are under more pressure than girls to behave in gender-appropriate ways. (*Can you explain why this is true?*)

THE ADOLESCENT
Adhering to Gender Roles
Adolescents tend to adhere more strictly to gender roles than do younger children. (*Why is this the case?*) In the process of gender (18) _____, increased pressure among adolescents to conform to gender roles magnifies differences between males and females.

Explaining Gender-Role Development
There are several theories that try to explain the development of gender roles. Money and Ehrhardt proposed a (19) _____ theory that focuses on the interaction of biological and social influences. According to this theory, several critical events contribute to gender-role development. One is receiving an X or Y chromosome, and the second event is the release of (20) _____, which stimulates the development of a male internal reproductive system. A third event occurs at 3 to 4 months after conception when testosterone triggers development of male external genitals or, in its absence, development of female external genitalia. This hormone also affects development of the (21) _____ and nervous

system. Hormones released during (22) _____ will stimulate the growth of the reproductive system and secondary sex characteristics. These biological events trigger a number of (23) _____ reactions that will further differentiate males and females.

Evidence from several sources indicates that biological factors do influence the development of males and females. Children who are chromosomally XX but who were exposed to male hormones prenatally are called (24) _____. (***How are these girls behaviorally different from other girls?***) The level of male hormones may also relate to (25) _____ in animals and humans. Social labeling also has an impact on gender development. Evidence suggests that there may be a sensitive or (26) _____ period between 18 months and 3 years of age when gender identity is established. (***Can you explain the evidence that suggests this?***)

According to Freud's psychoanalytic theory, both biology and environment contribute to gender-role development. Preschool-age children are in the (27) _____ stage of psychosexual development. A boy in this stage experiences a(n) (28) _____ complex and a girl is said to experience a(n) (29) _____ complex. In both cases, the children experience love for their parent of the other sex and as a result of this, experience jealousy and conflict with the same-sex parent. The conflict is resolved through (30) _____ with the same-sex parent. (***What is the psychoanalytic rationale for why boys seem to learn gender stereotypes and gender-typed behaviors faster than girls?***)

Social learning theorists believe that gender-role development occurs through (31) _____ where children are reinforced for sex-appropriate behaviors and punished for behaviors considered appropriate for members of the other sex. (***How can differential treatment lead to differences in ability?***) According to this view, sex-role development also occurs through (32) _____ where children adopt attitudes and behaviors of same-sex models. (***What are some likely sources of gender-stereotyped behavior that children observe?***)

Cognitive-developmental theorists argue that gender-role development depends on a child's level of cognitive development. Children must first acquire basic gender (33) _____, or the recognition of being male of female. They must also acquire gender (34) _____, the understanding that gender identity is constant across time, and (35) _____, or knowing that gender is constant across situations. (***What level of cognitive development is needed for these understandings?***) According to this view, once children understand that biological sex is unchanging, they actively socialize themselves by seeking out same-sex models. (***What are criticisms of this view of gender-role development?***)

An information processing model proposed by Martin and Halverson suggests that children acquire (36) _____, which are organized sets of expectations and beliefs about males and females and these beliefs influence the things that children pay attention to and remember. According to this theory, children classify people and things as belonging to a simple in-group or out-group. Children then construct an (37) _____ by collecting more elaborate information about the role of their own sex. (***What evidence supports this perspective?***)

Together, the biosocial, social learning, and cognitive theories help explain how gender-typed behaviors develop. Biological factors guide development, people react to a child's gender, and children actively socialize themselves to act in ways consistent with their understandings of their gender.

THE ADULT
Changes in Gender Roles
In adulthood, male and female roles are often similar until marriage and parenthood begins to differentiate the roles. The roles become more similar again during middle age when child care responsibilities decline.

Masculinity, Femininity, and Androgyny
Sandra Bem argues that masculinity and femininity are two separate psychological dimensions. Someone who is (38) _____ has masculine-stereotyped traits as well as feminine-stereotyped traits. Gutmann refers to demands placed on a person by parenthood as the (39) _____. The demands often mean that men emphasize their masculine qualities and women emphasize their feminine qualities. Gutmann proposes that when no longer constrained by the parental imperative, psychologically masculine men adopt more (40) _____ qualities and psychologically feminine women adopt more (41) _____ qualities. A related hypothesis is that a midlife (42) _____ occurs, and adults retain their gender-typed qualities but add qualities associated with the other gender. Gutmann's hypothesis is partially supported. Parenthood does tend to make people more traditionally sex-typed, but they tend to become (43) _____ in the postparental phases of life, rather than replacing sex-typed traits with other-sex traits. Thus, they experience the androgyny shift.

Androgynous people tend to be more flexible in their (44) _____ than traditionally sex-typed persons. However, it is not androgyny per se, but a person's (45) _____ traits that are associated with high self-esteem and good adjustment. And while androgynous parents seem to raise children who are androgynous, some evidence suggests that these children are less competent and less socially responsive and assertive than children of traditionally sex-typed parents. (***What other characteristics are associated with androgyny?***)

SEXUALITY OVER THE LIFE SPAN
Are Infants Sexual Beings?
According to Freud, infants who are in the oral stage of psychosexual development gain pleasure from activities such as sucking and biting. The genitals of infants are sensitive to stimulation and both male and female infants have been observed to engage in masturbation-like activities, although these are not interpreted sexually in the same way that they are for adults.

Childhood Sexuality
Children's understanding of sex and reproduction has been related to their level of (46) _____ development. They often interpret information about sex and reproduction in terms of what they already know (assimilation). According to Freud, preschoolers in the (47) _____ stage are interested in their genitals, and school-aged children are in a (48) _____ in which sexuality is repressed.

Contrary to what Freud believed, sexual interest and experimentation do not decrease during childhood. Some research indicates that age (49) _____ is an important milestone when children experience their first sexual attraction. Children's sexual behaviors are influenced by parental and societal attitudes. In countries classified as (50) _____, early sex is accepted whereas in countries classified as (51) _____, early sex is discouraged. (***Where does the U.S. fit in this classification?***)

Children who are sexually abused exhibit a variety of problems common to emotionally disturbed individuals, such as anxiety and depression. In particular, lack of self worth and distrust of others affect victims' abilities to build successful relationships. One problem among victims of sexual abuse is their tendency to act out sexually, called (52) _____. A second problems is (53) _____, a clinical disorder involving flashbacks and nightmares about the event.

Adolescent Sexuality

As part of establishing their sexual identity, adolescents must become aware of their sexual (54) _____. Many establish a heterosexual orientation without much thought. Others may experiment with homosexual activities, but do not necessarily end up with an enduring homosexual orientation. (***What factors influence the development of sexual orientation?***)

Sexual morality of adolescents has changed during the past century. Most adolescents believe that sex with (55) _____ is acceptable. The (56) _____ regarding sexual behavior of males and females is declining but has not disappeared. There is increased confusion about sexual (57) _____ since individuals must now decide for themselves what is right or wrong, rather than adhering to general rules.

Sexual behaviors have also changed during the last century. Adolescents engage in sexual behaviors at earlier ages and more adolescents are having sexual intercourse. Since many sexually active adolescents fail to use (58) _____, there are a number of unplanned pregnancies.

Adult Sexuality

People continue to be sexual beings throughout middle and late adulthood. Frequency of sexual intercourse declines with age for both single and married individuals. In part, this decline results from (59) _____ changes in men and women as they get older. Sexual capacity can also be affected by diseases and use of prescribed drugs, which both increase as a person gets older. Societal attitudes and lack of a (60) _____ also contribute to the decline of sexual activity of older adults.

REVIEW OF KEY TERMS

Below is a list of terms and concepts from this chapter. Use these to complete the following sentence definitions. You might also want to try writing definitions in your own words and then checking your definitions with those in the text.

agency
androgenized female
androgyny
androgyny shift
communality
double standard
Electra complex
gender consistency
gender identity
gender intensification
gender role
gender-role norms

gender-role stereotypes
gender schema
gender segregation
gender stability
gender typing
identification
Oedipus complex
parental imperative
posttraumatic stress disorder
sexual orientation
social-role hypothesis

1.   Understanding that gender identity is stable over time is _____.

2.   A behavior pattern or trait that defines how to act as female or male in a particular society is called a _____.

3.   The _____ refers to the belief that sexual behaviors that are acceptable for males are not acceptable for females.

4.   A _____ is an organized set of beliefs and expectations about males and females that influence the type of information that is attended to and remembered.

5.   _____ refer to generalizations about what males and females are like.

6.   _____ is the understanding that gender is constant despite changes in appearance or activities.

7.   The process by which children learn their biological sex and acquire the motives, values, and behaviors considered appropriate for members of that sex is _____.

8.   The masculine gender role revolves around _____, which is an orientation toward dominance, independence, assertiveness, and competitiveness.

9.   Societal standards about what males and females should be like are contained in _____.

10.   The requirements or demands imposed on a person by parenthood are referred to as the _____.

11.   _____ is the awareness of one's self as male or female.

12. The possession of both masculine-stereotyped traits and feminine-stereotyped traits is called _____.

13. Gender-role norms that encourage connectedness to others are the major focus of _____.

14. A female who was exposed prenatally to male hormones and has external genitals that appear masculine is labeled a(n) _____.

15. Through the process of _____, children internalize the attitudes and behaviors of the same-sex parent.

16. _____ refers to one's preference for sexual partners of the same or other sex.

17. The Freudian term for a boy's feelings of love toward his mother and fear of his father is _____.

18. _____ consists of a cluster of symptoms, including nightmares and flashbacks, associated with an extremely traumatic experience.

19. The concept of _____ refers to the addition of characteristics typically associated with the other sex to traditionally gender-typed characteristics already held by an individual.

20. The Freudian term for a girl's feelings of love toward her father and rivalry with her mother is _____.

21. _____ refers to the separation of people into groups of males and females.

22. In the process of _____, there is an increase in sex differences as a result of pressure to conform to gender roles.

23. According to the _____, differences in the societal roles of men and women help create and maintain gender-role stereotypes.

For each multiple choice question, read all alternatives and then select the best answer.

1. The process by which children learn their biological sex and acquire the motives, values, and behaviors considered appropriate for the members of that sex is called
    a.   gender typing.
    b.   gender-role norms.
    c.   gender differences.
    d.   gender consistency.

2. Which one the following is <u>true</u> regarding psychological differences between males and females?
    a.   Males and females do not actually differ on any psychological traits or abilities.
    b.   Wherever there is a difference between males and females, males outperform females.
    c.   There are no differences between males and females throughout childhood, but beginning in adolescence, males outperform females in most areas.
    d.   Females tend to outperform males on verbal tasks and males tend to outperform females on tests of mathematical reasoning.

3. Females in our society have historically been encouraged to adopt traits that emphasize
    a.   sexuality.
    b.   agency.
    c.   communality.
    d.   androgyny.

4. Most children can correctly label themselves as males or females by age _____ and begin to understand that one's sex does not change around age _____.
    a.   5 years; 11 years
    b.   3 years; 6 years
    c.   18 months; 3 years
    d.   2 years; 3 years

5. Money and Ehrhardt's biosocial theory of gender-role development suggests that
    a.   there are real biological differences between boys and girls and these differences influence how people react to the children.
    b.   biological differences between males and females cause them to behave differently and to have different levels of expertise in areas such as math and verbal skills.
    c.   biological differences males and females may exist, but these differences have no impact on psychological differences between males and females.
    d.   biological factors affect males' behavior but not females' behavior.

6. A woman who receives male hormones while she is pregnant may deliver a child who is
   a. genetically XY and has external genitals that appear feminine.
   b. genetically XX and has external genitals that appear masculine.
   c. genetically XX and becomes very masculine appearing following puberty.
   d. mentally retarded.

7. According to Freud's psychoanalytic explanation, boys resolve their Oedipus complexes and girls resolve their Electra complexes
   a. when they move into the phallic stage of development.
   b. out of love for their parents.
   c. by identifying with the parent of the other sex.
   d. by identifying with the same-sex parent.

8. Social learning theorists explain sex-typing as the result of
   a. the child's understanding of gender identity and gender constancy.
   b. the child's desire to be like his or her parents.
   c. the parents differentially reinforcing behaviors and the child's observation of same-sex models.
   d. chromosomal and hormonal differences between males and females.

9. According to cognitive-developmental theorists, gender-role development
   a. begins with children's understanding that they are girls or boys.
   b. begins with children imitating same-sex models.
   c. begins when parents differentially reinforce boys and girls.
   d. depends on observational learning.

10. When children realize that their gender is stable over time, they have achieved _____, and when they realize that their gender is stable over situations, they have achieved _____.
    a. gender stability; gender identity
    b. gender identity; gender consistency
    c. gender consistency; gender stability
    d. gender stability; gender consistency

11. Gender schemas
    a. determine a child's behavior in ambiguous situations.
    b. influence the kinds of information that children attend to.
    c. refer to the child's understanding that their gender is stable over time.
    d. reflect the fact that children have difficulty understanding their appropriate gender roles.

12. Which of the following accurately characterizes developmental changes in thinking about gender roles?
    a. Preschoolers are the most rigid in their thinking about gender roles.
    b. The period of young adulthood is when people hold the most rigid beliefs about gender roles.
    c. Children in early elementary school and adolescence hold the most rigid beliefs about gender roles.
    d. Children in middle childhood hold the most rigid beliefs about gender roles.

13. Which of the following is <u>true</u> regarding changes in sexual attitudes?
    a. Regardless of how they may act, most adolescents believe that premarital sex is wrong.
    b. Most adolescents are quite knowledgeable about sex and clearly understand today's sexual norms.
    c. The "double standard" for males and females sexual behavior no longer exists.
    d. Most adolescents believe that sex with affection is OK.

14. In Sandra Bem's model, an androgynous individual is a person who is
    a. high in both masculine and feminine traits.
    b. high in masculine traits and low in feminine traits.
    c. low in masculine traits and high in feminine traits.
    d. low in both masculine and feminine traits.

15. With respect to androgyny, research indicates that
    a. androgynous people are less flexible in their behavior than sex-typed people.
    b. children of androgynous parents are more socially responsible and assertive than children of sex-typed people.
    c. the possession of masculine traits leads to higher self-esteem and good adjustment.
    d. the possession of feminine traits by men leads to better adjustment.

COMPARE THEORIES OF GENDER-TYPING

For each theory of gender typing listed below, note the contribution that it has made to our understanding of the development of gender typing. Use the description of the theories in the text and Table 12.2 on page 347 to check your answers.

THEORY	CONTRIBUTION
Biosocial Theory	
Social Learning Theory	
Cognitive-Developmental Theory	
Gender Schema Theory	

CRITICAL THINKING QUESTIONS

By answering the following questions, you will strengthen your understanding of the material in this chapter. These questions require higher level thinking skills such as integration and application of concepts. Sample answers are provided for three of the questions. These illustrate one possibility, but there are other answers you could provide that might be just as good. For the other questions, you can check yourself by referring to the text (a hint is provided), or by asking a peer or your instructor to review your answer.

1. One issue debated by scholars in the field of gender roles is the existence of actual differences between males and females. Are there "real" gender differences? Discuss all sides of this issue and provide evidence to support each position.
    [Sample answer provided.]

2. Use the research on gender-role development to illustrate the nature/nurture issue.
    [Sample answer provided.]

3. What are the most significant developments or changes in our sexual selves across the lifespan?
    [Sample answer provided.]

4.   Which ideas of Freud seem to be accurate regarding early sexuality and gender-role development, and which ideas of Freud have not been supported?
[Hint: There are references to Freud throughout the sections on sexuality, so review this part of the chapter with Freud's theory and stages of psychosexual development in mind.]

5.   What happens to gender roles and gender differences during adulthood?
[Hint: Review the section on "The Adult."]

ANSWERS

Chapter Summary and Guided Review (Fill-in the blank)

1.	chromosomes	31.	differential reinforcement
2.	hormones	32.	observational learning
3.	gender roles	33.	identity
4.	norms	34.	stability
5.	stereotypes	35.	consistency
6.	gender typing	36.	gender schemata
7.	communality	37.	own-sex schema
8.	agency	38.	androgynous
9.	verbal	39.	parental imperative
10.	mathematical	40.	feminine
11.	spatial	41.	masculine
12.	aggressive	42.	androgyny shift
13.	stereotypes	43.	androgynous
14.	social role	44.	behavior
15.	gender identity	45.	masculine
16.	stereotypes	46.	cognitive
17.	segregation	47.	phallic
18.	intensification	48.	latency period
19.	biosocial	49.	ten
20.	testosterone	50.	teen permissive
21.	brain	51.	sexual conservatives
22.	puberty	52.	sexualized behavior
23.	social	53.	posttraumatic stress disorder
24.	androgenized females	54.	orientation
25.	aggression	55.	affection
26.	critical	56.	double standard
27.	phallic	57.	norms
28.	Oedipus	58.	contraception
29.	Electra	59.	physiological
30.	identification	60.	partner

Review of Key Terms

1.	gender stability	2.	gender role

3.	double standard	14.	androgenized females
4.	gender schema	15.	identification
5.	gender-role stereotypes	16.	sexual orientation
6.	gender consistency	17.	Oedipus complex
7.	gender typing	18.	posttraumatic stress disorder
8.	agency	19.	androgyny shift
9.	gender-role norms	20.	Electra complex
10.	parental imperative	21.	gender segregation
11.	gender identity	22.	gender intensification
12.	androgyny	23.	social-role hypothesis
13.	communality		

Multiple Choice Self Test

1.	A (p. 324)	6.	B (p. 331)	11.	B (p. 337)
2.	D (pp. 324-25)	7.	D (p. 333)	12.	C (pp. 328-29)
3.	C (pp. 323-324)	8.	C (pp. 333-34)	13.	D (p. 346)
4.	B (pp. 327; 336)	9.	A (p. 336)	14.	A (pp. 339-340)
5.	A (p. 330)	10.	D (pp. 336-37)	15.	C (p. 340)

Critical Thinking Questions

1.   *Some people would argue that there are no "real" differences between men and women other than their different reproductive systems and genitals. People on this side of the issue insist that there are no meaningful psychological, intellectual, or behavioral differences between men and women. They argue that what may appear to be gender differences are actually the result of socialization differences, not inherent differences. Consequently, they believe that if society treated men and women similarly, they would behave similarly.*

    Other people believe that there are some differences between males and females. They cite the four "well-established" sex differences that Maccoby and Jacklin reported in their classic review: Math ability, spatial ability, and aggression (all in favor of males), and verbal ability (in favor of females). Some people believe that these four differences result from socialization. Others, however, believe there is evidence that there are intrinsic differences. For example, differences in aggression show up very early in life and are observed cross-culturally, which suggests there may be a biological or genetic component to sex differences in aggression.

    Finally, there are still others who believe that there are additional differences between men and women, including activity level, compliance, cooperativeness, nurturance, and others. Again, some of these people believe these differences result from socialization but others think that men and women are different because of physiological differences.

2.   *There are biological differences between males and females, starting prenatally with different chromosome patterns (XX for girls and XY for boys) and different levels of hormones. These lead to differences in internal organs and external genitals. Studies of individuals who have been exposed prenatally to unusually high or low levels of hormones exhibit some differences from individuals who were exposed to normal levels of hormones. For example, androgenized females were exposed to excess levels of the male hormone androgen. Even when their genitals were corrected to appear feminine and they were raised as girls, they behaved*

more tomboyish than other girls and they were more likely to describe themselves as homosexual or bisexual.

In addition, some research shows that there are small differences between the behavior of male and female infants. Male infants, for example, are more active and seem to focus more on physical objects. These differences show up very early in life, before the environment would be able to socialize them into different behaviors.

On the nurture side of the issue, it is clear that society treats boys and girls differently— reinforcing them for behaving in ways that are consistent with their gender and discouraging or even punishing them for behaving in gender inconsistent ways. Boys are allowed to get away with more aggressive behavior than girls because stereotypes "allow" boys to be more aggressive. Children are also exposed to many, many gender-stereotypic messages in the world around them. In their homes, parents' activities usually fall into gender-stereotypic patterns with dads doing the outside chores and moms doing the inside chores and more of the child rearing. On TV, children see many gender-stereotypic models and see that people who act in ways that are gender inconsistent often get ridiculed or otherwise punished.

3.   *The biggest changes in our sexual selves occur during adolescence as we go through puberty. There are dramatic changes in boys' and girls' bodies as they develop secondary sex characteristics and become sexually mature. These changes have psychological implications, depending on whether the timing of maturity is early, late, or on time. For boys, being early or on time is better than being late. For girls, being on time or late has more advantages (or fewer disadvantages) than maturing early. Adolescents spend a great deal of timing thinking about and worrying about their sexual selves. Some come to the realization that they are homosexual, which is a dramatic insight at any age.*

Another significant change in the sexual selves of women would be going through menopause, the cessation of menstruation. This is likely to trigger a reevaluation of what it means to be a sexual being. Men may go through a similar process during andropause, but it much more gradual and doesn't have the same conclusion. Men can continue to father children well into old age, whereas women are unable to bear children once they go through menopause (unless they turn to one of the new assisted reproductive technologies).

CHAPTER THIRTEEN

SOCIAL COGNITION AND MORAL DEVELOPMENT

OVERVIEW

Whether you realize it or not, you use social cognitive skills every day when you think about your own or another person's thoughts, behaviors, motivations, or emotions. This chapter discusses what these skills are, how they change across the life span, factors that can foster these skills, and the importance of these skills to other areas of development.

A large portion of this chapter is devoted to moral development, including the theoretical explanations of moral affect (Freud's psychoanalytic theory), moral reasoning (Kohlberg's and Piaget's cognitive-developmental theories), and moral behavior (social-learning theory). Each theory is evaluated in light of research findings. Particularly interesting in this chapter are the discussions of how to foster moral maturity and increase social cognitive skills and the correlates of antisocial behavior.

LEARNING OBJECTIVES

After reading and studying the material in this chapter, you should be able to answer the following questions.

1. What is a theory of mind? How is it assessed? What developmental changes occur in the understanding of a theory of mind and what factors affect its emergence?

2. How do person perception and role taking skills develop? Why are these skills important?

3. What is morality? What are the three basic components of morality?

4. What is Freud's explanation for the development of morality?

5. How did Kohlberg assess moral reasoning? What are the important characteristics of each level and stage of Kohlberg's theory? What are examples of responses at each stage of reasoning?

6.   How do social learning theorists explain moral behavior?

7.   What do infants understand about morality and prosocial behavior?

8.   What changes in moral reasoning and behavior occur during childhood?

9.   What parenting characteristics contribute to the development of morality? Which parenting style is "best"?

10.   What changes in moral reasoning occur during adolescence? How is moral development related to antisocial behavior of adolescents? What other factors influence antisocial behavior?

11.   What changes in moral reasoning and behavior occur during adulthood?

12.   How does Kohlberg's theory of moral reasoning fare in light of research findings? In what ways might the theory be biased or incomplete?

CHAPTER SUMMARY AND GUIDED REVIEW

The following summary provides an overview of the main points contained in this chapter of the text. Fill-in the blanks with terms that appropriately complete the sentence. Scattered throughout the summary are questions in parentheses. These are meant to encourage you to think actively as you are reading and connect this summary to the more detailed information provided in the text. You can answer these questions as you are filling in the blanks or you can complete all the blanks, then go back and reread the entire summary, addressing the questions in order to provide more depth of understanding.

SOCIAL COGNITION

Social cognition involves the ability to think about thoughts, emotions, motives, and behaviors of one's self and others.

Developing a Theory of Mind

Using a task called the (1) _____, researchers assess children's understanding that people can have incorrect beliefs and be influenced by these beliefs. *(Can you explain how this task works?)* This task has been used to determine whether children have a (2) _____, which is the understanding of mental states and the role of mental states on behavior. Research shows that many children with autism lack this understanding, which may limit their abilities to have successful social interactions.

Precursors of a theory of mind can be seen as young as 9 months, when infants and care givers look at the same object together, showing (3) _____. Other research shows that two year olds develop a desire psychology based on what they want. By age four, they show (4) _____ psychology, which incorporates an understanding of beliefs. The development of a theory of mind seems to involve biological/maturational factors as well as normal interactions with other people. *(What evidence supports the nature and nurture components of theory of mind?)*

Describing Other People

How do children perceive other people? Young children describe people in terms of (5) _____ traits and behaviors. By age seven or eight, children use psychological traits to describe others, and by eleven or twelve years, they can use psychological characteristics to make social comparisons of people.

Role-Taking Skills

Role-taking skill is the ability to assume another person's perspective. Selman has concluded that role-taking skills develop in stages. Preschool children tend to be (6) _____ and have trouble assuming another person's perspective. With concrete operational thought, children can understand that there are different perspectives even if people have received the same information. With the development of formal operational thought, adolescents can simultaneously consider two different perspectives and how they fit with the perspective of the broader social group. *(What are the implications of good social cognition skills such as role-taking?)*

Social-Cognition in Adulthood

Social cognitive skills of adults are advanced in some ways, but also may show some losses. Elderly adults who continue to use their social cognition skills show no decline in these abilities.

PERSPECTIVES ON MORAL DEVELOPMENT

The ability to distinguish right from wrong, act on this distinction, and experience the accompanying emotion implies morality. Morality includes an emotional or (7) _____ component, a behavioral component, and a (8) _____ component that focuses on how a person reasons and makes decisions about moral dilemmas.

Moral Affect: Psychoanalytic Theory and Beyond

Freud's psychoanalytic theory focused on emotions or (9) _____. A child who has done something wrong typically feels some negative emotion such as guilt or shame. Being able to experience another person's feelings, or (10) _____, is another moral affect, which can lead to positive social acts or (11) _____ behaviors. Freud believed that morality was not present until the (12) _____ developed during the phallic stage of psychosexual development. At this time, children (13) _____ the moral standards of the same-sex parent. The specifics of Freud's theory are not well supported. *(**List some of the problems with Freud's explanation of morality.**)*

Moral Reasoning: Cognitive-Developmental Theory

Cognitive developmental theorists such as Piaget and Kohlberg focused on moral reasoning. According to Piaget, preschool children are premoral and show little awareness of rules. Elementary school-age children take rules very seriously and believe that consequences are more important than intentions. They are in Piaget's stage of (14) _____ morality. Older children view rules as agreements between individuals and believe intentions are more important than consequences. This is Piaget's stage of (15) _____ morality.

Kohlberg developed a theory of moral reasoning that consists of three levels, each with two stages. Progress through these stages follows an (16) _____, or fixed order. The first, or (17) _____, level consists of stage 1, the punishment-and-obedience orientation, where the emphasis is on the (18) _____ of an act, and stage 2, called (19) _____, where an act is judged by whether it satisfies personal needs or results in personal gain. The (20) _____ level consists of stage 3, the "good boy" or "good girl" morality, where actions are right if they please others or are approved by others, and stage 4, the authority and social-order-maintaining morality with its focus on conforming to (21) _____. The last level of moral reasoning is (22) _____ morality, which includes stages 5 and 6. Stage five is the morality of contract, individual rights, and democratically accepted law, and stage six is the morality of individual principles of conscience. *(**Can you provide responses that portray these six different stages?**)*

Moral Behavior: Social Learning Theory

Social learning theorists focus mainly on moral behaviors. According to this view, moral behavior is learned the same way everything else is learned—through reinforcement (or punishment) and through (23) _____. According to Bandura's social cognitive theory, moral thinking is connected to moral action through cognitive (24) _____ mechanisms. Normally, such monitoring and evaluation keeps our behavior in line with our internalized standards. But sometimes, we exercise (25) _____ in which we ignore or distances ourselves from moral standards, opening the door to immoral behavior. A major difference between social learning theory and the other theories of moral development is that social learning theorists view morality as (26) _____ behavior rather than a general trait.

THE INFANT

Infants in our society are often viewed as lacking any sense of morality, or as being (27) _____.

Early Moral Training

Although infants are not held morally responsible for their actions, they are learning lessons about what is right and wrong. Children must learn to experience negative emotions when they do something wrong and to exert self-control when tempted to violate rules. Research suggests that moral development is fostered by a close, warm, cooperative relationship between child and parent, otherwise known as a (28) _____. In addition, emotion-centered discussion is an important component of moral learning.

Prosocial Behavior

Infants display some rudimentary signs that they understand another person's feelings, known as (29) _____. They are not yet able to share or help another person or otherwise engage in (30) _____ behaviors until sometime during the second year of life.

THE CHILD
Weighing Intentions

Research on Piaget's theory of moral reasoning indicates that he underestimated young children. When Piaget's moral reasoning tasks are simplified, even young children can consider a person's (31) _____ when making moral judgments.

Understanding Rules

Young children may not view rules as sacred. Turiel reports that young children distinguish between two kinds of rules in daily life. (32) _____ rules focus on basic rights and privileges of individuals and (33) _____ rules focus on what social consensus deems right or wrong. Even young children understand the difference between these two types of rules and understand that violating a (34) _____ rule is the more serious transgression.

Applying Theory of Mind

The emergence of a theory of mind helps children better understand how their actions influence other people.

Thinking Through Kohlberg's Dilemmas

School-aged children typically reason at the (35) _____ level when tested with Kohlberg's moral dilemmas.

Behaving Morally

Research with children on resistance to temptation indicates that moral behavior is not consistent across (36) _____. (***How have researchers studied resistance to temptation?***) Moral inconsistency due to situation-specific differences supports (37) _____ theory.

Nurturing Morality

Social learning theorists recommend that parents foster moral maturity using the same principles that apply to other behaviors: reinforcement and punishment, and observation of moral behavior. In addition, fostering empathy can help develop moral behavior.

Research has linked moral development to parental discipline styles. Disciplining by withholding attention, love, or approval is called (38) _____.
(39) _____ is the use of physical power to gain compliance to rules. Explaining to a child why a behavior is wrong and pointing out how it affects other people is
(40) _____. The use of (41) _____ is associated with higher levels of moral maturity than use of the other two discipline styles. (*Can you explain why this is true?*) The use of (42) _____ is often associated with immature moral responses, although it may be useful if used sparingly. Use of (43) _____ has been found to have mixed effects. The way children respond to moral training may depend on their (44) _____. The interaction of children's temperaments with their social environments illustrates the concept of (45) _____.

THE ADOLESCENT
Changes in Moral Reasoning

Most adolescents reason at the (46) _____ level of Kohlberg's model, and they begin to view morality as an important part of their identity.

Antisocial Behavior

Some adolescents engage in antisocial and delinquent behaviors. There is a weak connection between these behaviors and level of moral reasoning. According to Kenneth Dodge, the way that social cues are processed may provide a better explanation of these behaviors. There are six steps in processing information, starting with encoding and then
(47) _____ of the information. Clarifying goals, searching for possible responses and evaluating these options are followed by the last step, (48) _____.
Aggressive adolescents are likely to have problems with every step of processing information. (*Can you provide some examples of faulty information processing that might lead to aggressive behavior?*)

This model helps us to understand the behavior but does not fully explain why someone processes information in this maladaptive way. According to Gerald Patterson,
(49) _____ family environments, where members try to control one another, are associated with antisocial children. Aggression is likely determined by a combination of genetic and environmental influences. (*Can you explain how genes and environments interact or correlate to determine aggression?*)

THE ADULT
Moral Development

Some adults move into Kohlberg's (50) _____ level of moral reasoning. Moral reasoning does not deteriorate in old age, and indeed it may improve.

Influences on Moral Development

An increase in (51) _____, or search for meaning in life, often occurs between middle and later adulthood. Along with postconventional reasoning, this is connected with the attainment of (52) _____.

Cognitive developmental theorists claim that cognitive growth and relevant social experiences contribute to moral development. Research suggests that general cognitive abilities are necessary but not sufficient for moral development. (***Can you specify how different levels of cognitive reasoning are related to different levels of moral reasoning?***) Kohlberg believed that one important social experience was interacting with others, particularly peers, in order to be exposed to different levels of moral reasoning, which could create cognitive (53) _____. This was thought to be necessary in order to advance to higher levels of reasoning. (***What are some other important social experiences that affect moral development?***)

Kohlberg's Theory and Beyond

There is support for Kohlberg's claim that moral development is stage-like. However, Kohlberg has been criticized for several reasons. One important criticism is that his theory is biased in several ways. It may be biased against people from different cultures, people with conservative values, and against women. In some studies, women reason at stage (54) _____ whereas men reason at stage (55) _____. Carol Gilligan argues that women reason using a morality of (56) _____ and men reason using a morality of (57) _____. (***Can you explain what these perspectives mean?***) Gilligan claims that neither focus is "right;" they are simply different ways to reason, and reflect differences in how boys and girls are traditionally raised in our society. Gilligan's theory is not well supported by research.

Another criticism of Kohlberg's theory is that it is incomplete because it ignores moral affect and behavior. Kohlberg would predict that moral behavior is related to level of moral reasoning. Overall, however, this relationship is weak.

REVIEW OF KEY TERMS

Below is a list of terms and concepts from this chapter. Match each one with its appropriate definition. You might also want to try writing definitions in your own words and then checking your definitions with those here in the Study Guide or in the text.

amoral
autonomous morality
belief-desire psychology
coercive family environment
conventional morality
desire psychology
empathy
false belief task
heteronomous morality
induction
joint attention
love withdrawal

moral affect
moral disengagement
morality
morality of care
morality of justice
moral reasoning
moral rules
mutually responsive orientation
postconventional morality
power assertion
preconventional morality
premoral period

prosocial behavior   social-conventional rules
role-taking skills   spirituality
social cognition   theory of mind

1.   The _____ is used to assess the understanding that people can have incorrect
      beliefs that influence their behavior.

2.   _____ are standards of what behaviors are right or wrong based on rights and
      privileges of individuals.

3.   Kohlberg's fifth and sixth stages are part of the _____ in which judgments
      are based on broad principles of justice that have validity separate from the views of any
      particular person or group.

4.   _____ is the cognitive process of deciding whether an act is right or wrong.

5.   _____ is a type of discipline style based on physical power of the adult over
      the child.

6.   Kohlberg's first two stages of moral reasoning are part of the _____ in which
      the personal consequences of a person's actions are used as the basis for judgments.

7.   Infants show _____ when they look at an object with a caregiver.

8.   A moral perspective that emphasizes one's responsibility for the welfare of others is
      called _____.

9.   Thinking about the thoughts, behaviors, motives, and emotions of oneself and others is
      called _____.

10.   _____ is a type of discipline style based on explanations that focus on how
      the misbehavior affects other people.

11.   _____ is a set of principles that allow a person to distinguish right from
      wrong, and act on this distinction.

12.   Understanding that people have mental states that influence behavior shows the presence
      of a _____.

13.   Kohlberg's third and fourth stages are part of the _____ in which actions are
      judged by whether they conform to the rules set forth by others.

14.   Experiencing another person's feelings is _____.

15. The ability to take another person's perspective and understand their thoughts and feelings is _____.

16. _____ is the emotional component of morality, consisting of feelings about right and wrong actions.

17. The lack of any sense of morality is referred to as being _____.

18. A discipline style that is based on threatened or actual loss of love or attention is _____.

19. _____ includes an understanding that a person's beliefs do not always accurately reflect reality.

20. _____ includes positive social acts that show a concern for the welfare of others.

21. _____ are standards for defining what behaviors are right or wrong based on social consensus.

22. A moral perspective that emphasizes the laws defining individual rights is _____.

23. Family interactions that are characterized by power struggles where members try to control each other exist in _____.

24. According to _____, young children understand what they want and often use wants to explain behavior.

25. The view that rules are unalterable and handed down by authority figures is part of Piaget's stage of _____.

26. The search for ultimate meaning in life is a significant component of _____.

27. According to Piaget, preschool-age children have little understanding of rules and are in a _____.

28. Early moral socialization can be enhanced by a close, warm, and cooperative relationship between parent and child, known as a _____.

29. Employing mechanisms of _____ allows people to avoid feeling bad when they engage in immoral behavior.

30. Piaget's final stage of moral development in which children understand that rules can be changed by consensus and pay attention to intentions is called _____.

For each multiple choice question, read all alternatives and then select the best answer.

1. Having a theory of mind shows an understanding that
   a. people's behavior is guided by a set of internalized set of rules about right and wrong.
   b. more than one person is looking at an object at a particular time.
   c. people have mental states that influence their behavior.
   d. other people experience different emotions.

2. Children who are popular and have close friends
   a. reason at the "good boy" "good girl" stage of moral reasoning.
   b. tend to use more reactive aggression than proactive aggression.
   c. are more likely to have an intuitive theory of emotions.
   d. tend to have more advanced role-taking skills than other children.

3. Social cognitive skills
   a. reach a peak as adolescents finish their formal schooling and then slowly decline.
   b. remain high in socially active older adults.
   c. relate specifically to a person's educational level.
   d. decline from young to older adulthood for most adults.

4. According to Freud's psychoanalytic theory
   a. children reach moral maturity around age 6 or 7 when they resolve their Oedipal (or Electra) conflicts.
   b. girls are more morally mature than boys since they have less to fear during the phallic stage of development.
   c. children reach moral maturity in adolescence when they enter the genital stage of development.
   d. the reasons behind an act are more important than how one feels about a moral action.

5. Research on Freud's explanation of morality shows that all of the following are PROBLEMS with the explanation EXCEPT
   a. males do not have stronger superegos than females.
   b. children do not achieve moral maturity by resolving the conflicts of the phallic stage.
   c. children do not develop greater moral maturity by interacting with cold, punitive parents.
   d. children do not experience feelings in conjunction with moral transgressions.

6. A child who says that it is wrong to cheat because he or she might get caught would be in Kohlberg's _____ stage.
   a. punishment-and-obedience orientation (stage 1)
   b. instrumental hedonism (stage 2)
   c. "good boy" or "good girl" morality (stage 3)
   d. authority and social-order-maintaining morality (stage 4)

7. A teenager who begins smoking because all his friends are doing it is probably in Kohlberg's _____ stage.
   a. instrumental hedonism (stage 2)
   b. "good boy" or "good girl" morality (stage 3)
   c. authority and social-order-maintaining morality (stage 4)
   d. morality of contract, individual rights, and democratically accepted law (stage 5)

8. Social learning theorists argue that morality is
   a. a generalized trait inherent to the person and subject to little change.
   b. a situation-specific trait that is subject to change.
   c. an emotional reaction and cannot be directly observed.
   d. established in early childhood and changes little after this.

9. Piaget argued that elementary school children
   a. are largely unaware of moral rules and so do not always act appropriately.
   b. base decisions on both consequences of an action and intentions of the actor.
   c. believe that rules can be changed at any time.
   d. believe that the consequences of an action are more important than intentions of the actor.

10. Standards of what behaviors are right or wrong based on rights and privileges of individuals are termed
    a. postconventional rules.
    b. social-conventional rules.
    c. moral rules.
    d. altruistic rules.

11. Recent studies of Kohlberg's and Piaget's theories of moral reasoning suggest that
    a. there is no relationship between level of cognitive development and moral reasoning.
    b. they underestimated children's moral reasoning capabilities.
    c. they overestimated children's moral reasoning capabilities.
    d. they focused too much attention on children's actions in a moral situation.

12. Parents who discipline their children by making them anxious about whether they will receive affection or approval are using
    a. love withdrawal.
    b. power assertion.
    c. emotional assertion.
    d. induction.

13. Parents who use an inductive style of discipline
    a. indoctrinate their child with their own values and beliefs.
    b. withhold attention until their child complies with rules.
    c. use their power to get their child to comply with rules.
    d. explain to their child why the behavior is wrong and emphasize how it affects other people.

14. Moral maturity can be fostered by
    a. using an inductive style of discipline.
    b. using love-withdrawal as the major disciplinary method.
    c. using power assertion as the major disciplinary method.
    d. harsh discipline that leaves the child in no doubt about whether a behavior is acceptable or not.

15. Carol Gilligan claims that men and women score at different levels on Kohlberg's moral dilemmas because
    a. males operate on the basis of a morality of justice and women do not.
    b. Freud was right—females are less morally mature.
    c. males are more concerned about the needs of others.
    d. males reason about real life dilemmas while women reason about hypothetical moral issues.

REVIEW KOHLBERG'S SIX STAGES OF MORAL REASONING

For this exercise, indicate how a person in each of Kohlberg's six stages would respond to the following Kohlberg dilemma. Use the Exploration box on page 364 of the text to check your answers.

Once there was man named Henry, who lived in a small town. Early one morning Henry and his wife were driving to town along a winding country road. It was still very early in the morning, and the sun was just beginning to rise. A very heavy fog still covered the road. It was difficult for Henry to see where he was driving. Suddenly, there was a sharp curve in the road. Henry lost control of the car. Henry was not hurt, but his wife was lying unconscious on the floor of the front seat. Henry did not know how badly she was hurt, but worried because it might be hours before another car came along the isolated road. Henry's car was completely smashed, and there were no other cars passing by on the road. There were no houses in sight. But Henry did see a small farm truck with keys locked in it. So he broke the truck's window, put his wife into the truck, and drove her to the hospital. Should Henry have stolen the truck?

MORAL STAGE	EXPLANATION
Stage 1: Punishment & obedience orientation	
Stage 2: Instrumental hedonism	
Stage 3: "Good boy" or "good girl" morality	
Stage 4: Authority & social-order-maintaining morality	
Stage 5: Morality of contract, individual rights, and democratically accepted law	
Stage 6: Morality of individual principles of conscience	

CRITICAL THINKING QUESTIONS

By answering the following questions, you will strengthen your understanding of the material in this chapter. These questions require higher level thinking skills such as integration and application of concepts. Sample answers are provided for three of the questions. These illustrate one possibility, but there are other answers you could provide that might be just as good. For the other questions, you can check yourself by referring to the text (a hint is provided), or by asking a peer or your instructor to review your answer.

1. What is it about raising a child using an induction approach to discipline that leads to greater moral maturity in comparison to children raised with power assertion or love withdrawal?
   [Sample answer provided.]

2. On Halloween night, several of your friends try to talk you into going out with them to pull some pranks in the neighborhood (e.g., soaping the neighbor's windows, scaring

young children, and knocking over gravestones). You are considering it. What preconventional, conventional, and postconventional answers might you give (either to join in or to abstain)?
[Sample answer provided.]

3. What factors lead some adolescents to engage in antisocial behaviors while many other adolescents do not? What are some protective factors against antisocial behaviors and what are some of the risk factors?
[Sample answer provided.]

4. What can parents do to increase a child's social cognitive skills and foster moral maturity?
[Hint: There is information on this issue in several places throughout the chapter, including within the discussion of "Theory of mind," "Role-taking skills," "Early moral training," and "How does one raise moral children?" In addition, the Application box on page 376, "Combating youth violence," provides useful information.]

5. Considering the research that has been conducted on moral reasoning, how has Kohlberg's theory fared?
[Hint: Review the section on "Kohlberg's theory and beyond," which starts on page 378.

ANSWERS

Chapter Summary and Guided Review (Fill-in the blank)

1.	false belief task	22.	postconventional
2.	theory of mind	23.	observation
3.	joint attention	24.	self-regulatory
4.	belief-desire	25.	moral disengagement
5.	physical	26.	situation-specific
6.	egocentric	27.	amoral
7.	affective	28.	mutually responsive orientation
8.	cognitive	29.	empathy
9.	moral affects	30.	prosocial
10.	empathy	31.	intentions
11.	prosocial	32.	moral
12.	superego	33.	social-conventional
13.	internalize	34.	moral
14.	heteronomous	35.	preconventional
15.	autonomous	36.	situations
16.	invariant	37.	social learning
17.	preconventional morality	38.	love withdrawal
18.	consequences	39.	power assertion
19.	instrumental hedonism	40.	induction
20.	conventional	41.	induction
21.	laws or rules	42.	power assertion

43. love withdrawal
44. temperaments
45. goodness of fit
46. conventional
47. interpretation
48. enactment
49. coercive
50. postconventional

51. spirituality
52. wisdom
53. disequilibrium
54. three
55. four
56. care
57. justice

Review of Key Terms
1. false belief task
2. moral rules
3. postconventional morality
4. moral reasoning
5. power assertion
6. preconventional morality
7. joint attention
8. morality of care
9. social cognition
10. induction
11. morality
12. theory of mind
13. conventional morality
14. empathy
15. role taking skills

16. moral affect
17. amoral
18. love withdrawal
19. belief-desire psychology
20. prosocial behavior
21. social-conventional rules
22. morality of justice
23. coercive family environments
24. desire psychology
25. heteronomous morality
26. spirituality
27. premoral period
28. mutually responsive orientation
29. moral disengagement
30. autonomous morality

Multiple Choice Self Test
1. C (p. 352)
2. D (p. 358)
3. B (pp. 358-59)
4. A (p. 360)
5. D (pp. 360-61)

6. A (p. 362)
7. B (p. 362)
8. B (p. 363)
9. D (p. 361)
10. C (p. 362)

11. B (pp. 367-68)
12. A (p. 368)
13. D (p. 369)
14. A (pp. 368-69)
15. A (p. 380)

Critical Thinking Questions
1. *Induction encourages children to think about how their actions affect other people. This gets them away from thinking egocentrically and focusing solely on how things benefit or harm themselves. This also fosters empathy. By pointing out why a child's behavior was wrong, parents can communicate standards of behavior that children can incorporate into their future actions. All these things help advance morality, particularly in children with temperaments that are high in emotionality and low in impulsivity.*

2. *A preconventional thinker would provide answers that focus on doing something in order to avoid punishment (stage one) or doing something for personal gain (stage two). In this example, an individual might say that they are not going to participate in Halloween night pranks because they could get caught and punished. Or they might decide to participate because they think their status among their friends will increase following their daring acts (i.e., they*

personally benefit from participating).

A conventional thinker would provide answers that focus on acting in ways that are approved by others (stage 3) or acting in ways that conform to the rules of the group (stage 4). An individual might decide to go along with their friends for the pranks because they believe they would receive approval from their peers for doing so. They might decide to not participate because it would be breaking the law to deface another person's property.

Postconventional thinkers would concentrate on actions that are morally right, not just legally right. They might argue that pulling Halloween pranks violates other individual's rights, even if there is not a specific law prohibiting what they plan on doing.

3.   *There are many factors that contribute to antisocial behavior. According to Dodge's social information-processing model, people who engage in antisocial acts processing information differently than people who do not engage in these acts. They don't always encode all the relevant information or they encode it in ways that highlight the disadvantages to them. They are also likely to think that others hold hostile intentions toward them; that any little infraction is motivated by a desire to hurt them. In response, they lash out. They often act impulsively, without thinking through all the consequences. When they do think of consequences, they are more likely to believe that aggressive acts are a positive solution to their problem.*

In addition to how they process information, aggressive youth often come from coercive family environments. These are families in which family members threaten, yell, and hit each other in order to control one another. Children learn this way of interaction, which makes them unpopular with the regular peer group, so they drift toward a peer group that is similar. Once they are in the habit of hanging out with other antisocial, rejected youth, it reinforces their aggressive tendencies, making it more likely that they will engage in antisocial acts.

It's also possible that some people are more genetically predisposed to aggression and antisocial behaviors than others. This might be mediated through temperament and personality characteristics. Certain personalities traits may provoke more coercive parenting, which in turn, leads to peer rejection and drifting toward a delinquent peer group.

CHAPTER FOURTEEN

ATTACHMENT AND SOCIAL RELATIONSHIPS

OVERVIEW

Relationships with others have a tremendous influence on our lives. As noted in the text, close relationships provide learning opportunities that affect all areas of development. They also provide social support that helps us celebrate positive events and protects us from negative events.

This chapter discusses the first major relationship—the one that develops between infants and their caregivers—and how the quality of this relationship influences later development. Also covered are peer relations and friendships, including how they evolve and change over the life span and factors that contribute to the quality of social relationships (for instance, why are some children more popular than others?). For children, play is particularly important because it provides opportunities to interact with others and learn skills for successful social relationships. In particular, pretend play is associated with better performance on some tests of cognitive development, language, and creativity.

The section on adolescents provides an interesting look at attachment relationships between adolescents and their parents. It also covers the transition from platonic, largely same-sex social interactions to romantic, opposite-sex interactions. The discussion of romantic relationships is continued in the section on adults, with an examination of factors that contribute to mate selection.

LEARNING OBJECTIVES

After reading and studying the material in this chapter, you should be able to answer the following questions.

1.   How do relationships with others contribute to development?

2.   How does Bowlby's attachment theory explain attachment? In this model, how do nature and nurture contribute to the development of attachment?

3.   In what ways are infants emotional beings? How are emotions socialized and regulated?

4.   How do infants become attached to a caregiver? What are some observable signs of infant attachment?

5.   What types of attachment relationships can develop between infants and caregivers? What infant, caregiver, and contextual factors determine the quality of early attachments? How do these early relationships relate to later development?

6.   What features characterize peer relations and friendships at different points of the life span?

7.   What different types of play evolve during the first few years of life? What are the developmental benefits of play?

8.   What factors contribute to peer acceptance and popularity, or to peer rejection, during childhood?

9.   How do relationships with peers and parents change during adolescence? How do peers and parents influence adolescents' lives?

10.   How do social networks and friendships change during adulthood?

11.   How do early attachment styles relate to romantic relationships?

CHAPTER SUMMARY AND GUIDED REVIEW

The following summary provides an overview of the main points contained in this chapter of the text. Fill-in the blanks with terms that appropriately complete the sentence. Scattered throughout the summary are questions in parentheses. These are meant to encourage you to think actively as you are reading and connect this summary to the more detailed information provided in the text. You can answer these questions as you are filling in the blanks or you can complete all the blanks, then go back and reread the entire summary, addressing the questions in order to provide more depth of understanding.

PERSPECTIVES ON RELATIONSHIPS

Social relationships are important because they provide us with learning experiences and with emotional and practical help, called (1) _____ that provides strength and helps protect us from stress. People who provide support are said to be part of a (2) _____ that changes across the life span.

Attachment Theory

John Bowlby developed an influential theory of parent-child attachment. According to Bowlby, attachment is a strong affection that binds one person to another. Infants express attachment by trying to maintain (3) _____ to the figure of their attachment and by showing a preference for this person. Bowlby claims that infants are biologically predisposed to form attachments. Some species experience (4) _____, an innate form of learning where the young will follow and become attached to the first moving object they encounter during a (5) _____ early in life. Bowlby believes that early attachments between parent and infant affect later development because infants develop (6) _____ models, or representations, of what relationships should be like.

Peers and the Two Worlds of Childhood

Relationships with members of one's social group, or (7) _____, are also important and are quite different from relationships with parents, forming two distinct social worlds during childhood. Theorist Harry Sullivan placed special emphasis on the significance of (8) _____, or close friendships with peers of the same sex that emerge at around 9-12 years of age. In her book, *The Nurture Assumption*, Judith Harris argues that parents influence their children through the genes they pass along to them, but not through their behavior. (***Is there evidence to support this position? What evidence contradicts Harris's argument?***)

THE INFANT

Infants are social creatures right from the start, although the nature of social relationships changes substantially throughout infancy.

Early Emotional Development

Research confirms that infants show a wide range of emotions, which emerge in a predictable order starting with (9) _____ emotions of contentment, interest, and distress. These earliest emotions may be (10)_____ predisposed because they emerge in all infants at about the same time. Secondary or (11) _____ emotions emerge around 18 months of age when infants have acquired a sense of self. Environment and culture influence expression of emotions. For example, infants in our culture learn that (12) _____ emotions are more accepted than (13)_____ ones. Infants also monitor the emotional reactions of other people in ambiguous situations to regulate their own reactions, which is called (14) _____. To manage their own emotions, infants must develop strategies for (15) _____, the process of initiating, maintaining, and altering emotional responses. (***What are some of these early strategies?***)

An Attachment Forms

       Just as infants become attached to caregivers, caregivers become attached to their infants. Infants have a number of features that seem to facilitate the development of attachment. (***What are some of these features?***) Infants and caregivers learn to take turns responding to each other's leads in (16) _____ routines or interactions.

       Infants progress through several phases as they develop a relationship with their caregivers. In the first phase, called (17) _____ responsiveness, infants are responsive to social stimuli but show no preference for one person over another. In the second phase, (18) _____ responsiveness, infants begin to show preferences for familiar companions. In the third phase, active (19) _____, or true attachment, infants will actively pursue the object of their attachment. The final phase represents a more goal-corrected (20) _____ between child and attachment figure.

       One sign that an attachment has formed is (21) _____, which is when infants show distress when separated from the object of their attachment. Infants may also show a wary response to the approach of an unfamiliar person, called (22) _____. (***What factors can affect this response?***) Once infants have formed an attachment, they often use that attachment figure as a (23) _____ for exploration. Thus, attachment facilitates exploratory behavior.

Quality of Attachment

       To measure the quality of an infant's attachment, Mary Ainsworth created the (24) _____ in which an infant's reactions to a series of mildly stressful events are observed. Infants who are classified as (25) _____ attached show distress when separated from their caregiver, joy when reunited, and use of caregiver as a secure base. Infants who show (26) _____ attachment show distress when separated from their caregiver, but are ambivalent about being reunited, and do not really use the caregiver as a secure base. Infants characterized by (27) _____ attachment show little distress at separation from caregiver, avoid the caregiver when reunited, and do not use the caregiver as a secure base. Infants who have been abused often show a fourth pattern of attachment called (28) _____, which is a combination of elements from the resistant and avoidant styles of attachment.

       What factors influence the quality of early attachment? Freud claimed that feeding is critical for the development of attachment because of the oral pleasure it provides. However, research with monkeys does not support this. Harlow used the term (29) _____ to describe the pleasurable sensations provided by clinging to something soft and warm. Research indicates that the availability of contact comfort contributes more to attachment than feeding.

Also, infants develop secure attachments to caregivers who are generally responsive to their needs. (***Which theories are supported by these findings? Explain how they are supported***.) Inconsistent parenting is associated with (30) _____ attachment, and inappropriate (too much or too little) amounts of stimulation are associated with (31) _____ attachment. In addition to the way parents interact with their infants, an infant's level of cognitive development and their (32) _____ influence the quality of infant-caregiver attachments. Secure attachment can occur with any temperament style as long as there is a good fit with the caregiver's behavior. Finally, cultural context influences attachment behaviors. (***Can you explain how culture influences attachment?***)

Implications of Early Attachment

Research with infants who have been raised in deprived environments shows that social isolation early in life has an adverse effect on development. The negative effects persist into childhood and adolescence, especially among those who were deprived for six months or more. Normal development seems to require sustained interactions with responsive caregivers.

For infants raised at home, having a secure or insecure attachment affects later development. Children who had formed secure attachments during infancy are more socially competent, more curious and eager to learn, and more emotionally healthy than children without secure attachments. In addition, secure attachments helped infants cope with stress and regulate emotions later on. (***How robust, i.e., strong and long-lasting, are these connections between infant attachment and later development?***) Finally, research shows that children who had secure attachments as infants process information differently than children who had insecure attachments. This supports Bowlby's idea that infants form (33) _____ of attachment relationships.

First Peer Relations

Infants are interested in other infants and begin to interact socially with them around six months of age through smiles, vocalizations, and gestures. By the end of their second year, infants are able to distinguish between infants as well as adults and act more sociable in the presence of familiar infants.

THE CHILD
Parent-Child Attachments

Children's attachments to their parents change throughout childhood. Interactions become more like a (34) _____ partnership where children are able to take the goals and plans of another person into consideration and act on the basis of this information.

Peer Networks

Children increasingly spend more time with their peers and in these interactions, children spend more and more time in (35) _____ groups playing with same-sex peers.

Play

Children between the ages of two and five play quite a bit, which provides opportunities to interact with others and sharpen their social skills. Their play becomes more (36) _____ and more imaginative. According to Parten's scale for classifying children's play, children who are engaged in no particular activity are in the category of (37) _____ play. Children who play alone are engaged in (38) _____ play. (39) _____ play involves watching others as they play and (40) _____ play is when two children play next to each other but not with each other. In (41) _____ play, children interact with one another, but only in (42) _____ play are children really united toward a common goal. Children increasingly engage in more associative and cooperative play, which are the most social of these play categories.

Play of preschool-aged children also becomes more imaginative. They engage in (43) _____ play when they use one thing to symbolize something else. They increasingly engage in (44) _____ play, combining their capacity for imaginary play with their social play.

Elementary school children engage in less symbolic play and more in organized games with (45) _____. According to Piaget, children must be in the (46) _____ stage of cognitive development to play games with rules.

Play is important for a number of reasons. It contributes to cognitive and social development because children get an opportunity to role play, cooperate with others, and resolve conflicts. Play enhances (47) _____ development because children can express feelings that they might otherwise keep to themselves.

Peer Acceptance and Popularity

Peer acceptance is often studied through (48) _____ techniques where likes and dislikes among the members of a group are examined. Based on this, children can be classified into five district categories of social status. Children well liked by others are (49) _____, whereas children who are rarely liked are (50) _____. Children who are (51) _____ are not really liked or disliked, they are ignored by classmates. Children who are both liked by many and disliked by many are (52) _____. Children classified as (53) _____ are in the middle on both the liked and disliked scales.

Several factors influence popularity, including some personal characteristics that the child has little control of (e.g. physical appearance and names.) A child's competencies are also important. (***Can you describe specific factors that have been found to be related to whether a child is popular or rejected, neglected, or controversial?***)

Friendships

Popular children are more likely than unpopular ones to have friends. Children with friends are better off than those without friends. Peer interactions contribute to social and emotional development.

THE ADOLESCENT

Adolescents spend even more time with peers than children do, and the quality of peer interactions changes.

Attachments to Parents

Adolescents remain attached to their parents and may experience anxiety when separated. Those who are securely attached to their parents show better adjustment to transitions such as going to college. (***What are other benefits of a secure attachment between adolescents and parents?***)

Friendships

Friendships during adolescence focus on (54) _____ and (55) _____ between the partners. Adolescents tend to choose friends who are similar in (56) _____ traits. (***How do males and females differ in their friendships during adolescence?***)

Changing Social Networks

In late childhood, children are often members of same-sex (57) _____ and interact little with the other sex. Collections of several cliques constitute a (58) _____, which serves mainly as a vehicle for structured social activities. Peers generally foster positive behaviors, but this depends on the type of crowd that adolescents belong to.

After interacting with other-sex peers in a group setting, adolescents often begin to form couples and the existence of crowds begins to dissolve. Adolescents begin to move from same-sex peer groups to dating relationships and most have dated by age 15. Adolescent romantic relationships progress through four phases from initiation to (59) _____, to affection, and finally, to (60) _____. (***Can you describe each of these phases?***) Dating among young adolescents often has (61) _____ consequences, while dating among older adolescents often has (62) _____ consequences. (***How does dating affect same-sex friendships and personal adjustment?***)

Parent and Peer Influence

Researchers have used (63) _____, or the tendency to yield to the opinions of another person, to study parent and peer influence on adolescents. Conformity to adults tends to decrease with age. Conformity to peers to engage in (64) _____ behavior increases with age, levels off, and then decreases by the end of high school. Despite the influence of peers during adolescence, parents and peers are not typically in conflict since adolescents consult peers and parents on different issues, not the same issues. (***How can parents help maintain good relationships with their teenagers?***)

THE ADULT

Social Networks

Friendships continue to be important during adulthood, although the nature of the social network changes somewhat over time. Young adults spend a great deal of time interacting with members of the other sex. They also have more friends than middle-aged or older adults. The social network of most adults seems to shrink as they marry and as they get older. The (65) _____ hypothesis suggests that we narrow our social network to include people who are most important to us and this may result in an increase in the (66) _____ of the relationship. (***Is this theory supported by research?***)

Attachment Styles

There may be some similarities between infants who are attached to a parent and adults who are in love with a romantic partner. As infants, we construct internal working models for attachment relationships that influence our adult relationships. Adults with a (67) _____ working model of attachment feel good about themselves and others and feel comfortable entering into relationships. Adults with a (68) _____ working model feel positive about others but not about themselves. They desperately want a relationship but fear abandonment. Adults with a (69) _____ working model feel positive about themselves but not about others. They deny any need for relationships and are very self-reliant. Adults with a (70) _____ working model of attachment hold negative views of themselves and others, and while they express a need for relationships, they also have a fear of closeness. (***Can you describe the implications of these attachment styles for adults?***) There is some continuity in attachment styles across the lifespan. The internal working models developed during infancy influence the quality of later relationships.

Adult Friendships

Friendships continue to be important to adults. Men and women continue to show different styles of interacting with friends. (***What are these differences?***) Adults especially value friendships that have lasted many years, even if the friends live geographically distant from one another. Adults typically perceive friendships as most satisfying when they involve (71) _____, meaning that the contributions of both members are balanced.

Adult Relationships and Adult Development

Just as attachment is critical for normal infant and child development, friendships are important for normal adult development. However, it is the (72) _____ of friendships that is important, not the quantity of friendships. It seems important that adults have a (73) _____ or person to whom they are particularly close and to whom they express their feelings and thoughts.

REVIEW OF KEY TERMS

Below is a list of terms and concepts from this chapter. Use these to complete the following sentence definitions. You might also want to try writing definitions in your own words and then checking your definitions with those in the text.

attachment
attachment theory
avoidant attachment
chumships
clique
confidant
conformity
contact comfort
crowd
disorganized/disoriented attachment
emotion regulation
equity
imprinting

internal working models
peer
pretend play
resistant attachment
secure attachment
secure base
self-conscious emotions
separation anxiety
social convoy
social pretend play
social referencing
social support
socioemotional selectivity theory

sociometric techniques   Strange Situation
stranger anxiety   synchronized routines

1. _____ is an innate form of learning in which the young of a species will follow and become attached to a moving object (usually the mother) during a critical period early in life.

2. A caregiver-infant relationship characterized by distress at separation, ambivalence at being reunited, and little use of caregiver as a secure base is called a(n) _____.

3. When separated from a caregiver to whom they are attached, many infants show wariness or fear called _____.

4. A _____ is a small, same-sex friendship group.

5. _____ is the sense that there is a balance of contributions and benefits in relationships between spouses, friends, and other intimates.

6. A close friendship with peers of the same age that emerges at about age 9 to 12 is a _____.

7. In adolescence, teens from several heterosexual cliques often congregate, forming a _____.

8. Harlow used the term _____ for the pleasure derived from clinging to something soft and warm.

9. A caregiver-infant relationship characterized by little distress at separation, avoidance of caregiver when reunited, and little exploration is a(n) _____.

10. A _____ is a member of one's social group and is usually of similar age and behavioral functioning.

11. A _____ is someone to whom an individual feels an especially close attachment and with whom thoughts and feelings can be shared.

12. The _____ consists of a series of mildly stressful events designed to measure the quality of an infant's attachment to a caregiver.

13. Infants may exhibit wariness or _____ when approached by an unfamiliar person.

14. _____ attempts to explain the bond that develops between parent and child as well as the emotional ties between other people.

15. The emotional and practical assistance that helps protect individuals from stress is _____.

16. _____ is the tendency to change or develop opinions to go along with those of another person or group.

17. _____ are the integrated interactions between partners who take turns responding to each other's leads.

18. Infants must learn strategies for _____ in order to successfully initiate, maintain, and alter their emotional responses.

19. An attachment figure who serves as a safe place from which an infant can explore the environment is considered to be a _____.

20. _____ is a strong affectionate tie that binds a person to an intimate companion.

21. A caregiver-infant relationship characterized by distress at separation, joy at being reunited, and use of caregiver as a secure base indicates the presence of a _____.

22. Using one thing to represent something else in a playful context is _____.

23. _____ are methods of studying social groups by determining likes and dislikes among the members of the group.

24. The changing composition of one's social support system over the life span is reflected in one's _____.

25. A combination of resistant and avoidant styles of attachment in which infants are confused about whether to approach or avoid a parent is a _____.

26. According to the _____, we narrow our social contact to the people who are most important to us.

27. A(n) _____ is a cognitive representation about social interactions, which shapes expectations for future relationships.

28. Social play and symbolic play are combined in _____.

29. Researchers refer to secondary emotions such as embarrassment as _____.

30. Infants engage in _____ when they monitor the reactions of their companion in order to help them decide how to act or feel.

For each multiple choice question, read all alternatives and then select the best answer.

1. Infants show attachment through which of the following behaviors?
   a. showing a preference for one person over another
   b. trying to maintain proximity to a person
   c. showing distress when a person leaves
   d. all of the above

2. According to Bowlby's attachment theory
   a. infants must develop an attachment during a critical period early in life or they will not form later attachments.
   b. infants become attached to the caregiver who feeds them.
   c. infants are biologically predisposed to form attachments.
   d. through reinforcement, infants learn to form attachments.

3. In the discriminating social responsiveness phase of developing attachment, infants
   a. respond to many different social stimuli such as voices and faces.
   b. respond differently depending on the social situation.
   c. show preferences for familiar companions.
   d. show clear attachment by following the object of their attachment and protesting when this person leaves.

4. Stranger anxiety would be greatest in which of the following situations?
   a. Seated on mother's lap at the doctor's office while mom warmly greets the doctor.
   b. Seated on mother's lap at home while mom warmly greets the next door neighbor.
   c. Seated on mother's lap at home while mom neutrally greets a salesperson.
   d. Seated across from mom at the doctor's office while mom neutrally greets the doctor.

5. According to Freud, infants become attached to their mothers because
   a. mothers become associated with pleasurable sensations.
   b. mothers are generally responsive to their needs.
   c. they are innately predisposed to form attachments.
   d. mothers provide oral pleasure.

6. Which of the following describes infants who have resistant attachment?
   a. Infants use their mother as a secure base, they are upset when she leaves them, and welcome her when she returns.
   b. Infants are upset when their mother leaves them and ambivalent when she returns.
   c. Infants are not really distressed when their mother leaves them and do not welcome her back when she returns.
   d. Infants are not really distressed when their mother leaves them and express joy when reunited with mother.

7. With respect to the relationship between security of attachment during infancy and social competence during adulthood, research suggests that
   a. quality of infant attachment does not predict adult social competence as well as peer relations during adolescence do.
   b. quality of infant attachment has no relation to social competence during adulthood.
   c. quality of infant attachment to parents is the most important predictor of adult social competence.
   d. individuals who were securely attached as infants always have positive social relationships.

8. The finding that infant monkeys in Harlow's research preferred the cloth surrogate over the wire surrogate regardless of which one provided food
   a. supports Erikson's claim that general responsiveness is important to development of attachment.
   b. shows that there is an innate predisposition to form attachments.
   c. shows that Freud's emphasis on feeding behavior cannot fully explain development of attachment.
   d. supports learning theory explanations of attachment since infants become attached to the mother who reinforced them with food.

9. Casey is securely attached to her mother and her father. When she enters preschool, she is MOST LIKELY to
   a. strenuously resist separating from her parents.
   b. cling to her teacher in her parents' absence.
   c. be very popular with her peers.
   d. be socially immature.

10. Effects of early social deprivation in human infants
    a. cannot be overcome.
    b. can be overcome if the infants are placed with affectionate and responsive caregivers.
    c. can be overcome if the infants are exposed to multiple caregivers.
    d. are usually not significant.

11. The capacity for pretend play emerges
    a. at birth.
    b. around 6-7 months of age.
    c. around 1 year.
    d. around 3 years.

12. Children who do not actually participate in play with others but watch others play are engaged in _____ play.
    a. solitary
    b. unoccupied
    c. parallel
    d. onlooker

13. Pretend play
    a. can be used to assess children's level of intellectual functioning.
    b. can provide children the opportunity to work through problems.
    c. shows the same pattern in all children.
    d. increases when children enter elementary school.

14. With respect to conformity to pressure during adolescence
    a. there is no difference between conformity to pressure from adults and pressure from peers.
    b. conformity to peer pressure for antisocial acts increases, peaks around ninth grade, and then decreases.
    c. adolescents are more likely to conform to peer pressure for prosocial acts than antisocial acts.
    d. adolescents are more likely to conform to parental pressure than peer pressure.

15. Steve, a 32-year-old, is fiercely self-sufficient and refuses to accept help from others. He claims that he has no time for relationships and when he does date, he feels that his partner wants more out of the relationship than he does. Steve's internal working model of attachment is BEST characterized as
    a. secure.
    b. preoccupied.
    c. dismissing.
    d. fearful.

CRITICAL THINKING QUESTIONS

By answering the following questions, you will strengthen your understanding of the material in this chapter. These questions require higher level thinking skills such as integration and application of concepts. Sample answers are provided for three of the questions. These illustrate one possibility, but there are other answers you could provide that might be just as good. For the other questions, you can check yourself by referring to the text (a hint is provided), or by asking a peer or your instructor to review your answer.

1. What are the likely outcomes for children who, as infants, were insecurely attached to their caregiver? What factors influence the outcome for these children?
   [Sample answer provided.]

2. What aspects of children's development are fostered by engaging in pretend play?
   [Sample answer provided.]

3. What factors influence whether a child is popular or rejected in peer relationships?
   [Sample answer provided.]

4.   What similarities exist between the attachments of infants-caregiver and the romantic relationships of adults?
      [Hint: Read the section on "Attachment styles" in the Adult section, starting on page 413 of the text.]

5.   What influences do peers and parents have on adolescents?
      [Hint: Review the section on "Parent and peer influence" in the Adolescent section on page 410 of the text.]

ANSWERS

Chapter Summary and Guided Review (Fill-in the blank)

1.	social support	33.	internal working models
2.	social convoy	34.	goal-corrected
3.	proximity	35.	gender segregated
4.	imprinting	36.	social
5.	critical period	37.	unoccupied
6.	internal working	38.	solitary
7.	peers	39.	onlooker
8.	chumships	40.	parallel
9.	primary	41.	associative
10.	biologically	42.	cooperative
11.	self-conscious	43.	pretend
12.	positive	44.	social pretend
13.	negative	45.	rules
14.	social referencing	46.	concrete operations
15.	emotion regulation	47.	emotional
16.	synchronized	48.	sociometric
17.	undiscriminating social	49.	popular
18.	discriminating social	50.	rejected
19.	proximity seeking	51.	neglected
20.	partnership	52.	controversial
21.	separation anxiety	53.	average
22.	stranger anxiety	54.	intimacy
23.	secure base	55.	self-disclosure
24.	Strange Situation	56.	psychological
25.	securely	57.	cliques
26.	resistant	58.	crowd
27.	avoidant	59.	status
28.	disorganized/disoriented	60.	bonding
29.	contact comfort	61.	negative
30.	resistant	62.	positive
31.	avoidant	63.	conformity
32.	temperament	64.	antisocial

65.	socioemotional selectivity	70.	fearful
66.	quality	71.	equity
67.	secure	72.	quality
68.	preoccupied	73.	confidant
69.	dismissing		

Review of Key Terms

1.	imprinting	16.	conformity
2.	resistant attachment	17.	synchronized routines
3.	separation anxiety	18.	emotion regulation
4.	clique	19.	secure base
5.	equity	20.	attachment
6.	chumship	21.	secure attachment
7.	crowd	22.	pretend play
8.	contact comfort	23.	sociometric techniques
9.	avoidant attachment	24.	social convoy
10.	peer	25.	disorganized/disoriented attachment
11.	confidant	26.	socioemotional selectivity hypothesis
12.	Strange Situation test	27.	internal working model
13.	stranger anxiety	28.	social pretend play
14.	attachment theory	29.	self-conscious emotions
15.	social support	30.	social referencing

Multiple Choice Self Test

1.	D (p. 392)	6.	B (p. 394)	11.	C (p. 403)
2.	C (p. 386)	7.	A (pp. 400-01)	12.	D (p. 403)
3.	C (p. 392)	8.	C (p. 395)	13.	B (pp. 404-405
4.	D (pp. 392-93)	9.	C (p. 400)	14.	B (p. 410)
5.	D (p. 397)	10.	B (pp. 397-400)	15.	C (pp. 413-14)

Critical Thinking Questions

1.   *Infants with insecure attachments tend to have parents who are inconsistent with their caregiving or provide inappropriate amounts (too much or too little) of caregiving. Characteristics of the infant also influence whether a secure or insecure attachment develops between parent and child. In situations where there is a poor fit between the infant's temperament and the parent's caregiving style, an insecure attachment may develop and have long lasting effects. Children who had been insecurely attached as infants tend to be less curious and less likely to pursue their goals than children who had been securely attached. They also tend to be socially withdrawn and less likely to draw other children into play. This carries through to adolescence, with insecure children less adjusted in terms of both intellectual and social skills. These differences may relate to how children process information. Children who have formed insecure attachments develop internal working models that lead them to have negative expectations of interactions with others. In contrast, securely attached children tend to remember positive events and have more positive expectations of interactions.*

2.   *During childhood, there is more to play than just having fun. Pretend play helps children understand and prepare for adult roles. Children who engage in lots of pretend play tend to score better*

on measures of cognitive development, language development, and creativity than children who don't engage in much pretend play. Pretend play helps children work through all sorts of possible scenarios so that when they are faced with a real problem, they have some experience to draw upon in formulating a response. Pretend play with others also forces children to see other perspectives, which helps their role taking skills and the development of theory of mind. Because of this, children who engage in more pretend play often have skills that make them more popular with other children. Engaging in pretend play may also help children act out their emotions in safe situations and allow them to cope with stresses in their lives.

3.   *Children who are popular are well-liked by most members of their group and are rarely disliked. In contrast, children who are rejected are rarely liked and often disliked. To some extent, whether a child ends up popular or rejected depends on characteristics of the child that are difficult to change. For example, physically attractive children and those who are intelligent are more likely to be popular than children who are physically unattractive or are not very bright. Bright kids likely know how to successfully orchestrate a social interaction. Temperament and personality characteristics also contribute to popularity. Children with easy-going temperaments are likely to be more popular than children with difficult temperaments. Children who are argumentative and not very good at "reading" social signals (i.e., weak social cognition skills) are more likely to be rejected.*

CHAPTER FIFTEEN

THE FAMILY

OVERVIEW

We all live in some sort of family, whether it is our family of origin with our mother and/or father and siblings, or in a family with our spouse and possibly our own children. Or we might be a member of a gay or lesbian family or a single adult who thinks of friends as family. What effects do these family systems have on our development? This chapter focuses on this question, looking at both traditional and nontraditional types of families. At the beginning of the chapter, it is noted that traditional families of a working father and a stay-at-home mother are no longer typical. Cultural changes of the 20th century have led to many different family configurations.

Have you ever wondered what life is like for parents after their children are grown and leave home? Or perhaps you are curious about whether siblings, amid the rivalry and fighting, have any positive influences on one another? Do fathers interact any differently with their babies than do mothers? Are adolescents and their parents consistently battling it out with one another? These are the sorts of questions addressed in this chapter on the family. In reading the research about family systems across the life span, you may gain some insight into processes within your own family.

LEARNING OBJECTIVES

After reading and studying the material in this chapter, you should be able to answer the following questions.

1. How is the family viewed by the family systems theory? How do individual family systems change and how have families changed across recent generations?

2. How is the father-infant relationship similar to and different from the mother-infant relationship?

3. What are two basic dimensions of parenting? What patterns of child rearing emerge from these dimensions? How do these parenting styles affect children's development?

4.   What effects do parents have on their children and what effects do children have on their parents? How do parents and children influence one another reciprocally?

5.   What features characterize sibling relationships across the life span? How do siblings contribute to development?

6.   What are relationships like between adolescents and their parents?

7.   How does marriage and parenthood affect adults? What changes occur in the family as the children mature and leave home?

8.   What sorts of roles do grandparents establish with their grandchildren?

9.   How do various family relationships change during adulthood?

10. What sorts of diversity exist in today's families? What is the life satisfaction of people in these different types of families?

11. How does divorce affect family relationships?

12. How can spouse abuse and child abuse be reduced?

The following summary provides an overview of the main points contained in this chapter of the text. Fill-in the blanks with terms that appropriately complete the sentence. Scattered throughout the summary are questions in parentheses. These are meant to encourage you to think actively as you are reading and connect this summary to the more detailed information provided in the text. You can answer these questions as you are filling in the blanks or you can complete all the blanks, then go back and reread the entire summary, addressing the questions in order to provide more depth of understanding.

UNDERSTANDING THE FAMILY

The Family as a System

According to family systems theory, the family is a social system, meaning that it is a whole unit consisting of interrelated parts. The (1) _____ family consists of a mother, father, and at least one child. Parents and their children live with other relatives in a(n) (2) _____.

The Family as a System within Other Systems

Families exist within a larger social system, and the cultural context influences the experiences within families, consistent with Bronfenbrenner's (3) _____ model.

The Family as a Changing System

Family membership changes over time and the relationships within families also develop and change over time. One family development theory uses the concept of a family (4) _____ to characterize the sequence of changes in family membership and relationships that occur over time. According to this view, there are eight distinct stages of family life. *(What are the roles or developmental tasks associated with each stage?)*

A Changing System in a Changing World

The changing family exists within a changing world and several social changes of the 20th century have significantly affected the family. Our society has a greater number of (5) _____ adults and more adults are delaying marriage and childbearing than in the past. More women are participating in the labor force and our society has seen a rise in the divorce rate and in the number of children living in poverty. There are more single-parent families and, as more divorced adults remarry, there are more (6) _____ families. For a variety of reasons, adults today spend more years without children than in past generations, and increased longevity contributes to longer relationships with parents, grandparents, and even great-grandparents. These multigenerational (four or more) families are referred to as (7) _____ families.

THE INFANT

Mother-Infant and Father-Infant Relationships

Despite the stereotype of mothers as the primary caregivers for infants, fathers are as capable as mothers when it comes to caring for infants. Still, mothers do spend more time with children than do fathers. Mothers' interactions with their children tend to be related to providing care while fathers' interactions are more likely to be (8) _____ oriented. Boys and girls both benefit from having fathers who are involved in their development.

Mothers, Fathers, and Infants: The System at Work

In addition to these effects, parents have many (9) _____ effects on their children through their ability to influence their spouses. (*Can you provide several examples of this type of effect?*) Children benefit from a three-person system in which parents support each other, allowing each to be good parents.

THE CHILD

Parenting Styles

One dimension of parenting, called (10) _____, describes how supportive, affectionate, and sensitive parents are toward their child. A second dimension of parenting, (11) _____ describes the degree of autonomy that parents allow their children. Four basic patterns of child rearing emerge from crossing these two dimensions. A(n) (12) _____ parenting style is a very restrictive style where parents impose many rules without explaining their importance, and often use physical means to gain compliance to the rules. A(n) (13) _____ parenting style is one where children are allowed a fair amount of freedom, but rules are clearly stated, explained, and enforced. A(n) (14) _____ parenting style is a lax style of parenting where few rules are imposed on children and children are encouraged to express their feelings and impulses. Finally, (15) _____ parenting occurs when parents are uninvolved in their children's upbringing. (*What are the characteristics of children raised with each of these styles? Which of these styles of parenting seems to have the "best" outcome in our society and which is associated with the worst outcomes?*)

Parenting styles are related to socioeconomic factors. (*Can you describe differences in parenting or goals associated with social class?*) Differences might result because of stresses associated with economic problems, or because of differences in skills useful or necessary to parents in blue-collar versus white-collar jobs. Culture and ethnic variations also lead to differences in parenting styles.

Models of Influence in the Family

According to the (16) _____ model, parents influence their child's behavior. But children can also influence their parents, according to the (17) _____ model. In addition, a child's age, competence level, and (18) _____ can all elicit a particular style of parenting and a compatible discipline method from the parent. According to a (19) _____ model of family influence, parents and children influence each other in an ongoing reciprocal manner. (*What are the roles of nature and nurture in family influence?*)

Sibling Relationships

A second child in the family often creates (20) _____, or feelings of competition, jealousy, and resentment between siblings. Many sibling relationships are also characterized by ambivalence. While sibling relationships can involve negative conflicts, siblings also have many positive effects on one another. For example, siblings help by providing (21) _____ for one another. In addition, older siblings often provide (22) _____ services for younger siblings and serve as (23) _____ for new behaviors.

THE ADOLESCENT
Ripples in the Parent-Child Relationship
Some people believe that adolescence is a particularly stressful period for parent-child relationships. Most teenagers, however, view their relationship with their parents as positive and close.

Renegotiating the Relationship
A major task of adolescence is to achieve (24) _____, or the ability to function independently. This creates some conflict with parents until adolescents and parents renegotiate the power and rules between them. While adolescents work to achieve autonomy, they also try to maintain a close attachment with their parents. (***How can parents help adolescents successfully achieve autonomy?***)

THE ADULT
Establishing the Marriage
Most adults in our society marry and they typically marry for (25) _____. Marriage is a major adjustment for both partners, and some deterioration in the relationship occurs during the first year. Married couples who end up unhappy often started out with more negativity and problems than couples who remain satisfied over time.

New Parenthood
Many couples have children within a few years of getting married and this is another major life transition with both positive and negative changes. Marital satisfaction tends to (26) _____ following the birth of a child and this change is more pronounced for women than men. Some babies are more difficult than others, which increases stress, and some adults are less equipped to deal with the stress of parenthood. A lack of resources, especially weak (27) _____ can also increase stress of parenthood. (***How is the transition to parenthood influenced by attachment styles?***)

The Child-Rearing Family
Having a second child is another stressful event for the family and marital satisfaction typically remains somewhat depressed with the addition of more children to the family. Despite these declines, couples are more satisfied than dissatisfied with their family situation.

The Empty Nest
As children reach maturity and leave their parent's home, the family system changes once again. "Empty nest" is used to describe the family structure after all children have left the home. Marital satisfaction tends to (28) _____ following the departure of children. (***Why do parents react this way to their children leaving home?***)

Grandparenthood

Many adults become grandparents in middle-age and do not fit the stereotyped image of white-haired elderly grandparents. Researchers have identified three major styles of grandparenting. Grandparents who are (29) _____ are largely symbolic figures who do not interact a great deal with grandchildren. (30) _____ grandparents frequently see their grandchildren and enjoy sharing activities with them. Grandparents who are (31) _____ assume a parent like role and provide some degree of child care for their grandchildren. Relationships between grandchildren and their (32) _____ grandmothers tend to be the closest.

Changing Family Relationships

As noted above, marital satisfaction appears to decline when children enter the family and increases when children leave the family. Women tend to be more affected by changes in the family structure than men. Many factors other than stage of family life cycle determine marital satisfaction. (***What are some of these factors?***)

Sibling relationships also change across the life span. Adult siblings typically keep in touch with each other, but the relationship is less intense than when siblings were young, and adult siblings rarely discuss intimate problems with each other. Nevertheless, siblings often report feeling close to one another, particularly as they get older.

Parents and children develop new relationships as the children become adults and leave home. The relationships are often more (33) _____, with recognition that each is an individual and has roles other than parent or child. Middle-aged adults continue to feel close to their parents. Many families are part of a (34) _____ family where they live in separate households but have close and frequent interaction with other relatives. The relationships among different generations tend to be (35) _____, which means that each contributes something to the relationship and gets something back in return. In most cases, we do <u>not</u> see (36) _____ in which parents become dependent on their children and their middle-age children take on the caregiving role. Middle-aged adults may also experience (37) _____ because of the demands from both their children and their parents. This can lead to (38) _____ as their personal resources become stretched by providing care for aging parents who may have impairments. Many adult children fulfill their (39) _____, or obligations to take care of their aging parents.

DIVERSITY IN FAMILY LIFE

Adult lifestyles in our culture have become quite diverse. Many adults delay marriage, remain single, or become single through divorce or death of a spouse.

Singles

There are an increasing number of adults who never marry. Living with a romantic partner without being married, or (40) _____, is more common than it used to be. Some couples use living together as a test of compatibility before marrying. However, couples who live together before marrying actually seem to be more dissatisfied with the marriage and more likely to (41) _____ than couples who marry without first living together.

Childless Married Couples

More couples are choosing not to have children than in the past, although for many couples, childlessness is not a choice, but a result of infertility. Childless couples tend to have somewhat higher marital satisfaction than couples with children during the child-rearing years. Following the child-rearing years, couples with and without children are similar in their levels of marital satisfaction. As older adults, individuals who have lost their spouse and never had children may experience a lack of (42) _____.

Dual-Career Families

In many families, both mothers and fathers work outside the home. Events from home can affect work and vice versa, known as (43) _____. These effects can be positive as well as negative. When both parents work, school-aged children may become part of the large group of (44) _____ children who must care for themselves after school.

Gay and Lesbian Families

Overall, gay and lesbian couples are more similar to heterosexual couples than they are different. The division of labor between these couples tends to be more (45) _____ than that of married couples.

Divorcing Families

Divorce is a series of experiences, not a single event that has finite beginning and end points. It is unclear what processes cause divorce, but there are several factors that seem to place some couples at a greater risk for divorce than other couples. (***What are some factors that increase the likelihood of divorce?***) Families experiencing a divorce typically go through a (46) _____ period during which there is much disruption. The stress of a divorce places individuals at greater risk for depression, physical problems, and even death. Adults experiencing divorce often have problems parenting. Custodial mothers tend to become less accepting and responsive, as well as less consistent in their discipline. While custodial mothers often use a more restrictive style of parenting, noncustodial fathers tend to be (47) _____. Most of the problems between parents and children dissipate in the two years following a divorce, but the divorce continues to affect both children and adults. (***What factors influence family members' reaction to divorce?***)

Remarriage and Reconstituted Families

Most divorced parents remarry within five years after a divorce, often creating (48) _____ families. While boys seem to suffer more than girls when parents divorce, they apparently benefit more than girls when their custodial mothers remarry. (***What are some possible reasons for this finding?***)

THE PROBLEM OF FAMILY VIOLENCE

Unfortunately, some families experience violence in the forms of child abuse, spouse abuse, and elder abuse.

<u>Why does family violence occur?</u>

Many child abusers were abused or neglected themselves as children. They may also be intolerant of normal behaviors of young children. Some children may have characteristics that make them more likely targets of abuse than other children. In addition to parent and child characteristics, the surrounding social climate and lack of social (49) _____ may contribute to the likelihood of abuse in the family.

<u>What are the Effects of Family Violence?</u>

Child abuse negatively affects its victims in a number of ways. (***Can you describe some developmental consequences of abuse?***) By identifying families that are high-risk candidates for family violence, it may be possible to provide the support necessary to prevent abuse from occurring.

REVIEW OF KEY TERMS

Below is a list of terms and concepts from this chapter. Use these to complete the following sentence definitions. You might also want to try writing definitions in your own words and then checking your definitions with those in the text.

acceptance/responsiveness	indirect effects
authoritarian parenting	latchkey children
authoritative parenting	middle generation squeeze
autonomy	modified extended family
beanpole family	neglectful parenting
caregiver burden	nuclear family
child effects model	parent effects model
cohabitation	permissive parenting
demandingness/control	reconstituted family
empty nest	role reversal
extended family household	sibling rivalry
filial responsibility	spillover effects
family life cycle	transactional model
family systems theory	

1.   A family that consists of parent, stepparent, and at least one child from a previous marriage is called a _____.

2.   A flexible parenting style in which parents set clear rules and provide explanations for rules but allow children some freedom and input is _____.

3.   According to the _____, children influence their parents.

4.   A _____ consists of a mother, father, and at least one child.

5. In a _____, nuclear families live in separate households but have close ties and frequent interaction with other relatives.

6. _____ refers to the feelings of competition, jealousy, and resentment that can develop between siblings.

7. When single adults live with a romantic partner without being married, they are in an arrangement called _____.

8. A dimension of parenting that describes the degree of autonomy that parents allow their children is referred to as _____.

9. In a(n) _____, a family unit lives with other relatives.

10. A critical task of adolescence is achieving _____, in which adolescents must develop independence in various realms.

11. The _____ consists of the sequence of changes in family composition, roles, and relationships that occur from the time people marry to the time they die.

12. _____ is a restrictive parenting style in which parents impose many rules and use power tactics to ensure obedience to these rules.

13. According to a _____, parents and children influence one another reciprocally.

14. After children are grown and leave home, parents may experience the _____ syndrome.

15. A dimension of parenting that describes how affectionate and responsive parents are toward their child is called _____.

16. Middle-aged adults who experience demands from both younger and older generations may experience the _____.

17. _____ is a parenting style in which adults make relatively few demands, encourage children to express their feelings, and rarely exert control over their behavior.

18. The effects that parents have on their children through their influence on their spouse's behavior are _____.

19. _____ occurs in situations where aging parents become dependent on their children and the children become caregivers for their parents.

20. Grown children's obligation to their parents is called their _____.

21.   _____ is a style of parenting in which parents are uninvolved in their children's upbringing.

22.   The _____ is one where there are three or more generations, usually small, all living at one time.

23.   According to _____, the family is whole unit, with interrelated parts that influence each other.

24.   According to a _____, parents are assumed to influence their children, but not vice versa.

25.   Middle-aged adults who must care for a parent with an impairment may experience _____ as they try to incorporate this with their other family responsibilities.

26.   With _____, events at work can affect home life and events at home can influence work.

MULTIPLE CHOICE SELF TEST

For each multiple choice question, read all alternatives and then select the best answer.

1.   The family life cycle
        a.   refers to the sequence of changes in family membership and roles between marriage and death.
        b.   refers to family units that consist of a parent, a stepparent and at least one child.
        c.   refers to the changes that have occurred in the family system during the 20th century.
        d.   undergoes dramatic changes every 10 years.

2.   A family unit consisting of a mother, father, and at least one child is called a _____ family.
        a.   reconstituted
        b.   extended
        c.   nuclear
        d.   beanpole

3.   Compared to mothers, fathers in general
        a.   spend as much time with their children.
        b.   spend less time with their children.
        c.   treat boys and girls more similarly.
        d.   serve as disciplinarian in the family.

4. Which type of parenting style places few demands on children and allows them to express their desires freely?
   a. permissive
   b. authoritative
   c. authoritarian
   d. neglectful

5. In which style of parenting do parents value obedience for its own sake and impose many rules that are typically not fully explained to children?
   a. permissive
   b. authoritative
   c. authoritarian
   d. neglectful

6. Children of parents who use a(n) _____ style of parenting are typically more self-reliant and achievement oriented than children raised with other styles of parenting
   a. permissive
   b. authoritative
   c. authoritarian
   d. neglectful

7. Feelings of rivalry or jealousy following the birth of a new sibling
   a. are strongest if parents maintain the same regular schedule they had for the first-born before the arrival of the new baby.
   b. can be minimized if the first-born had already established a good relationship with parents.
   c. can be minimized if the parents lavish the first child with attention.
   d. are always worse if the first-born is a boy.

8. With respect to adolescent-parent relationships, research indicates
   a. there is a huge gap between generations in their values and attitudes.
   b. adolescents generally report being unhappy with the relationship.
   c. boys are much more dissatisfied with the relationship than girls.
   d. adolescents are strongly influenced by their parents on important issues.

9. The relationship between adult siblings
   a. disintegrates once the siblings leave school.
   b. remains close although less intense than during childhood.
   c. involves a great deal of sharing and discussing feelings.
   d. continues to be as intense as during childhood.

10. Which of the following is true regarding marital satisfaction?
    a. Marital satisfaction is highest following the birth of a child.
    b. Because of the adjustments that must be made, marital satisfaction is lowest right after marriage.
    c. Marital satisfaction declines following the birth of a child.
    d. Marital satisfaction declines across middle and older adulthood.

11. Cohabiting couples who later marry
    a. are more dissatisfied with their marriages than couples who had not lived together before marrying.
    b. are more satisfied with their marriages than couples who had not lived together before marrying.
    c. are less likely to divorce than couples who had not lived together before marrying.
    d. are basically no different from couples who had not lived together before marrying.

12. Adults who never marry
    a. typically have some psychological problem.
    b. are lonely and maladjusted.
    c. are much happier and better adjusted than married adults.
    d. are somewhat less happy than married adults.

13. Evidence indicates that following a divorce
    a. both boys and girls settle quickly into a new lifestyle with few adjustment problems.
    b. boys take longer to adjust than girls and exhibit more behavior problems.
    c. girls take longer to adjust than boys and exhibit more depression.
    d. neither boys or girls adjust to the new lifestyle within several years of the divorce.

14. Reconstituted families where children in a mother-headed family acquire a stepfather
    a. seem to benefit boys more than girls.
    b. seem to benefit girls more than boys.
    c. seem to benefit boys and girls equally.
    d. do not benefit any of the children, just the adults.

15. Child abuse is less likely in families where
    a. the parents had been abused themselves and so they know the negative impact that abuse can have.
    b. there are multiple sources of stress.
    c. there is a strong support network available to parents.
    d. parents have difficulty "reading" their child's signals.

CRITICAL THINKING QUESTIONS

By answering the following questions, you will strengthen your understanding of the material in this chapter. These questions require higher level thinking skills such as integration and application of concepts. Sample answers are provided for three of the questions. These illustrate one possibility, but there are other answers you could provide that might be just as good. For the other questions, you can check yourself by referring to the text (a hint is provided), or by asking a peer or your instructor to review your answer.

1. What type of parenting dimensions and parent control have the best outcome for children? What makes these parenting styles effective?
   [Sample answer provided.]

2. What are the effects of divorce from the perspective of parents and children?
   [Sample answer provided.]

3. What factors increase/decrease the likelihood of family violence?
   [Sample answer provided.]

4. What affects can children have on their parents across the life span?
   [Hint: There is a little information on this topic scattered throughout the chapter, including the sections on "Models of Influence in the Family" and "The child-rearing family."]

5. What are potential advantages and disadvantages for individuals who marry, individuals who remain single, couples who have children, and those who do not have children?
   [Hint: Review the section in the text on "Diversity in Family Life."]

ANSWERS

Chapter Summary and Guided Review (Fill-in the blank)

1.	nuclear	12.	authoritarian
2.	extended	13.	authoritative
3.	bioecological	14.	permissive
4.	life cycle	15.	neglectful
5.	single	16.	parent effects
6.	reconstituted	17.	child effects
7.	beanpole	18.	personality
8.	play	19.	transactional
9.	indirect	20.	sibling rivalry
10.	acceptance/responsiveness	21.	emotional support
11.	demandingness/control	22.	caretaking

23.	teachers	37.	middle generation squeeze
24.	autonomy	38.	caregiver burden
25.	love	39.	filial responsibility
26.	decline	40.	cohabitation
27.	spousal support	41.	divorce
28.	increase	42.	social support
29.	remote	43.	spillover effects
30.	companionate	44.	latchkey
31.	involved	45.	egalitarian
32.	maternal	46.	crisis
33.	mutual	47.	overpermissive
34.	modified extended	48.	reconstituted
35.	equitable	49.	support
36.	role reversal		

Review of Key Terms

1.	reconstituted family	14.	empty nest
2.	authoritative parenting	15.	acceptance/responsiveness
3.	child effects model	16.	middle generation squeeze
4.	nuclear family	17.	permissive parenting
5.	modified extended family	18.	indirect effects
6.	sibling rivalry	19.	role reversal
7.	cohabitation	20.	filial responsibility
8.	demandingness/control	21.	neglectful parenting
9.	extended family household	22.	beanpole family
10.	autonomy	23.	family systems theory
11.	family life cycle	24.	parent effects model
12.	authoritarian parenting	25.	caregiver burden
13.	transactional model	26.	spillover effects

Multiple Choice Self Test

1.	A (p. 423)	6.	B (p. 426)	11.	A (p. 443)
2.	C (p. 422)	7.	B (p. 432)	12.	D (p. 443)
3.	B (p. 425)	8.	D (pp. 433-434)	13.	B (pp. 445-447)
4.	A (p. 427)	9.	B (p. 440)	14.	A (p. 448)
5.	C (p. 426)	10.	C (p. 439)	15.	C (pp. 449-450)

Critical Thinking Questions

1. *Parents who are warm and responsive foster more positive qualities in their children than parents who are insensitive and rejecting. These positive qualities include secure attachments to parents, high self-esteem, and competence in academic and social settings. It is also important for parents to have some degree of control with respect to decision making. Parents who set no rules (permissive parenting) have children who are impulsive, aggressive, low in self-control, and not very achievement oriented. On the other hand, parents who are overly controlling also tend to have children who exhibit some behavior difficulties. For*

example, authoritarian parents who set many rules without giving good explanations for why these rules are important and expect strict compliance to them, often have children who are moody, easily annoyed, and not very pleasant. The best child outcomes are seen when parents use authoritative styles of child rearing. Authoritative parents set rules but clearly explain why they are important, they are consistent in their enforcement of rules, and they allow their children to be involved in family decision making. Children raised in authoritative homes tend to be pleasant, self-reliant, cooperative, and achievement-oriented. These traits continue to be evident into adolescence.

Children raised in authoritative homes have learned the value of limits and have learned to control their own behavior. Children whose parents are overly permissive never have to learn self-control at home, which follows them into other settings. Similarly, when parents are very restrictive and demanding, they do all the controlling and do not give children the opportunity to learn to control their own behavior.

Finally, the worst child outcomes result when parents are neglectful; they are simply not involved in their children's lives and signal to their children that they don't really care. These children tend to be resentful, hostile, and prone to getting into trouble as a way of lashing out at uncaring adults.

2.　　*Divorce affects all members of the family, parents as well as children. For parents, there is a great deal of distress, as well as anger and perhaps some relief. The emotional turmoil puts them at greater risk of depression and physical health problems. Parenting skills tend to deteriorate during the divorce phase, which begins months, even years before the actual divorce and extends beyond the date of the official divorce decree. Both parents need to readjust their identities and take on different roles. Usually the mother becomes the custodial parent and has added responsibilities for child rearing. The father usually becomes the more distant parent and sees his children less often. Both parents may experience financial stress as they have to each manage separate households on single salaries rather than one household with (normally) two salaries.*

Children are similarly distressed by the divorce and the disruption in family life. They may experience anger, fear, and guilt. Their emotions make them more difficult, with increased behavior problems and emotionality (e.g., more crying, tantrums, and whininess). Children have to get used to going back and forth between two households

For both parents and children, divorce can have life-long effects. While some of these effects can be negative, especially those occurring during the period of the actual divorce, other effects can be positive. If families were dysfunctional when the parents were married but can become more functional following the divorce, then both parents as individuals and children can benefit.

3.　　*Researchers have identified several factors that predispose families to violence. For one, parents who abuse their children often grew up in families where they were abused or witnessed violence. Mothers who are abusive are often victims themselves of spousal abuse, so they may believe that abuse is a viable way of solving problems. Abusers are also more likely to have low self-esteem and deal with their insecurities by bullying others. Parents who are abusive may have unrealistic expectations of how children should behave at different ages. They may abuse their children for doing things that are developmentally normal. There is also some evidence that some children are more at-risk for abuse than others because of personal characteristics, such as a difficult temperament. Finally, abuse is more likely to occur in families experiencing stress and weak social support. Stress can result from numerous factors, including poverty, loss or change of jobs, and changes in family structure (e.g., divorce or addition of stepchildren).*

CHAPTER SIXTEEN

DEVELOPMENTAL PSYCHOPATHOLOGY

OVERVIEW

This is a substantial chapter, covering a variety of psychological disorders. Some of these disorders are fairly unique to a particular age period, such as eating disorders during adolescence and dementia among older adults. Other disorders, though, are prevalent throughout the life span, most notably depression. Before getting into these specific disorders, the chapter discusses how experts distinguish abnormal from normal behavior, and which criteria are used to diagnose psychological disorders. Then, psychopathologies for each major period of the life span are discussed, starting with autism during infancy. For childhood, attention-deficit hyperactivity disorder is highlighted. The section on adolescence covers eating disorders and drug use, and the section on adults discusses dementia. Throughout all the sections, there is discussion of depression. For each disorder, characteristics, suspected causes, typical treatments, and likely outcomes are presented.

LEARNING OBJECTIVES

After reading and studying the material in this chapter, you should be able to answer the following questions.

1.   What criteria are used to define and diagnose psychological disorders?   What sorts of questions or issues do developmental psychopathologists study?

2.   What are the characteristics, suspected causes, treatment, and prognosis for individuals with autism?

3.   In what ways to infants exhibit depression-like conditions? How is depression in infants similar to, or different from, depression in adults?

4.   What is the difference between undercontrolled and overcontrolled disorders?

5. What are the symptoms, suspected causes, treatment, and long-term prognosis for children with attention-deficit hyperactivity disorder?

6. How is depression during childhood similar to, or different from, depression during adulthood?

7. How do interactions of nature and nurture contribute to psychological disorders? Do childhood problems persist into adolescence and adulthood? Explain.

8. Are psychological problems more prevalent during adolescence than other periods of the life span? Explain.

9. What are the characteristics, suspected causes, and treatment of eating disorders?

10. What is the course of depression and suicidal behavior during adolescence? What factors influence depression during adulthood?

11. What are the characteristics and causes of dementia?

CHAPTER SUMMARY AND GUIDED REVIEW

The following summary provides an overview of the main points contained in this chapter of the text. Fill-in the blanks with terms that appropriately complete the sentence. Scattered throughout the summary are questions in parentheses. These are meant to encourage you to think actively as you are reading and connect this summary to the more detailed information provided in the text. You can answer these questions as you are filling in the blanks or you can complete all the blanks, then go back and reread the entire summary, addressing the questions in order to provide more depth of understanding.

WHAT MAKES DEVELOPMENT ABNORMAL?

There are three general ways to define abnormal behavior. The first criteria uses (1)_____, or whether a person's behavior falls outside the normal range of behavior. The second classification uses the extent to which a behavior interferes with personal and social adaptation, or the (2) _____ of the behavior. The third classification is whether or not a behavior causes (3) _____ for the individual.

DSM-IV Diagnostic Criteria

More specific diagnostic criteria have been described by the American Psychiatric Association in the *Diagnostic and Statistical Manual of Mental Disorders (DSM-IV)*. This manual specifies symptoms and behaviors associated with all psychological disorders. For example, *DSM-IV* defines (4) _____ as at least one episode of feeling profoundly depressed, sad, and hopeless, and/or losing interest in and the ability to derive pleasure from almost all activities.

Developmental Psychopathology

Developmental psychopathology is the study of the origins and course of abnormal behavior across the life span. Some developmental psychopathologists believe that DSM is too focused on problems as diseases and that instead, psychopathology should be viewed as a pattern of adaptation that emerges over time, or (5) _____. In addition, the expectations about how to act in a particular context, or the (6) _____, must be considered, along with societal expectations about what behaviors are appropriate at various ages, or (7) _____. A useful perspective on the contributions of nature and nurture to psychopathology is the (8) _____ model, which suggests that psychopathology results from the interaction of a predisposition to a disorder and the experience of stressful events. *(Can you use the case of depression to illustrate this model?)*

THE INFANT
Autism

Autism is a disorder beginning in infancy that is characterized by deviant social development, deviant language and communication skills, and repetitive, stereotyped behavior. This is classified as a (9) _____ disorder in the *DSM*. The language of autistic children may include (10) _____, where a child repeats or echoes sounds or words produced by someone else. There is great variability among individuals with autistic disorders. Those with (11) _____ have average or above average intelligence but have trouble establishing social relationships because of problems with mindreading and social skills. Other autistic children score in the mental retardation range on intelligence tests.

There are numerous theories about what causes autism. According to the (12) _____ hypothesis, autistic individuals are deficient in their understanding of mental states and the role of mental states in behavior. Another theory is that autistic children have trouble with (13) _____, the ability to plan and organize that permit integration of pieces of information into meaningful wholes. A third idea is the (14) _____ hypothesis, which posits that autistic individuals focus on detail and cannot generalize or see the "big picture." Finally, the (15) _____ hypothesis suggests that autism is the outcome of an exaggerated emphasis on systematizing rather than empathizing.

Autism appears to have both genetic and environmental causes, although no specific causes have yet been pinpointed. Long-term prognosis for autistic children can be poor for those who are also mentally retarded and/or those who do not develop good communication skills. Treatment usually focuses on intense (16) _____ training starting at an early age.

Depression

Infants are not capable of expressing the cognitive symptoms of depression, but can show behavioral symptoms and bodily or (17) _____ symptoms. Infants who have lost an attachment figure, those who are abused or neglected, and those whose mothers are depressed are most likely to show depressive symptoms. A condition called (18) _____ occurs when infants who are raised in a stressful situation fail to grow normally and become underweight for their age. If removed from the stressful situation, infants recover their weight very quickly.

THE CHILD

Children who have undercontrolled disorders, or (19) _____ problems, engage in behaviors that disturb other people and conflict with societal expectations. Children with overcontrolled disorders, or (20) _____ problems, focus their problems inward. There is a gender difference in expression of problems. In general, (21) _____ are more likely to show externalizing problems and (22) _____ are more likely to show internalizing disorders.

Attention-Deficit Hyperactivity Disorder

According to DSM-IV criteria, children with attention-deficit hyperactivity disorder show inattention, hyperactivity, and (23) _____. Although all young children show these behaviors to some extent, children who are diagnosed with the disorder show them to a marked degree. Many children with ADHD also have other conditions such as learning disabilities. This co-occurrence is called (24) _____. Behaviors associated with hyperactivity vary with age. (**Can you describe behaviors that might indicate ADHD in infants and children?**) ADHD seems to be caused by brain chemistry, or a (25) _____ problem, but it is unclear precisely what this is. One possibility is that the ability to plan and control behavior, controlled by (26) _____, is deficient. Many hyperactive children are treated with (27) _____ drugs that increase children's ability to concentrate and seem to improve academic performance. (**What are some concerns about using such drugs to treat ADHD?**)

Depression

It is now recognized that children can become depressed and can be diagnosed using the same criteria that are used with adults. This does not mean that children and adults display depression in exactly the same behaviors. Preschool children are more likely to display somatic and (28) _____ symptoms rather than (29) _____ symptoms that adults and older children display. Many clinically depressed children continue to experience some episodes of depression later in childhood, adolescence, or adulthood.

Nature, Nurture, and Childhood Disorders

Children with disorders often come from troubled families, which may suggest the influence of (30) _____ factors. But it is also possible that the disorder is (31) _____ based, or, applying the (32) _____ model discussed in the previous chapter, the child's disorder may have helped create a disordered environment.

Do Childhood Problems Persist?

In some children, problems persist into adulthood, showing (33) _____ of development. But many children with disordered behavior do not have problems as adults, illustrating (34) _____ in development. At risk children who overcome problems show resilience suggesting that there are (35) _____ factors that prevent them from developing disorders.

THE ADOLESCENT
Storm and Stress?

Adolescence is not really a period of storm and stress as G. Stanley Hall suggested. However, adolescents do seem to be more vulnerable to some forms of psychological disorders.

Anorexia Nervosa

Eating disorders are more prevalent in adolescence than during other periods, and are much more common among girls than boys. Refusal to maintain weight that is at least 85% of one's expected weight is termed (36) _____. Binging and purging is associated with (37) _____. Our society may increase the likelihood of eating disorders with its emphasis on thinness. In addition, some girls appear to have a genetic predisposition, or a (38) _____, to develop an eating disorder. Further, girls who develop eating disorders typically experience disturbed (39) _____ relationships and stress. (***What is the prognosis and treatment for adolescents with eating disorders?***)

Depression and Suicidal Behavior

Adolescents who are depressed display many of the same cognitive symptoms that depressed adults display, as well as other problem behaviors. The rate of (40) _____ has increased, making this the third leading cause of death among adolescents. Suicidal thoughts are common during adolescence. Adolescents are more likely than adults to attempt suicide, but are less likely to "succeed" at killing themselves. As with other behaviors, suicidal behavior results from an interaction of genetic and environmental factors. (***What are some of the factors that contribute to suicidal behavior?***)

THE ADULT

Most adults must cope with some degree of stress in their lives. Young adults seem to experience more stress than older adults, leaving them at greater risk for mental health problems.

Depression

Contrary to a popular belief, elderly adults are not more depressed than younger adults.

This may be because depression is often undiagnosed in the elderly. (*Why might this be the case?*) Women are more likely than men to be diagnosed with depression. (*Can you explain why there might be a gender difference in diagnosis of depression?*)

Aging and Dementia

Many people worry about developing senility or (41) _____ as they get older. This progressive deterioration of intellectual functioning and personality is not a part of normal aging. One form of dementia is caused by (42) _____ disease, which is progressive and irreversible deterioration of neurons, resulting in increasingly impaired mental functioning. A brain affected by Alzheimer's shows characteristic patterns of neurofibrillary tangles and (43) _____ plaques. These plaques are caused by a toxic protein called (44) _____. Early signs of Alzheimer's include trouble learning and remembering verbal material. Over time, Alzheimer's patients lose their ability to function independently. Some forms of this disease appear to have a (45) _____ basis. This is supported by the fact that this disorder often recurs in families, and by the finding that individuals with Down Syndrome, a chromosomal disorder, are very likely to develop Alzheimer's disease. (*What is being done to treat Alzheimer's disease?*)

Another irreversible dementia is (46) _____ dementia, which results from cardiovascular problems such as strokes. Some forms of dementia are reversible. (*What factors might cause a reversible dementia?*) Some elderly adults may be experiencing (47) _____, which is mistaken for dementia because of the similar symptoms. (*How can these two problems be distinguished from one another?*)

REVIEW OF KEY TERMS

Below is a list of terms and concepts from this chapter. Use these to complete the following sentence definitions. You might also want to try writing definitions in your own words and then checking your definitions with those in the text.

age norm
Alzheimer's disease
anorexia nervosa
Asperger syndrome
attention-deficit hyperactivity disorder
autism
beta-amyloid
bulimia nervosa
comorbidity
delirium
dementia
developmental psychopathology
diathesis/stress model
DSM-IV

echolalia
executive function hypothesis
externalizing problems
extreme male brain hypothesis
failure to thrive
internalizing problems
major depressive disorder
protective factors
social norm
somatic symptoms
storm and stress
theory of mind hypothesis
vascular dementia
weak central coherence hypothesis

1. _____ is the existence of more than one disorder in an individual.

2. _____ are problems that are disruptive to the individual and include conditions such as anxiety disorders, phobias, and severe shyness.

3. Alzheimer's patients develop senile plaques encrusted with _____, a toxic protein that damages neurons.

4. _____ refers to the notion that adolescence is a time of problems and emotional ups and downs.

5. The field of _____ concerns the study of the origins and course of maladaptive behavior.

6. Some individuals at risk for problems have _____ that help cushion them from harm.

7. A group of disorders characterized by progressive deterioration of intellectual functioning and personality is collectively called _____.

8. The term _____ is used to describe infants who are neglected, abused, or otherwise stressed fail to grow normally, becoming underweight for their age.

9. The _____ proposes that psychopathology results from the interaction of a predisposition to a disorder and the experience of stressful events.

10. A(n) _____ is a societal expectation about what behavior is appropriate or normal at various ages.

11. A disorder called _____ involves progressive and irreversible deterioration of neurons resulting in increasingly impaired mental functioning.

12. Clinicians use a manual called the _____ to diagnose psychological disorders.

13. Mental deterioration that results from cardiovascular problems such as strokes is diagnosed as _____.

14. _____ occur when individuals act in ways that disturb other people and conflict with societal expectations.

15. An expectation about how to behave that prevails in a culture or subculture is called a _____.

16. Refusal to maintain a weight that is at least 85% of the expected weight for one's height and age is diagnosed as _____.

17. Autistic children often exhibit _____, a form of language where a child echoes or repeats sounds or words made by someone else.

18. _____ is an explanation of autism suggesting that affected individuals have an exaggerated systematizing brain and a weak empathizing brain.

19. A diagnosis of _____ is made when individuals feel profoundly depressed, sad, or hopeless, and/or lose interest in activities, and are not able to derive pleasure from activities.

20. _____ is one of the autism spectrum disorders characterized by normal intelligence but deficient mindreading and social skills.

21. A theory of autism focused on the individual's poor understanding of mental states and the influence of mental states on behavior is the _____.

22. Repeated episodes of binging and purging are diagnosed as _____.

23. Bodily symptoms such as loss of appetite or changes in normal sleep patterns are called _____.

24. The disorder _____ begins in infancy or early childhood and is characterized by deviant social and language development, and repetitive, stereotyped behavior.

25. _____ is a theory of autism that focuses on deficits in higher-level control functions that allow individuals to plan, redirect, and inhibit actions.

26. According to the _____ hypothesis of autism, affected individuals focus on details and have trouble organizing information into the "big picture."

27. A(n) _____ is a reversible condition characterized by periods of disorientation and confusion alternating with periods of coherence.

28. _____ is diagnosed when there are significant problems with attention, impulsivity, and hyperactivity.

MULTIPLE CHOICE SELF TEST

For each multiple choice question, read all alternatives and then select the best answer.

1.   Age norms are defined as
     a.   the ages when it is appropriate to act in a deviant manner.
     b.   societal expectations about what behavior is appropriate at different ages.
     c.   societal expectations about how to behave in different contexts.
     d.   the average ages when people are most susceptible to various disorders.

2.   Which of the following persons is most likely to be diagnosed as having a psychological
     disorder?
     a.   a child who cannot fall asleep at night because he is worried about goblins under
          the bed
     b.   a woman who can no longer to work because she is so upset about her appearance
     c.   a man who quits his job because it is no longer challenging
     d.   a woman who is sobbing because her husband has recently died

3.   According to developmental psychopathologists, psychopathology is a
     a.   pattern of behavior that develops over time.
     b.   medical condition that you either have or do not have.
     c.   disease that can be treated with medicine.
     d.   developmental disorder that lies solely within the person.

4.   A disorder that begins in infancy and is characterized by deviant social development and
     communication skills is
     a.   anorexia.
     b.   dementia.
     c.   autism.
     d.   attention-deficit hyperactivity disorder.

5.   According to the diathesis-stress model, psychopathology results from
     a.   a defect that emerges according to a genetic blueprint.
     b.   an impoverished environment.
     c.   a conflict between two different value systems.
     d.   an interaction between a predisposition within the person and a stressful
          environment.

6.   Autistic children
     a.   typically outgrow the disorder as they get older and are indistinguishable from
          others during adulthood.
     b.   have a number of physical problems in addition to their deficits in social and
          communication skills.
     c.   may score in the mental retardation range on intelligence tests or may be within
          the average range if they have one of the milder forms of autism.
     d.   show marked improvement after they enter elementary school and begin
          interacting with other children.

7.   Which of the following seems to be a promising explanation of the cause of autism?
    a.   Autistic children have cold, distant parents.
    b.   Autistic children have inherited a recessive set of genes for the disorder.
    c.   Autistic children are unable to verbalize their thoughts.
    d.   Autistic children lack an understanding of mind and/or the ability to plan, redirect, or inhibit actions.

8.   Children who act in ways that conflict with rules and other people are said to have
    a.   an internalizing problem.
    b.   an externalizing problem.
    c.   masked depression.
    d.   autism.

9.   Attention-deficit hyperactivity disorder is
    a.   diagnosed on the basis of too much motor activity.
    b.   involves the triad of attention, impulsivity, and excess motor activity.
    c.   an overcontrolled disorder.
    d.   associated with mental retardation.

10.   Depression
    a.   is displayed in similar ways across the life span.
    b.   is not present until children are old enough to verbally express their feelings.
    c.   is an undercontrolled disorder.
    d.   can be present throughout the life span but is expressed in different behaviors.

11.   Problems that exist in early childhood
    a.   disappear when children enter elementary school.
    b.   are nonexistent by the time children leave school.
    c.   are more likely to disappear than persist, although some do persist.
    d.   typically are still present later in life.

12.   Eating disorders such as anorexia and bulimia
    a.   are caused by the body's inability to properly metabolize food.
    b.   develop, in part, as a result of a genetic predisposition interacting with stress and social pressure.
    c.   are easily controlled with a properly managed diet.
    d.   are present during adolescence and then disappear.

13. With respect to suicide,
    a. adolescents are more likely to attempt suicide than adults but less likely to succeed.
    b. adolescents successfully commit suicide at a higher rate than any other age group.
    c. males and females are equally likely to end up killing themselves.
    d. elderly adults commit suicide at a rate somewhat higher than adolescents and younger adults.

14. Which of the following is TRUE?
    a. Most children who have problems grow up to have problems as adults.
    b. Many adults who have problems also experienced problems as children.
    c. Children are most likely to overcome undercontrolled problems.
    d. There is very little change over time in the course of any psychological disorder.

15. One difference between Alzheimer's disease and delirium is that
    a. Alzheimer's disease affects mental functioning and delirium does not.
    b. Patients with Alzheimer's disease have periods of lucidity, while those with delirium do not.
    c. Alzheimer's disease occurs only in old age, while delirium occurs only at younger ages.
    d. Alzheimer's disease is irreversible, whereas delirium is reversible.

CRITICAL THINKING QUESTIONS

By answering the following questions, you will strengthen your understanding of the material in this chapter. These questions require higher level thinking skills such as integration and application of concepts. Sample answers are provided for three of the questions. These illustrate one possibility, but there are other answers you could provide that might be just as good. For the other questions, you can check yourself by referring to the text (a hint is provided), or by asking a peer or your instructor to review your answer.

1. What gender differences are found across the life span in the diagnosis or course of mental disorders? What factors might account for these differences?
   [Sample answer provided.]

2. How does depression manifest itself across the lifespan?
   [Sample answer provided.]

3. Are individuals with an autism spectrum disorder (ASD) qualitatively or quantitatively different from individuals without ASD?
   [Sample answer provided.]

4.   How would you explain the development of psychological disorders from the perspective of each of the major developmental theories (Freud and Erikson's psychoanalytic theories, Piaget's cognitive-developmental theory, Skinner and Bandura's learning theories, and Bronfenbrenner's ecological theory)?
[Hint: Go back and consult earlier chapters, particularly Chapter Two, to gather information about the theorists that will help you explain or interpret psychological disorders.]

5.   What are the current theories about the cause(s) of autism? What support is there for each theory?
[Hint: Review the subsection on "Suspected Causes" in the section on autism.]

ANSWERS

Chapter Summary and Guided Review (Fill-in the blank)

1.	statistical deviance	25.	neurological
2.	maladaptiveness	26.	executive functions
3.	personal distress	27.	stimulant
4.	major depressive disorder	28.	behavioral
5.	development	29.	cognitive
6.	social norms	30.	environment
7.	age norms	31.	genetically
8.	diathesis/stress	32.	child effects
9.	pervasive developmental	33.	continuity
10.	echolalia	34.	discontinuity
11.	Asperberger syndrome	35.	protective
12.	theory of mind	36.	anorexia nervosa
13.	executive functions	37.	bulimia nervosa
14.	weak central coherence	38.	diathesis
15.	extreme male brain	39.	family
16.	behavioral	40.	suicide
17.	somatic	41.	third
18.	failure to thrive	42.	dementia
19.	externalizing	43.	Alzheimer's
20.	internalizing	44.	senile
21.	boys	45.	beta-amyloid
22.	girls	46.	genetic
23.	impulsivity	47.	vascular
24.	comorbidity	48.	delirium

Review of Key Terms

1.	comorbidity	5.	developmental psychopathology
2.	internalizing problems	6.	protective factors
3.	beta-amyloid	7.	dementia
4.	storm and stress	8.	failure to thrive

9.   diathesis/stress model
10.   age norm
11.   Alzheimer's disease
12.   DSM-IV
13.   vascular dementia
14.   externalizing problems
15.   social norm
16.   anorexia nervosa
17.   echolalia
18.   extreme male brain hypothesis
19.   major depressive disorder

20.   Asperger syndrome
21.   theory of mind hypothesis
22.   bulimia nervosa
23.   somatic symptoms
24.   autism
25.   executive dysfunction hypothesis
26.   weak central coherence
27.   delirium
28.   attention-deficit hyperactivity disorder

Multiple Choice Self Test

1.   B (p. 458)
2.   B (p. 456)
3.   A (p. 457)
4.   C (p. 460)
5.   D (p. 459)

6.   C (p. 464)
7.   D (pp. 461-463)
8.   A (p. 467)
9.   B (p. 467)
10.   D (p. 469)

11.   C (p. 472)
12.   B (p. 473)
13.   A (pp. 475-476)
14.   B (pp. 477-478)
15.   D (p. 481)

Critical Thinking Questions

1.   *Overall, males and females are equally likely to have psychological disorders, although there are some differences in the types of disorders that affect males and females. In general, boys are more likely to show externalizing problems that put them in conflict with others, such as conduct disorders or hyperactivity. Girls are more likely to have internalizing problems that cause inner conflict, such as depression or eating disorders.*

    There may be genetic or biological reasons for these differences. For example, hormone levels differ for men and women and could contribute to different rates of depression. Think about the dramatic hormone changes following the birth of a baby that can lead to postpartum depression in women. Hormones cannot account for all the differences, though, between men and women. Socialization may also explain differences in depression. Women are socialized to internalize their problems and it is socially acceptable for women to seek help for their problems. Men are socialized to externalize their problems and are not encouraged to seek help. Men and women may also learn to cope with their problems differently. Some evidence suggests that women ruminate about their problems more than men, which tends to prolong the problem, while men distract themselves from their problems, which tends to curtail the problem.

2.   *Depression can occur at any point throughout the lifespan. Infants who have lost a caregiver or who haven't formed a secure attachment can display behavioral and bodily symptoms of depression. These include loss of interest in activities and loss of appetite. If these persist, it can lead to failure to thrive, in which the infant doesn't grow normally, loses weight, and becomes underweight.*

    Depression during childhood is uncommon, but still possible. Children can show the same depressive symptoms as adolescents and adults. Among children who meet the criteria for depression, many also meet the criteria for other disorders as well, especially anxiety disorder, ADHD, and conduct disorder. Young children are likely to display the behavioral and bodily symptoms of depression and less likely to express the cognitive symptoms. Thus, they may lose interest in favorite activities, have trouble sleeping, and eat poorly, but may not verbalize their feelings.

Adolescents are more vulnerable to depression and express the cognitive symptoms (e.g., hopelessness) as well as the behavioral and bodily symptoms, just as adults do. They often have other problems along with their depression, such as substance abuse (which may be their way of "medicating" their depression), eating disorders, anxiety, and antisocial behavior. The rate of attempted suicides escalates during adolescence, but the rate of committed suicides is higher among older adults.

Depression is one of the most common psychological problems of adulthood. More women than men are diagnosed with depression, and younger adults are more vulnerable than older adults. Depression in elderly adults is often overlooked because some of the symptoms of depression (e.g., fatigue, sleeping problems, memory problems) are mistaken for "symptoms" of old age. The underdiagnosis of depression during older adulthood may help explain why the suicide rate is higher among this age group.

3.   *There are numerous theories about what causes autism. According to some of these theories, autism represents a qualitative difference from "normal" or average. For example, according to the theory of mind hypothesis, individuals with autism are different from individuals without autism because they are not able to form a theory of mind, which limits their ability to understand mental states and how mental states affect behavior. And according to the executive dysfunction hypothesis, autism is a deficit in executive functions, which are the processes that allow us to plan and inhibit actions. In contrast, scientists such as Baron-Cohen argue that autism is just an extreme version of the male brain. Thus, it is a quantitative difference: people with autism just have more of what characterizes the male brain (e.g., analyzing things to figure out how they work and extracting rules). At this point, there doesn't seem to be a single, best explanation of autism. This might mean that autism can stem from multiple sources, and might contain elements that are qualitatively distinct from others as well as elements that are quantitatively different from others.*

CHAPTER SEVENTEEN

THE FINAL CHALLENGE: DEATH AND DYING

OVERVIEW

      This chapter covers some of the physical realities of death, such as biological definitions, factors that affect life expectancy, and leading causes of death at different ages. But the focus of the chapter is on psychological interpretations and reactions to death. How do people of different ages understand death? How do they grieve and cope with death? Two theories that are prominent in this chapter are Kübler-Ross's theory and the Parkes/Bowlby attachment model of bereavement. Kübler-Ross proposed that our reaction to death goes through a series of five stages. Although flawed, the theory has been instrumental in highlighting different emotional responses to death. Parkes and Bowlby proposed four overlapping responses to grief that are similar to the separation anxiety experienced by infants. The chapter closes by looking at factors related to coping and ways to lessen the grief associated with death.

LEARNING OBJECTIVES

After reading and studying the material in this chapter, you should be able to answer the following questions.

1.   How is death defined? Why is the definition of death controversial? How does the social meaning of death vary across cultures and how has it changed over time?

2.   What factors influence life expectancy?

3.   What is the difference between programmed theories of aging and damage theories of aging? What is an example of each type of theory?

4.   What are Kübler-Ross's stages of dying? How valid and useful is this theory?

5. What is the Parkes/Bowlby attachment model of bereavement?

6. What is the infant's understanding of separation and death?

7. How do children's conceptions of death compare to a "mature" understanding of death? What factors might influence a child's understanding of death?

8. What is a dying child's understanding of death? How do dying children cope with the prospect of their own death? How do children cope with the death of a loved one?

9. What is the adolescent's understanding of death?

10. How do family members react and cope with the loss of a spouse, a child, and a parent?

11. What factors contribute to effective and ineffective coping with grief?

12. What can be done for those who are dying and for those who are bereaved to better understand and face the reality of death?

CHAPTER SUMMARY AND GUIDED REVIEW

The following summary provides an overview of the main points contained in this chapter of the text. Fill-in the blanks with terms that appropriately complete the sentence. Scattered throughout the summary are questions in parentheses. These are meant to encourage you to think actively as you are reading and connect this summary to the more detailed information provided in the text. You can answer these questions as you are filling in the blanks or you can complete all the blanks, then go back and reread the entire summary, addressing the questions in order to provide more depth of understanding.

LIFE AND DEATH ISSUES

What is death?

Biological death is not a single event but a (1) _____. According to the "Harvard" definition, biological death is defined as (2) _____ death. This means an irreversible loss of functioning in the entire brain. To be judged dead by this definition, a person must be totally unresponsive to (3) _____; fail to move for one hour and fail to breathe for three minutes after disconnection from life support systems; show no (4) _____; and show no electrical activity in the (5) _____ of the brain. (***Why is there debate over when someone is actually dead?***) Hastening someone's death when that person is terminally ill is referred to as (6) _____.

The meaning of death, and reactions to death, vary greatly across cultures and subcultures. (***What are some examples of cultural differences in the social meaning of death?***)

What Kills Us and When?

The average number of years that a person is expected to live, or one's (7) _____, is about 76 years in the United States. Life expectancies have increased in recent centuries. (***What accounts for this increase?***) The leading causes of death in the United States change across the life span. Infants typically die of complications surrounding birth or from (8) _____. Children typically die from (9) _____. Adolescents and young adults are generally healthy, but susceptible to accidents and violent deaths (homicides and suicides). Middle-aged adults are more likely to die from (10) _____ diseases, such as cancer and heart disease.

Theories of Aging: Why Do We Age and Die?

Theories of aging fall into two main categories. The (11) _____ theories of aging focus on the genetic control of aging, whereas (12) _____ theories of aging focus on the cumulative effects of damage to cells and organs over time.

An assumption of the programmed theories is that all species have a (13) _____ life span, or ceiling on the number of years that any member of that species can live. This figure varies across species, suggesting that (14) _____ genes may control how long we live. Genetics influence aging, possibly because human cells can only divide a certain number of times, a restriction known as the (15) _____. Cell division may be restricted because the stretch of DNA at the end of chromosomes, called the (16) _____ does not replicate itself like the rest of the chromosome does. Children with the condition (17) _____ age prematurely and provide evidence of a genetic component to aging.

According to a damage theory called the (18) _____ theory, normal metabolic processes produce toxic by-products that damage normal cells. It may be possible to inhibit free radical activity with (19) _____ such as vitamins E and C.

Many factors, both genetic and environmental, interact to produce aging and bring about death. One technique that may extend life is (20) _____, or substantially limiting the number of calories consumed.

THE EXPERIENCE OF DYING

Kübler-Ross's Stages of Dying

Kübler-Ross proposed that people who are dying progress through a common sequence of five stages. In the first stage, (21) _____ and isolation, a person responds to the news that he or she is dying by refusing to believe that it is true, a common defense mechanism to keep anxiety-provoking thoughts out of conscious awareness. In the second stage, the dying person responds with feelings of rage or (22) _____. In the third stage, the person tries to (23) _____ to gain more time and be given a second chance. When it becomes apparent that death is really going to occur, the dying person experiences (24) _____ and, if the person can work through the earlier responses to death, he or she may come to the final stage, which is (25) _____ of their death. Throughout all the stages, Kübler-Ross believed that people retained a sense of (26) _____ regarding their death.

Criticisms and Alternative Views

A major problem with Kübler-Ross's characterization of death is that dying people really do not experience these reactions as (27) _____. For example, some experts believe that dying patients alternate between denial and (28) _____, rather than moving systematically from one reaction to another. Another problem with Kübler-Ross's theory is that it does not account for how the path or (29) _____ of an illness affects one's perceptions. A third problem with Kübler-Ross's theory is that it ignores how a person's (30) _____ affects their response to dying. (***Can you explain how this factor can impact one's experience of dying?***)

THE EXPERIENCE OF BEREAVEMENT

The term (31) _____ is used to refer to a state of loss, whereas the emotional response to loss is called (32) _____. Culturally defined ways of displaying reactions to loss is referred to as (33) _____. Many people experience (34) _____ prior to the actual death of a loved one, unless the death is quite sudden.

The Parkes/Bowlby Attachment Model

Parkes and Bowlby characterize grieving as a reaction to (35) _____ from a loved one that progresses through several overlapping phases. The first reaction is (36) _____, which occurs in the first hours and days following a death. The second phase is (37) _____, which is most intense about 5 to 14 days after the death, and is accompanied by restlessness and preoccupation with thoughts of the loved one. Anger and guilt are also common reactions during this phase. The third phase is (38) _____ and despair when the person realizes that the loved one is gone forever. Finally, in the fourth phase of (39) _____, a person begins to move on with life by forming new relationships and getting involved in new activities.

Some Evidence

The reality is that bereavement is more complicated than what can be conveyed by a model. Some people cope effectively and can be characterized as (40) _____, whereas others experience serious and long-term grief and can be characterized as

(41) _____.

THE INFANT

      Infants experience death of a loved one as that person's (42) _____
from their life, but do not understand death as the ending of life. Infants separated from their
attachment figures show reactions that are similar to the reactions of bereaved adults, including
protest and despair.

THE CHILD
Grasping the Concept of Death

      Young children are curious about death and begin to show some understanding of death,
but have not reached a "mature" understanding. According to the mature adults view, death is:

* (43) _____ because it involves the end of all life processes;
* (44) _____, or cannot be undone;
* happens to everyone, or is (45) _____; and
* caused by internal or biological factors.

Preschool-aged children tend to think dead people retain some of their living capabilities and that
death can be reversed. Between the ages of 5 and 7, children begin to realize that death involves
cessation of life, it is irreversible, and it is universal. It takes children a few more years,
however, to fully understand that death is caused by biological factors, even if triggered by
external factors. Children's understanding of death is affected by their level of
(46) _____ development and by their cultural and life experiences. (*What life
experiences affect understanding of death?*)

The Dying Child

      Terminally ill children are typically aware that they are dying and experience a variety of
emotions such as anger and depression. (*How do terminally ill children of different ages
respond to their situation?*)

The Bereaved Child

      Children who lose a loved one grieve, but express their grief differently than adults do.
They may display a variety of problems, including problems with sleeping, eating, and other
daily routines. Because children are very dependent on their parents and do not have adult-level
coping strategies, they are particularly vulnerable to long-term problems following the loss of a
parent. (*What factors can help bereaved children cope with their loss?*)

THE ADOLESCENT

      Adolescents have developed a mature understanding of death and may spend time
contemplating death and its meaning. Adolescents grieve similarly to adults, but are influenced
by general themes or concerns of the adolescent period.

THE ADULT
Death in the Family Context

      Adults who lose a spouse often experience other changes as well and are at greater risk
for illness and physical symptoms. Recent research has identified five copying patterns among

those who have lost a spouse: common grief, chronic grief, chronic depression, depression-improved, and resilient. (*Can you describe these patterns?*) The loss of a child seems particularly difficult to cope with, in part because we do not expect children to die before their parents. The (47) _____ of the child does not really affect the intensity of a parent's grief. For an adult, the death of a parent may not be as disruptive as the loss of a spouse or child, because in some ways, it is expected.

Challenges to the Grief Work Perspective

According to the grief work perspective, bereaved people must (48) _____ their loss and work through the accompanying emotions in order to cope adaptively. Further, we believe that there are several forms of "complicated" or (49) _____ grief. This view has been challenged by cross-cultural research because what might be considered "pathological" grief in our society may be perfectly normal expression of grief in other societies.

Who Copes and Who Succumbs?

Some people cope more effectively with the loss of a loved one than others. The ability to cope is influenced by several factors. Bowlby argues that early (50) _____ relationships affect our later ability to cope with grief. (*Can you describe the relationship between early experience and later coping ability?*) An individual's (51) _____ and overall coping style also influence how well they cope with death, as does the closeness of the relationship between the bereaved person and the deceased. Reactions to death are also affected by the suddenness or unexpectedness of the death. Finally, the (52) _____ of death also influences how a person responds to the loss. Grief at any age can be positively affected by the presence of (53) _____, and negatively affected by the presence of additional (54) _____.

Bereavement and Human Development

Bereavement is painful, but can also have positive effects on development. For instance, many bereaved individuals feel more confident and independent after recovering from their loss than prior to their loss.

TAKING THE STING OUT OF DEATH

For the Dying

Some people who are dying are cared for by a (55) _____, a program that supports the dying person. (*What are the characteristics of these programs?*)

For the Bereaved

Therapy and support groups are available and beneficial to bereaved individuals.

REVIEW OF KEY TERMS

Below is a list of terms and concepts from this chapter. Use these to complete the following sentence definitions. You might also want to try writing definitions in your own words and then checking your definitions with those in the text.

anticipatory grief
antioxidants
assisted suicide
bereavement
caloric restriction
damage theories of aging
denial
euthanasia
frcc radical theory
grief
grief work perspective
Hayflick limit

hospice
life expectancy
Living Will
maximum life span
mourning
Parkes/Bowlby attachment model of
    bereavement
progeria
programmed theories of aging
telomere
total brain death

1.   The _____ suggests that there is a limited number of times that a human cell
      can divide.

2.   _____ is a defense mechanism where anxiety-producing thoughts are kept
      out of conscious awareness.

3.   The technique of _____, eating a highly nutritious but very restricted diet,
      may increase life span.

4.   _____ is the act of killing or allowing a person who is terminally ill to die.

5.   _____ is the emotional response to loss.

6.   A _____ program supports dying persons and their families through a caring
      philosophy.

7.   _____ explain aging through systematic genetic mechanisms.

8.   Substances that may increase longevity by inhibiting the activity of free radicals are
      _____.

9.   _____ refers to an irreversible loss of functioning in the entire brain.

10.   According to the _____, bereaved individuals must confront their loss and
      work through their painful emotions.

11.   A _____ is a tiny piece of DNA on the end of chromosomes.

12.   _____ is the ceiling on the number of years that anyone lives.

13.   Culturally prescribed ways of displaying one's reaction to death are known as
      _____.

14. According to the _____ theory, molecules with an extra electron react with other molecules to produce substances that damage normal cells.

15. According to _____, damage to cells and organs accumulates over time and eventually causes a person's death.

16. Our _____ is the average length of time we can expect to live.

17. A _____ is a document used to indicate whether someone wants extraordinary medical procedures used to extend life when he or she is hopelessly ill.

18. Grieving that begins before a death occurs in anticipation of what will happen is called _____.

19. _____ refers to a state of loss.

20. Helping someone else bring about their own death is _____.

21. A genetic disorder that causes premature aging and early death is called _____.

22. The _____ describes loss of an attachment figure in terms of numbness, yearning, disorganization and despair, and reorganization.

MULTIPLE CHOICE SELF TEST

For each multiple choice question, read all alternatives and then select the best answer.

1. The Harvard definition of biological death is
   a. the point at which the heart stops beating.
   b. irreversible loss of functioning in the cerebral cortex.
   c. irreversible loss of functioning in the entire brain.
   d. failure to breathe without life support systems.

2. Cross-cultural research on death and dying indicates that
   a. cultures have evolved different social meanings of death.
   b. all cultures have similar ways of coping with death.
   c. people of some cultures do not experience grief.
   d. there is universal agreement on the definition of death.

3. The average length of time that a person can expect to live is called
   a. life span.
   b. life expectancy.
   c. age norm.
   d. maximum life span.

4. The leading cause of death in childhood is _____ and in middle age, the leading cause of death is _____.
    a. congenital abnormalities; chronic diseases
    b. accidents; suicides
    c. hereditary defects; violent acts such as homicides
    d. accidents; chronic diseases

5. The Hayflick limit is
    a. the number of times that a gene can "turn on" or "turn off" to bring about maturational changes.
    b. the ceiling on the number of years that anyone lives.
    c. the speed with which the body can repair damaged cells.
    d. the limited number times that a human cell can divide.

6. Theories that focus on the genetic control of aging are called _____ theories and those that focus on gradual deterioration of cells are called _____ theories
    a. genetic; environmental
    b. programmed; damage
    c. damage; programmed
    d. biological; psychological

7. According to Kübler-Ross's stages of dying, a person who expresses resentment and criticizes everyone is in the stage of
    a. denial and isolation.
    b. anger.
    c. bargaining.
    d. depression.

8. According to Kübler-Ross's stages of dying, a dying person who agrees to stop smoking and drinking in return for a little more time is in the stage of
    a. denial and isolation.
    b. anger.
    c. bargaining.
    d. depression.

9. One of the biggest problems with Kübler-Ross's stages of dying is that
    a. dying is not really stage-like.
    b. patients go through the stages in order but at different rates.
    c. they are focused on a person's cognitive understanding of death rather than the person's affective response.
    d. they describe a person's response to death of a spouse or parent but not the response to one's own impending death.

10. The emotional response to death is referred to as
    a. bereavement.
    b. grief.
    c. mourning.
    d. depression.

11. In the first few days following the death of a loved one, the bereaved person
    a. is usually unable to function.
    b. experiences anticipatory grief.
    c. experiences the worst despair of the mourning process.
    d. is typically in a state of shock and numbness.

12. Preschool-aged children are likely to believe that
    a. death is inevitable and will happen to everyone eventually.
    b. dead people still experience sensations and perceptions, just not as intensely as live people.
    c. people die because of changes in internal bodily functioning.
    d. death is irreversible.

13. Terminally ill children typically
    a. accept their impending death with equanimity.
    b. have no idea that they are dying or what it means to die.
    c. go through Kübler-Ross's stages of dying in sequential order.
    d. experience a range of negative emotions and express a number of negative behaviors.

14. Grief over the loss of a child
    a. is greatest if the child is young.
    b. does not differ in intensity as a function of the age of the child.
    c. is less intense if the child dies from an accident beyond the parent's control.
    d. is more intense for fathers than mothers since mothers in our culture are encouraged to express grief more openly than fathers.

15. Children's grief
    a. can be reduced by not talking about death and the deceased.
    b. can be reduced if they have a number of other stressors to deal with at the same time.
    c. can be reduced if appropriate social support systems are in place.
    d. is always expressed openly through behavior such as crying.

CRITICAL THINKING QUESTIONS

By answering the following questions, you will strengthen your understanding of the material in this chapter. These questions require higher level thinking skills such as integration and application of concepts. Sample answers are provided for three of the questions. These illustrate one possibility, but there are other answers you could provide that might be just as good. For the other questions, you can check yourself by referring to the text (a hint is provided), or by asking a peer or your instructor to review your answer.

1. In general, what factors contribute to the process of aging and death?
    [Sample answer provided.]

2. Integrate the understanding of death with Piaget's stages of cognitive development and apply this to the practical situation of coping with the death of a pet or the death of a parent. For example, how would you help a child in the preoperational stage understand and cope with death of a parent? How would you explain that the pet dog has died? How would your conversations with children in the concrete operational stage and adolescents or adults in the formal operational stage differ from the conversation that you have with the preoperational child?
    [Sample answer provided.]

3. What factors influence how someone copes with the loss of a loved one?
    [Sample answer provided.]

4. How does the Parke/Bowlby model use attachment theory to characterize grieving? Is there any evidence for this view?
    [Hint: Review the section on "The Experience of Bereavement," starting on page 495 of the text.]

5. What are the advantages and disadvantages of viewing the experience of dying with Kubler-Ross's theory?
    [Hint: Review the section on "The Experience of Dying," starting on page 491 of the text, with special attention to the subsection on "Criticisms and Alternate Views."]

ANSWERS

Chapter Summary and Guided Review (Fill-in the blank)

1.	process	9.	accidents
2.	total brain	10.	chronic
3.	stimuli	11.	programmed
4.	reflexes	12.	damage
5.	cortex	13.	maximum
6.	euthanasia	14.	species-specific
7.	life expectancy	15.	Hayflick limit
8.	congenital abnormalities	16.	telomere

17.	progeria	37.	yearning
18.	free radical	38.	disorganization
19.	antioxidants	39.	reorganization
20.	caloric restriction	40.	resilient
21.	denial	41.	chronic grievers
22.	anger	42.	disappearance
23.	bargain	43.	final
24.	depression	44.	irreversible
25.	acceptance	45.	universal
26.	hope	46.	cognitive
27.	stages	47.	age
28.	acceptance	48.	confront
29.	trajectory	49.	pathological
30.	personality	50.	attachment
31.	bereavement	51.	personality
32.	grief	52.	cause
33.	mourning	53.	social support
34.	anticipatory grief	54.	stressors
35.	separation	55.	hospice
36.	numbness		

Review of Key Terms

1.	Hayflick limit	13.	mourning
2.	denial	14.	free radical theory
3.	caloric restriction	15.	damage theories of aging
4.	euthanasia	16.	life expectancy
5.	grief	17.	Living Will
6.	hospice	18.	anticipatory grief
7.	programmed theories of aging	19.	bereavement
8.	antioxidants	20.	assisted suicide
9.	total brain death	21.	progeria
10.	grief work perspective	22.	Parkes/Bowlby attachment model of bereavement
11.	telomere		
12.	maximum life span		

Multiple Choice Self Test

1.	C (p. 485)	6.	B (p. 489)	11.	D (p. 495)
2.	A (p. 487)	7.	B (p. 493)	12.	B (p. 498)
3.	B (p. 488)	8.	C (p. 493)	13.	D (p. 499)
4.	D (p. 489)	9.	A (p. 494)	14.	B (p. 503)
5.	D (p. 490)	10.	B (p. 495)	15.	C (p. 500)

Critical Thinking Questions

1.   *Aging and death result from a combination of genetic and environmental factors. Research with twins shows that genes contribute to life expectancy—identical twins show similar patterns of aging. Laboratory research indicates that human cells are limited in the number of*

times that they can replicate, suggesting that there might be a genetically programmed clock for aging and death. Other research suggests that damage to the cells from environmental toxins and free radicals produced by normal metabolic processes accumulates over time and eventually kills us. Unfortunately, we do not have much control over genetic factors and we all breathe and metabolize food and live in environments with some degree of pollution, pesticides, etc. At this point, the only method that has been shown to extend the life span (of animals in the laboratory) is dietary restriction: eating a highly nutritious, but very limited diet. It has yet to be demonstrated that this method works with humans.

2.　　*According to Piaget, children interpret the world differently depending on their stage of cognitive development. Infants in the sensorimotor stage would have little understanding of death. Towards the end of the sensorimotor stage, when they acquire object permanence, they would be able to recognize that someone who had been present is currently missing, but they would not be able to really understand what this means. Children in the preoperational stage would not be able to think logically about death, but would instead, try to understand death in terms of their limited cognitive abilities. Just as they struggle with the concept of reversibility on conservation tasks, they may illogically believe that death can be reversed. They may apply transductive reasoning and argue that two things are connected when in fact they are not. For example, they may believe that they caused their goldfish to die because they slammed the door to the room with the fishtank.*

　　Children's understanding of death becomes much more advanced when they move into the concrete operations stage. They can now reason logically and understand that death is not reversible and is final. They no longer attribute life-like characteristics to dead people (e.g., they know they can't feel the cold and don't get hungry). They may still struggle with understanding the biological causality of death, however, because this requires some understanding of abstract concepts. Children in the concrete operational stage still have trouble thinking about abstract or hypothetical ideas—ideas that are not concrete and haven't been personally experienced. Once they achieve formal operational thought, however, they can imagine all sorts of possibilities, including how the death of a loved person will affect multiple areas of their life and how it will impact on others as well.

3.　　*How well you cope with the loss of a loved one will depend on several factors. One obvious factor is the relation or attachment to the person prior to death. For example, coping with the loss of a child would be very difficult for a parent because parents don't normally anticipate that their children will die before them. Coping with the death of a parent who is old might be easier for a grown child than coping with the death of a parent while still young. Personal resources are also important. Some people are more resilient than others and have better coping strategies. They think of life issues in a way that is more productive in terms of getting on with their own lives. Other people have a life perspective that might be more counterproductive and make it difficult to move on after the death of a loved one. Social support is another important factor in determining how well people cope with loss. People with strong social support are generally better able to cope. On the other hand, people with less social support or people with additional stressors cope less well.*

EPILOGUE

FITTING THE PIECES TOGETHER

OVERVIEW

There are two major objectives of this chapter. One is to summarize developments of each major age or stage of the life span by chronologically organizing the topical information presented in the earlier chapters of the text. You should be able to describe the physical, cognitive, personal, and social developments of infants, preschool children, school-aged children, adolescents, young adults, middle-aged adults, and older adults. A second objective is to pull out and summarize the major developmental themes running throughout the text. These themes help us understand the developmental changes occurring throughout the life span. You should be able to describe the major themes and apply or give examples of each one.

LEARNING OBJECTIVES

1.   What are the significant trends (physical, cognitive, personal, and social) of each major age or stage of the life span (infants, preschool children, school-aged children, adolescents, young adults, middle-aged adults, and older adults)?

2.   What are the major developmental themes running throughout the text?

CHAPTER SUMMARY AND GUIDED REVIEW

The following summary provides an overview of the main points contained in this chapter of the text. Fill-in the blanks with terms that appropriately complete the sentence. Scattered throughout the summary are questions in parentheses. These are meant to encourage you to think actively as you are reading and connect this summary to the more detailed information provided in the text. You can answer these questions as you are filling in the blanks or you can complete all the blanks, then go back and reread the entire summary, addressing the questions in order to provide more depth of understanding.

MAJOR TRENDS IN HUMAN DEVELOPMENT
Infants (Birth to Age 2)
      Infant development is remarkably (1) _____, changing relatively helpless newborns into fairly sophisticated toddlers. Newborns come equipped with inborn or automatic (2) _____ and (3) _____ capabilities that allow

them to respond to their environment. Many (4) _____ reflexes disappear as infants mature during the first year and are replaced by voluntary motor behaviors. According to Piaget, infants are in the (5) _____ period of cognitive development. During this period, they acquire (6) _____, or the understanding that objects exist even when they are not being perceived. They also acquire the (7)_____, which allows them to mentally represent ideas. Along with cognitive developments, infants are developing a sense of self and showing signs of distinct temperaments. According to Erikson, infants face the first (8) _____ conflict of trust vs. mistrust and must somehow resolve this conflict. Infants are also forming (9) _____ with caregivers that can influence their later relationships.

Preschool Children (Ages 2 through 5)

Preschool children acquire gross motor control and fine motor skills necessary for many important tasks. According to Piaget, they are in the (10) _____ stage of cognitive development, where they often use perceptually salient features to solve a problem rather than the (11) _____ used by older children. They master the basics of language using the (12) _____ acquired at the end of the sensorimotor period. Preschool children have short attention spans and they typically lack (13) _____ skills that would help them learn and remember more effectively. Preschool children are often characterized as (14) _____ because they have difficulty understanding another person's perspective. According to Erikson, preschool children wrestle with two conflicts. In the stage of (15) _____ versus shame and doubt, they must learn to assert themselves and in the stage of (16) _____ versus guilt, they try to implement bold plans. They develop (17) _____, which allows them to predict and explain behavior in terms of mental states. Although still very close to parents, preschool children begin to spend more time with peers.

School-Age Children (Ages 6 through 11)

School-age children are typically more self-controlled, serious, and (18) _____ than younger children. They also have developed better (19) _____ skills, allowing them to participate in a wider range of sports and activities. They are in Piaget's (20) _____ stage, which means they can reason logically about concrete problems. They master the finer points of language and communication, and can take the perspective of their listener. According to Vygotsky, they use (21) _____ as a tool for problem solving. School-aged children show a greater understanding of self and others. They are faced with Erikson's conflict of (22) _____ versus inferiority, as they struggle to master scholastic and personal tasks. We also see the formation of a more stable (23) _____ during this period, parts of which are evident in adulthood. Some school-aged children move from Kohlberg's (24) _____ level of moral reasoning to (25) _____ moral reasoning as they realize that rules are agreements among people. The social world expands and socialization of children is increasingly affected by agents outside the home.

<u>Adolescents (Ages 12 through 19)</u>

Adolescents undergo dramatic physical changes as they go through (26) _____ and experience their growth spurt. As a result, many adolescents are preoccupied with appearance. There are also significant cognitive changes. Adolescents can think more systematically and (27) _____ about hypothetical situations or problems as they progress in Piaget's (28) _____ stage. They are able to think about self and others in more sophisticated ways. According to Erikson, a major developmental task of this period is developing a sense of (29) _____. Adolescents are more serious about preparing for adult roles than younger children and they increasingly participate in making decisions about their lives. They are more involved with their (30) _____ group, which can influence them in both positive and negative ways.

<u>Young Adults (Ages 20 through 39)</u>

Young adults are at peak physical capacity and peak (31) _____ functioning. Some will move from Kohlberg's level of (32) _____ moral reasoning to (33) _____ reasoning. They face Erikson's conflict of (34) _____ versus isolation, and experiment with romantic relationships and marriage. Many become parents and most face a number of family and career responsibilities.

<u>Middle-Aged Adults (Ages 40 through 64)</u>

Middle-aged adults show gradual physical declines, and are more susceptible to heart disease and other chronic illnesses. Women experience (35) _____ around age 50. Intellectual capabilities during this period are relatively stable. Expertise on the job and at home allows adults to effectively solve everyday problems. Creative achievement is often at its peak during this period. Middle-aged adults struggle with Erikson's conflict of (36) _____ versus stagnation as they raise their families and make contributions to society. As children leave home, middle-aged adults often pursue other interests and find satisfaction in watching their children live adult lives.

<u>Older Adults (Age 65 and Up)</u>

Older adults experience some losses and declines in functioning. They take more time to learn things and may experience some (37) _____ lapses. They have difficulty solving (38) _____ problems, but experience no big change in cognitive and linguistic skills that are used everyday. Older adults face Erikson's conflict of (39) _____ versus despair as they review their lives and try to find meaning from their accomplishments. It is difficult to describe a single pattern of development, since there is immense (40) _____ among capabilities of older adults

MAJOR THEMES IN HUMAN DEVELOPMENT

1. <u>Nature and nurture truly interact in development</u>. Biological and environmental factors together explain both universal trends in development and individual differences in development. Our experiences influence whether we realize our genetic potentials; our genes influence what experiences we seek and our response to these experiences.

2. <u>We are whole people throughout the life span.</u> Physical, cognitive, personal, and social developments are intertwined during each period of the life span.

3. <u>Development proceeds in multiple directions.</u> Development becomes increasingly differentiated and integrated. It involves gains, losses, and changes that are simply different but not gains or losses.

4 <u>There is both continuity and discontinuity in development.</u> This issue raises questions about whether change is stagelike (qualitative changes) or not (quantitative changes), and whether or not early experiences predict later traits (or carry over to adulthood).

5. <u>There is much plasticity in development.</u> Human beings have the capacity to change in response to their experiences.

6. <u>We are individuals, becoming even more diverse with age.</u> There is an incredible amount of diversity among humans, which makes it difficult to form generalizations about them. And as we age, human development becomes less and less predictable.

7. <u>We develop in a cultural and historical context.</u> Development is affected by broad cultural and historical contexts, as well as the individual's immediate environment.

8. <u>We are active in our own development.</u> We actively explore the world and create our own understandings of the world rather than being passively molded by the world around us. The person and environment reciprocally interact and influence one another.

9. <u>Development is a lifelong process.</u> Development in any one phase of life is best understood by viewing it as part of a lifelong process.

10. <u>Development is best viewed from multiple perspectives.</u> Development may be best understood by integrating multiple theories and adopting a contextual perspective that emphasizes variations in development.

MULTIPLE CHOICE SELF TEST

For each multiple choice question, read all alternatives and then select the best answer.

1. Which advance in cognition is instrumental in helping the child move from random problem-solving to a point where s/he can mentally devise a solution to a problem and then try it out?
   a. transformational logic
   b. acquisition of symbolic capacity
   c. movement from concrete-operational to formal-operational thought
   d. the ability to conserve

2. Preschoolers are MOST likely to be in which of the following stages?
   a.   autonomy vs. shame and doubt; latency
   b.   initiative vs. guilt; conventional morality
   c.   autonomy vs. shame and doubt; preconventional morality
   d.   industry vs. inferiority; preconventional morality

3. A marked weakness of the preoperational stage is the inability to
   a.   think logically.
   b.   use language effectively.
   c.   allow one thing to represent something else.
   d.   socially interact with their peers.

4. One drawback of concrete operational thinking is difficulty with
   a.   any sort of problem solving task.
   b.   tasks that require mental consideration of tangible objects.
   c.   abstract or hypothetical tasks.
   d.   tasks that require understanding the perspective of another person.

5. Erikson believed that young adults were struggling with the issue of
   a.   industry versus inferiority.
   b.   identity versus role confusion.
   c.   intimacy versus isolation.
   d.   generativity versus stagnation.

6. Older adults (age 65 and over) are typically
   a.   lower in self-esteem and life satisfaction than younger adults.
   b.   in Erikson's stage of generativity vs. stagnation.
   c.   superior to younger adults with regard to fluid intelligence, though their crystallized intelligence has deteriorated significantly.
   d.   suffering from some sort of physical limitations.

7. With the evidence in, it is MOST accurate to say that cognitive development is
   a.   discontinuous and stage-like, as Piaget asserted.
   b.   continuous, reflected in measures of quantitative change such as accumulation and loss of knowledge over time.
   c.   largely maturational and independent of environmental influence.
   d.   both stage-like and gradual, depending on the aspect being studied.

8. To say that there is discontinuity in development means that
   a.   changes smoothly and gradually occur across the life span.
   b.   changes occur in distinct steps.
   c.   early traits carry over and form the basis of later traits.
   d.   change is a matter of quantitatively adding to what is already present.

9.   We are MOST LIKELY to be similar to someone else our same age during
        a.   infancy.
        b.   childhood.
        c.   adolescence.
        d.   old age.

10.   Which is TRUE with regard to the course of development across the life span?
        a.   In general, there is growth throughout childhood and young adulthood, stability
                during middle-age, and a decline in functioning during old age.
        b.   In general, there is growth throughout childhood and young adulthood, followed
                by steady declines in functioning beginning with middle-age.
        c.   In general, growth proceeds in an incremental fashion throughout childhood and
                adolescence, levels off during young adulthood, and begins to decline by age 40.
        d.   There is evidence of growth, loss, and change at every stage of the life span.

CRITICAL THINKING QUESTIONS

*By answering the following questions, you will strengthen your understanding of
the material in this chapter. These questions require higher level thinking skills
such as integration and application of concepts. Sample answers are provided
for three of the questions. These illustrate one possibility, but there are other
answers you could provide that might be just as good. For the other questions,
you can check yourself by referring to the text (a hint is provided), or by asking a
peer or your instructor to review your answer.*

1.   One theme that runs throughout the text is "There is both continuity and discontinuity in
        development." Explain what this means and give a concrete example from any area of
        developmental psychology.
        [Sample answer is provided.]

2.   Another theme that runs throughout the text is "Nature and nurture both contribute to
        development." Explain what this means and provide evidence illustrating the influences
        of both nature and nurture.
        [Sample answer is provided.]

3.   Describe the major characteristics of a typical preschool-age child.
        [Sample answer is provided.]

4.   Discuss the social, cognitive, and physical changes that occur across adulthood.
        [Hint: Review the sections on "Young Adults," "Middle-Aged Adults," and "Older
        Adults," starting on page 514 of the text.]

5.   Compare and contrast the accomplishments of school-age children with those of
        adolescents.

[Hint: Review the sections on "School-age Children" and "Adolescents" on pages 513-514 of the text.]

ANSWERS

Chapter Summary and Guided Review (Fill-in the blank)

1.	rapid	21.	private speech
2.	reflexes	22.	industry
3.	sensory	23.	personality
4.	automatic	24.	preconventional
5.	sensorimotor	25.	conventional
6.	object permanence	26.	puberty
7.	symbolic capacity	27.	abstractly
8.	psychosocial	28.	formal operations
9.	attachments	29.	identity
10.	preoperational	30.	peer
11.	logical reasoning	31.	cognitive
12.	symbolic capacity	32.	conventional
13.	information processing	33.	postconventional
14.	egocentric	34.	intimacy
15.	autonomy	35.	menopause
16.	initiative	36.	generativity
17.	theory of mind	37.	memory
18.	logical	38.	novel
19.	motor	39.	integrity
20.	concrete operations	40.	diversity

Multiple Choice Self-Test

1.	B (p. 513)	6.	D (p. 517)
2.	C (p. 513)	7.	D (p. 519)
3.	A (p. 513)	8.	B (p. 519)
4.	C (p. 513)	9.	A (p. 520)
5.	C (p. 514)	10.	D (p. 519)

Critical Thinking Questions

1. *Continuity refers to growth that is gradual and incremental over time, while discontinuity refers to more abrupt, stage-like changes. Continuous growth is quantitatively adding more to something you already have (e.g., height), while discontinuous growth is qualitatively changing something (e.g., adding a new way to solve problems rather than just getting faster at using an old problem solving method).*

The research presented throughout the text makes it clear that there are some aspects of development that are continuous and others that are discontinuous. As one example of continuous and discontinuous development consider a language accomplishment noted in Chapter 10. At around 18 months of age, there is vocabulary spurt when acquisition of words increases dramatically. This occurs because toddlers come to realize that everything has a name and then want to learn all the names they can. The realization is a discontinuous change because it reflects a new understanding; the subsequent increase in vocabulary is continuous because children are adding more and more to what they already have.

2. *The nature-nurture issue is the major question facing scientists who study human development. All aspects of development involve some combination of nature (e.g., biological and genetic factors) and nurture (environmental factors). Further, nature can influence nurture and nurture can influence nature. For example, research with twins shows that intelligence has a genetic component: Children are similar to their parents in intelligence, whether they are raised in the same home with them or adopted and raised separately. Identical twins are more similar to one another in intelligence than are other pairs, again, whether they are raised together or apart. But one's environment also influences intelligence. Children who are moved from an impoverished home into an enriched home show an increase in their IQ scores. Scores on the HOME Inventory, which measures the quality of the home environment, are correlated with children's IQ scores. Further, as children get older, the intellectual profile that they have inherited will lead them to seek out certain environments that are a good fit with their profile. Thus, environments are related to genetic factors.*

3. *Preschool-age children are typically in Piaget's stage of preoperations, which is characterized by pre-logical reasoning based on symbols and intuition. Young children often draw conclusions based on the appearance of a problem rather than by logically thinking about the components of the problem. As a result, they fail traditional tests of conservation. Young children have mastered the basics of language and are increasing their vocabularies and sentence complexity. They tend to be egocentric because they have trouble holding multiple perspectives in their mind at the same time. Young children have limitations in their information processing; they don't use effective memory strategies and their short-term working memory is not as efficient as it will be when they are older. According to Erikson, preschool-age children face the conflicts of autonomy versus shame and initiative versus guilt. If these conflicts are resolved successfully, preschoolers emerge with the confidence to assert themselves. They also develop a theory of mind during this time, which allows them to understand mental states and how mental states affect behavior. Preschoolers are curious and, in many ways, seem eager to learn about the world around them.*